Migration and
Residential Mobility

MIGRATION AND RESIDENTIAL MOBILITY

Macro and Micro Approaches

Martin Cadwallader

The University of Wisconsin Press

The University of Wisconsin Press
114 North Murray Street
Madison, Wisconsin 53715

3 Henrietta Street
London WC2E 8LU, England

Library of Congress Cataloging-in-Publication Data
Cadwallader, Martin T., 1947–
Migration and residential mobility: macro and micro approaches /
Martin Cadwallader.
292 p.   cm.
Includes bibliographical references (p. 239) and index.
ISBN 0-299-13490-3 (cloth).—ISBN 0-299-13494-6 (paper)
1. Population geography—Econometric models. 2. Migration,
Internal—Econometric models. 3. Residential mobility
—Econometric models. I. Title.
HB1951.C25   1992
304.8'01'5195—dc20   92-50246

For
Lorraine, Evan,
and Meredith

Contents

Figures

Tables

Preface

The purpose of this book is to explore the phenomenon of human migration, especially as it occurs within the so-called developed countries of the world. The approach is analytical, and various kinds of migration models are described and explained. These models are primarily statistical in nature, involving for the most part different applications of the general linear model. In particular, structural equation models are used to specify the interrelationships among sets of variables that are hypothesized to explain migration. Although the ideas and concepts have been culled from a a variety of disciplines, there is a unifying geographic emphasis on the relationship between socioeconomic processes and spatial patterns.

The book is organized according to two main axes of differentiation. First, a distinction is made between macro and micro approaches to explaining migration. The macro approach is concerned with explaining aggregate migration patterns by measured characteristics of the socioeconomic and physical environments, while the micro approach explains individual migration behavior within the framework of the psychological decision-making process. A second distinction is made between interregional migration and migration within cities, or residential mobility.

Parts of this book first appeared in academic journals, and I would like to thank the following journals and publishers for allowing me to reproduce some of my previously published material: *Area* (Institute of British Geographics), *Environment and Behavior* (Sage Publications), *Environment and Planning* (Pion), *Geografiska Annaler, Growth and Change,* Prentice-Hall, *Professional Geographer* (Association of American Geographers), *Progress in Human Geography* (Edward Arnold), Routledge, Chapman and Hall, *Transactions of the Institute of British Geographers*

(Institute of British Geographers), and *Urban Geography* (V. H. Winston and Son).

I am also grateful to the following publishers and authors for permission to reproduce copyrighted material: Ronald Abler for figure 4.1; the Association of American Geographers for figures 2.1, 2.2, and 2.4; the Canadian Association of Geographers for figures 3.8 and 3.9 and table 3.2; Pion for tables 3.4 and 3.5; *The Review of Economics and Statistics* for table 2.7; Sage Publications for table 2.10; Springer-Verlag for tables 2.8 and 2.9; the University of Chicago Press for figure 3.3; and the University of North Carolina Press for figure 3.2.

While writing this book I have been generously helped by a number of people and institutions. Bill Clark first stimulated my interest in migration and residential mobility when I was a graduate student in the Department of Geography at UCLA, some twenty years ago now. He encouraged me to approach the topic from an analytical prespective and made a number of valuable comments on a previous draft of the present book. I am also grateful to Jim Huff for his helpful comments. Much of the research was supported by grants from the National Science Foundation and the Graduate School of the University of Wisconsin–Madison. These grants enabled me to support a group of exceptionally talented graduate students. At one time or another David Kaplan, Russell Kirby, and Thomas Klak have all provided much-appreciated assistance with data collection and analysis. The maps and diagrams were drawn by the University of Wisconsin Cartography Laboratory. A special thanks goes to my colleagues in the Department of Geography at Madison for providing such a supportive intellectual and social environment. On a more personal note, I would like to thank my parents, Eric and Muriel Cadwallader. They sacrificed a great deal for my early education and have since been a constant source of encouragement. Finally, this book is for Lorraine, Evan, and Meredith— my three companions.

Migration and
Residential Mobility

1

Theoretical Frameworks

Human migration is both a cause and a consequence of social change. The demographic and socioeconomic composition of regions is determined by migration flows, and an understanding of interregional migration is thus mandatory for anyone attempting to analyze the general process of regional change. Similarly, within cities, the process of neighborhood change cannot be satisfactorily understood without reference to residential mobility. Pragmatically, our predictions of such diverse phenomena as energy consumption and school enrollments depend upon our ability to explain successfully the variation in migration behavior.

Migration has widespread consequences, both for the individuals involved and for the society within which it takes place. As a result, policymakers have become increasingly aware of the role of migration in the context of such issues as economic growth, social well-being, and political representation. For example, since World War II the United States has witnessed a series of profound changes in the distribution of its population. First, the immediate postwar years were dominated by migration from central cities to the surrounding suburbs, although this trend is now considerably muted, especially in those cities experiencing substantial gentrification. Second, during the 1970s there was a significant movement away from large metropolitan areas toward smaller cities and even distinctly rural areas. Finally, coincidental with this period of counterurbanization, there has been a dramatic shift of population out of the highly industrialized states in the Northeast to the less densely settled areas of the Southwest.

Given the critical role of migration in both determining and reflecting social change, it is hardly surprising that most of the social sciences are involved in its study. Indeed, research on migration represents one of the few truly interdisciplinary fields of endeavor, involving geographers, economists, sociologists, demographers, and others. Although each discipline projects a particular orientation—economists have tended to emphasize economic opportunities, sociologists have focused on the characteristics of migrants, and geographers have highlighted the spatial structure of migration flows—there has been a genuine convergence of the disciplinary foci. The present book reflects this convergence, in that the concepts and models have been culled from a variety of disciplinary perspectives.

As in most overviews of the migration literature, a distinction is made here between interregional migration and migration within cities, or residential mobility (W. A. V. 1982b; Cadwallader 1986a). Of perhaps greater importance, however, is the distinction between macro- and micro-level approaches (Stillwell and Congdon 1991). The macro approach is concerned with explaining aggregate migration behavior by measuring characteristics of the socioeconomic and physical environments, such as income, unemployment, and climate. The literature of this approach is firmly rooted within the rubric of neoclassical economics, with due attention being given to interregional wage differentials and investment in human capital. The micro approach, on the other hand, attempts to explain migration within the context of the psychological decision-making process and is concerned with how individuals choose between alternatives. Concepts such as place utility and the perception and evaluation of potential destinations are thus subsumed within the general framework of choice behavior developed by psychologists.

This philosophical dichotomy within migration research has been explored by White (1980b), who refers to an objective philosophy and a cognitive philosophy. While an objective philosophy involves analyzing the contextual determinants of migration without concern for intermediate states of mind, a cognitive philosophy explicitly considers the individual's storing and processing of information about potential destinations. For exponents of the cognitive approach, migration is best explained as a result of the perception of origin and destination characteristics, rather than according to the actual configuration of those characteristics. While both approaches have been partially successful, it is also true that a synthesis of the two approaches might afford greater insight than either approach offers on its own. To argue thusly is to suggest that these two lines of inquiry are complementary rather than com-

	Macro-level approaches	Micro-level approaches
Interregional migration	Chapter 2 Chapter 3	Chapter 4
Residential mobility	Chapter 5	Chapter 6

Figure 1.1. The organizational structure of the book.

petitive (Golledge 1980). The same types of explanatory variables are often used in both, but the methodological perspectives differ markedly.

Within this context, the organizational structure of the present book can be conveniently outlined in the form of a matrix (fig. 1.1). On the vertical axis, migration is divided, on the basis of spatial scale, into interregional migration and residential mobility. Similarly, on the horizontal axis a distinction is made between the macro- and micro-level approaches to studying migration. The five major chapters of the book fit into the four cells of this matrix, such that Chapter 2, for example, considers the macro approach to interregional migration, while Chapter 6 explores the micro approach to residential mobility. Throughout the book various kinds of migration models are described and explained. These models are primarily statistical in nature, involving for the most part applications of the general linear model, such as multiple regression, factor analysis, path analysis, and simultaneous equations. Most of the substantive examples are taken from the more developed countries of the world, including the United States, Canada, England, Sweden, and Australia.

Before proceeding further, however, it is important to consider the different theoretical frameworks that have been utilized in investigations of migration behavior, as these conceptualizations have played a major role in the formulation and interpretation of empirical analyses. Traditionally, most of the work on migration has been carried out within the context of an empirically based, hypothesis-testing approach to social science. As a result, the model-building paradigm, especially as exemplified by neoclassical economics, has been dominant. More recently, however, a variety of other perspectives have emerged, such as the behavioral, institutional, and political economy approaches. The purpose of the present chapter is to describe and evaluate these perspectives briefly, with a view toward suggesting how they might best be deployed to aid our understanding of the process of migration.

Theoretical pluralism and epistemological debate thus characterize contemporary work on migration. Many have welcomed this theoretical emphasis as a positive response to the somewhat sterile empiricism of previous work; they believe that the range of perspectives ensures that research is not imprisoned by a particular theoretical orthodoxy (Johnston 1980). Others, however, have suggested that this kind of eclecticism is potentially harmful and that it only serves to blur crucial distinctions between competing and incompatible doctrines. Fincher (1983), for example, argues that it is theoretically inconsistent to combine Marxist with non-Marxist categories in an attempt to selectively employ certain insights without using the whole "theoretical package."

The present book adopts the stance that theoretical pluralism should be encouraged, as there is no epistemology that can be used as a yardstick against which all other approaches can be measured for scientific adequacy. Each perspective can only provide a partial explanation of migration phenomena, but by focusing on the interstices between the various approaches and emphasizing their complementarity, we can begin the necessary integration that might lead to a higher order of synthesis. While it is true that convergence may mute the critique that different theories can provide for each other, each approach contains certain lacunae that can gain from contacts with new material. Moreover, it has been strongly argued that, despite a variety of epistemological differences, there is a basic similarity in the procedures for assessing empirical work (Chouinard, Fincher, and Webber 1984).

The current preoccupation with social theory does, however, highlight the often problematic relationship between theory and empirical reality (Cadwallader 1988). Structural Marxism, in particular, has been plagued by severe problems in its juxtaposing of formalism and empiricism. Constructing a formalized theoretical ensemble before conducting empirical research tends to accentuate the need for intermediate categories between the abstract and the observable. In other words, we must construct intermediate concepts that can weld theoretical structures to particular situations. The search for what Clark and Dear (1984:6) have termed "middle-level theory" is aimed at linking the level of appearances with the underlying social processes, creating a framework that allows us to move from the abstract to the concrete and back again. The challenge is to find an intermediate ground between a sometimes crude structural determinancy and a rather naive humanism. Put in current terms, we need a more balanced and integrated understanding of the interactions between human agency and social structure (Giddens 1984).

Neoclassical Economics

Neoclassical economics, developed in the latter half of the nineteenth century, signaled a shift from the emphasis on the production side of economic systems to a fuller consideration of consumer preferences. Indeed, a fundamental axiom of neoclassical economics is that individual preferences help to shape both the nature of the economy and the characteristics of the larger society within which that economy is embedded. Individual freedom, consumer sovereignty, and a reverence for market mechanisms are all implied within the framework of neoclassical economics, and this form of economics still constitutes the orthodox approach in most of Western Europe and North America.

In general, neoclassical economics conceives of the economy as comprising a large number of individual households and firms. Firms purchase land, labor, and capital, the so-called factors of production, from the factor market. They then combine these factors of production in such a way as to maximize their profits. In particular, the firm must choose a specific productive process and a specific volume of output, or scale of production. The finished products are then sold on the product market, where they are purchased by households, which are attempting to maximize utility or personal satisfaction. Households obtain the money to buy goods on the product market by selling their land, labor, and capital on the factor market. The interaction between supply and demand regulates prices on both factor and product markets.

Throughout, the neoclassical analysis emphasizes equilibrium conditions and views the market economy as a harmonious, self-regulating system. Households, firms, product markets, and factor markets are all inextricably interrelated, such that a change in one part of the economy will have implications for all of the other parts. For example, the price of labor on the labor market affects the costs of production, which in turn affect prices on the product market, and so on. In this sense, the phenomenon of excessive unemployment is often simply viewed as a temporary aberration that will eventually be corrected by market mechanisms.

A number of general assumptions are incorporated within the neoclassical perspective. First, individual firms and households are assumed to be too small to influence prices on either the factor market or the product market independently. Second, individual households allocate expenditures on the product market in order to maximize utility, subject to budgetary constraints and the prevailing set of prices. Third, individual firms behave in order to maximize profits. Fourth, both households and firms are assumed to possess perfect information about market conditions. Fifth, interchanging the factors of production is assumed to be unproblematic. Of course, subsequent modifications of neoclassical economics have addressed the unrealistic nature of these assumptions. For example, monopoly and oligopoly situations have been considered as it has been recognized that buyers and sellers are often large enough to influence prices. Also, the category of public goods has been introduced to account for those goods and services, such as police protection and education, which are not generated by market conditions but for which society accepts a collective responsibility.

Regarding migration, the neoclassical theory of factor mobility suggests that labor moves in response to interregional wage differentials, with the volume of movement increasing as the wage differential increases (Clark and Gertler 1983). More specifically, labor will migrate from low-wage to high-wage areas. Moreover, it is argued that this migration will lead to an optimal spatial allocation of the demand and supply of labor and that ultimately wage rates will be equalized across regional labor markets. As labor migrates to high-wage areas, the supply of labor is increased at the destination and decreased at the origin, thus equalizing wages. In this context, neoclassical models emphasize real wages rather than money wages; if commodity prices decline, a commensurate decline in money wages will not induce migration, as real wages would remain the same.

The assumptions of this macro-adjustment model are typical of those associated with neoclassical economics in general (Clark and Ballard 1980). First, workers are assumed to maximize income. Second, workers possess perfect information concerning employment opportunities and wage rates. Third, there are no barriers, either social or economic, to labor mobility. Fourth, workers are many in number and homogeneous with respect to skills and tastes. Finally, the macro-adjustment model implies a system that moves toward an equilibrium condition (Evans 1990). If wage differentials were near zero, then migration would also be near zero, as the system would be close to a state of equilibrium, characterized by equal levels of supply and demand for labor.

This notion of a system striving for equilibrium has encouraged the use of a systems approach to understanding migration. Systems analysis emphasizes the connectivity between phenomena and implies that once the system has been successfully modeled it can then be manipulated in a policy context (Huggett 1980). Most systems are conceptualized as consisting of three major components: a set of elements with certain attributes, a set of links representing the relationships between those elements, and a set of links representing the relationships between the system and its environment. If the latter set of links is absent, then the system is termed a closed one. Migration systems, however, are likely to be open. Systems analysis represents an attractive means of analyzing the variety of cause-and-effect relationships involved in migration, as well as capturing the associated feedback effects (Cordey-Hayes 1978). Migration can be viewed as an interconnected spatial system in which the effect of a change in one location will be felt in various other locations.

The major contribution toward a systems approach to migration was provided by Mabogunje (1970), who focused on the issue of rural-to-urban migration, especially in less-developed countries. Mabogunje postulated that the socioeconomic environment for such a system is one in which rural communities are becoming increasingly integrated into the national economy, thus stimulating a rural-to-urban movement as people search for better wages and employment opportunities. The two most important subsystems, within the overall system, are the rural and urban control subsystems. In the rural areas the nature of family commitments and the structure of the village community act as controls on the volume of migration. The urban control subsystem, on the other hand, influences the volume of migration by providing particular levels of housing and employment opportunities.

The neoclassical approach in general has been subjected to a number of criticisms, most of which relate to the empirical status of the assumptions (Gober-Meyers 1978a). First, the neoclassical model predicts long-run equilibrium, but some have argued that initial regional economic disparities are often reinforced and that divergence rather than convergence is the rule (Myrdal 1957). This argument draws upon the notion of migration selectivity. Since migrants tend to be younger and more highly skilled than the more stable segments of the population, high-wage regions that gain in population as a result of interregional migration will experience a favorable change in their population composition. Conversely, poorer, depressed regions tend to lose the younger and more highly educated segments of the population, thus experiencing an unfavorable change in population composition. In this way, the net out-migration from depressed regions might reduce unemployment in the short run, only to create greater unemployment in the long run.

Second, the assumption of no barriers to migration is obviously open to serious question. The relaxation of this assumption has generally involved the introduction of a distance variable, which acts as a surrogate for the costs of movement and represents an intervening obstacle between the positive and negative factors associated with the origin and destination (Lee 1966). The introduction of a migration cost variable, however, does not necessarily render the revised model inconsistent with the basic elements of the neoclassical perspective. An equilibrium condition can still occur, as long as the wage differential is equal to the cost of migration. In other words, migration will continue until wages in the destination region are no longer higher than the sum of wages in the origin region plus the economic and psychological costs of moving.

Third, the assumption of a homogeneous work force has become increasingly unrealistic with the progressive specialization of labor. In order to account for this heterogeneity, researchers have disaggregated the population in a variety of ways—according to race, education, occupational structure, and age (Barsby and Cox 1975; Clark and White 1990). For example, Hart (1973) analyzed the ability to predict the migration behavior of three different occupational groups. As the poorest predictions were obtained for the professional group, he concluded that the less-skilled occupational groups are more constrained by economic necessity. In general, however, the neoclassical paradigm has been criticized not only for ignoring the heterogeneity of labor but also for reducing the factors of production, such as labor and capital, to the status of abstract and mutually substitutable technical inputs and thus assuming that they are politically neutral (Scott 1980:81).

Fourth, the assumption of perfect information implies that all segments of the population have equal knowledge of job opportunities and wage rates. In reality, however, such knowledge greatly depends upon the structure of contact networks and previous migration flows (Amrhein 1985). Migrant stock, or the proportion of the population from the sender area residing in the receiver area, is often included in migration models as a means of calibrating information levels; this implies that previous out-migrants send back information concerning employment opportunities and wage rates. Kau and Sirmans (1977) corroborate this line of reasoning when they suggest that the migrant stock factor is especially important in explaining the behavior of those migrants making their first interstate move. The number of people migrating during a previous time period can also be used as a surrogate for information flows, but this method of measurement highlights the problems involved in interpreting the theoretical significance of information levels, as one would expect previous migration to be highly correlated with the current determinants of migration.

Finally, it is not at all clear that migrants attempt to maximize income. At the very least, allowance has to be made for the role of expected income differentials, as expressed in the more behaviorally oriented investment in human capital theory of migration (Ritchey 1976). Also, it can be hypothesized that migrants are influenced by the broader notion of place utility, rather than strictly adhering to income maximization. The concept of place utility, which can be defined as the overall level of attraction of a particular place for a particular individual, emphasizes the important role played by locational preferences and suggests the significance of noneconomic variables such as the quality of schools and health care services (Brown and Gustavus 1977). Indeed, the inclusion of such concepts as expectations and locational preferences characterizes the so-called behavioral approach to migration.

The Behavioral Approach

The emergence of the behavioral movement in human geography and its application in the field of migration are at least partly due to the search for alternative models of human beings (Golledge and Rushton 1984). In particular, behavioralists have attempted to replace the behaviorally unsatisfactory concept of "economic man" and its attendant assumptions of profit maximization and perfect information with a more realistic counterpart. Following Simon (1957), some have suggested that a more realistic model of human beings would combine the principles of satisficing behavior and bounded rationality. In other words, it is assumed that people are sometimes satisfied with less than optimal profit levels and that decisions are often made in a context of incomplete knowledge and uncertainty.

The rejection of "economic man" as a workable descriptive model of human beings appears eminently reasonable, as acting with complete rationality in the real world is but one of a range of possible behaviors. This line of reasoning does not deny that "economic man" is a powerful tool in a normative context but simply emphasizes that the behavioral approach is concerned with identifying regularities in actual, not optimal, behavior. As Harvey (1981) has pointed out, however, care must be taken to replace this conceptualization with an alternative that is both amenable to operationalization and theoretically useful. As yet, largely due to the difficulties involved in determining aspiration levels, the satisficer concept has proven very difficult to operationalize.

In comparison with the satisficing concept, the principle of bounded rationality appears to be more promising. It takes into account our simplified and distorted view of reality, thus attempting to explain behavior based on individual perceptions. In this context, Kirk (1963) made an important distinction between what he labeled the phenomenal and behavioral environments. The phenomenal environment refers to the objective physical environment in which behavior takes place, whereas the behavioral environment is the subjective psychological environment in which decisions are made that are then translated into overt action in the phenomenal environment. A fundamental axiom of the behavioral approach is that decision-making has its roots in the behavioral environment rather than in the phenomenal environment. In other words, a person's behavior is based on his or her perception of the environment, not on the environment as it actually exists (Golledge and Timmermans 1990).

Given this interest in individual differences, it is hardly surprising that the behavioral approach is characterized by the use of individual, or micro-level, data. Such data are prerequisites for those researchers interested in the variability of individual behavior, although this does not imply a preoccupation with the unique as opposed to the general. Rather, behavioralists accept that ecological fallacies can often occur when inferences about individual behavior are made from aggregated data. More important, however, the aim is not simply to obtain a more detailed picture of migration by focusing on individual flows and patterns, but rather to understand the individual decision-making process within a social psychological context. As a result, the behavioral approach to migration has emphasized such issues as information gathering and destination selection (Roseman 1983).

The attempt to focus on choice and decision-making in explaining migration has necessitated the development of a variety of behavioral concepts. Such concepts underline the interest in process rather than pattern and have expanded the range of traditional economic variables. For example, terms such as *action space* and *awareness space* have become accepted parts of the vocabulary for those investigating the process of residential search, and the concept of locational stress has been used to analyze the initial decision to move (Clark 1981b). In many respects, the contribution of the behavioral approach to the migration literature has been in the area of concept development, rather than in intensive empirical testing.

The concept of a cognitive map and the related process of cognitive mapping have particularly concerned behavioral geographers. Early in the present century Trowbridge (1913), in a paper addressing the cognition of direction, used the term *imaginary map*. This paper specifically focused on the cognitive representation of large-scale environments and implied that people possess spatial images of those environments. The term *cognitive map* itself was apparently coined by Tolman (1948).

His experimental data consisted of observations on rat behavior, but he believed that the results had significance for human behavior. In general, Tolman contended that during the learning process something akin to a field map of routes and paths becomes established in the rat's brain and that this map ultimately determines the rat's behavior.

A cognitive map represents, therefore, an individual's model of objective reality (Golledge and Stimson 1987:70). The use of the term *map*, however, is not meant to imply that our internal representations of the physical world are necessarily in cartographic form. Rather, the term indicates a functional analog, as the interest lies in a cognitive representation that has the functions of a cartographic map but not necessarily the physical properties of such a map (Downs 1981). In this respect, cognitive mapping refers to the process by which information about the spatial environment is organized, stored, recalled, and manipulated, while a cognitive map is simply the product of this process at any particular point in time (Downs and Stea 1977:6).

In general, cognitive maps contain two kinds of information that influence the decision-making process involved in migration. First, there is information concerning the location of places that is devoid of evaluative content. For example, work on the directional component of cognitive maps suggests that directional distortions can be analyzed by using the frame-of-reference concept employed in psychological investigations of the perception of verticality (Cadwallader 1977). Second, cognitive maps contain information concerning the value judgments we have about different places. That is, such maps can serve as a repository for our locational preferences and attitudes, the dynamic nature of which is reflected by various kinds of learning processes.

Despite its theoretical promise, the behavioral approach has been beset by difficulties. Behavioralists have postulated the importance of environmental images, but it has proved exceedingly difficult to capture and measure the properties of those images. For example, the form of the relationship between physical and cognitive distance is not independent of the methodology employed, while evidence of noncommututativity and intransitivity in distance estimates suggests that people do not possess internal representations of the environment that can be portrayed by Euclidean geometry (Cadwallader 1979b). Such calibration efforts are further confounded by aggregation problems. Although working at the level of individual data, behavioral researchers argue that there are significant similarities between individuals which can be used as a foundation for meaningful aggregation. The appropriate form and degree of aggregation, however, depends upon the type of behavior being analyzed.

The assumption that specific images can be legitimately extracted from the totality of such images has been seriously questioned (Bunting and Guelke 1979). Images are holistic, and the cognition of any particular environment or place is embedded within a set of cultural and ideological attitudes. It is exactly this kind of problem, however, that the empiricist tradition in cogitive psychology has attempted to address. A related problem involves the language of discourse. The categories traditionally used to characterize the real environment may have little relevance for the perceived environment.

Perhaps most important, criticisms of the behavioral approach have tended to focus on the implied assumption of subject-object separation (Cox 1981), the idea that the world can somehow be divided into an objective world of things and a subjective world of the mind, thus allowing the observer to be separate from the observed. Such a division is less critical, however, if one emphasizes the interrelationships between subject and object and stresses that cognitive representations are formed by transactions between the two. This viewpoint has given rise to a more humanistically oriented behavioral approach, focusing on human feelings and values, like the sense of place (Tuan 1977). Such an approach, however, with its illustrative use of facts and examples, is not easily integrated with the hypothesis-testing orientation of most research on migration. Rather, the humanist philosophy provides an important form of criticism that helps to counter some of the extreme abstractive tendencies of the positivist tradition (Entrikin 1976).

Because of its preoccupation with measurement and highly formalized methodology, the behavioral approach has sometimes been viewed as a mere appendage to the positivist tradition of neoclassical economics (Ley 1981). In all fairness, however, behavioral geographers never intended to produce a different disciplinary subfield, but rather to incorporate behavioral variables and concepts within the explanatory schema (Golledge 1981). Indeed, in many respects behavioral research has moved well beyond its original positivist underpinnings (Couclelis and Golledge 1983). With the recognition of mental reality as a primary objective of study, the tendency toward a reductionist philosophy of human behavior lost much of its impetus. The image of an objectively defined reality being passively observed by an impartial scientist has been replaced by an acceptance of the indivisibility of fact and value.

Like neoclassical economics, however, the behavioral approach is heavily oriented toward consumer preferences and the demand side of the economy. The behavioral viewpoint has thus been attacked for neglecting the societal constraints on individual human behavior. For example, it can be argued that an understanding of residential mobility cannot be divorced from a consideration of the urban housing market, as the operation of such a market provides the larger context for mobility (Short 1978). In particular, the demand and supply of housing are influenced by the interaction of various institutions. Indeed, the motives and behavior of these institutions, such as mortgage lending companies and real estate agents, constitute the subject matter of the institutional approach to migration and mobility. This approach thus provides a useful antidote to the consumer sovereignty implied by both neoclassical economics and the behavioral perspective.

The Institutional Approach

The institutional perspective emphasizes the effects of such institutions as governments, mortgage lending companies, and real estate agents on patterns of interregional migration and residential mobility (Flowerdew 1982). For example, McKay and Whitelaw (1977) argue that large private and governmental organizations are an important force in the generation of interregional migration flows in Australia and that the spatial structure of such organizations thus severely constrains the choices facing migrants. This approach, which is sometimes called the managerial perspective, referring to those individual actors who are primarily responsible for making the decisions that guide the behavior of the larger institutions they represent, was codified by Pahl (1969). He suggested that previous research had been preoccupied with understanding consumer choice, while giving insufficient attention to the associated constraints. As a result, he argued that research should emphasize the interplay of spatial and social constraints which determines the differential access to resources such as housing, education, and transportation. Moreover, he believed that these social constraints could be best understood by examining the activities and values of the so-called managers of the social system, including landowners, builders, real estate agents, and mortgage companies.

This kind of analysis owes a great deal to Weberian sociology, which emphasizes the motivations of individual "actors," or institutions, in various kinds of social systems. The issue of power was central to Weber's sociology, as conflicts inevitably arise when individual actors attempt to actualize their differing goals (Saunders 1981:123). Power emerges from the interrelationships between actors and is manifested when any one actor is able to realize his or her will over the opposition of others. This power over others is either economic or political in origin; unlike Marx, Weber argued that these two arenas of domination remain analytically distinct. Also unlike Marxist thought, the Weberian perspective identifies actors rather than classes as the basic units of analysis, and the Weberian notion of an ever-increasing bureaucracy lends confirmation to the growing importance of managers (Leonard 1982; Wilson 1989).

In the context of the urban housing market and residential mobility, the various managers of scarce resources include key actors from the spheres of finance capital, industrial capital, commercial capital, landed capital, and the public sector (Knox 1987:227). First, finance capital involves all the various savings and loan associations, banks, and mortgage companies that are involved in lending money for housing developments, purchases, and improvements. Such financial institutions play an important role in determining who lives where, as they regulate the flow of money into the housing market (Doling and Williams 1983; Murdie 1986). They often avoid neighborhoods perceived to have a high risk of declining property values, and the denial of funds to inner-city neighborhoods tends to encourage decay and stimulate decline. In its extreme form this practice is known as redlining (Darden 1980; Jones and Maclennan 1987) and involves financial institutions refusing to make mortgage funds available in certain parts of a city. In other circumstances, however, the policies of these financial institutions have revitalized inner-city areas by supporting the process of gentrification.

Second, industrial capital refers to builders and developers. Within the constraints of planning regulations, the decisions of various builders and developers greatly influence the type and quantity of housing supplied. The residential development process comprises three major stages: site selection, site preparation, and the housing construction itself (Baerwald 1981). While small companies tend to focus on the construction of single-family dwelling units on infill sites, the larger companies emphasize extensive suburban developments. Most new construction reflects the demands of upper-income groups, as they are most able to afford new housing. Low-income groups tend to obtain housing via the filtering of housing process, whereby older housing is successively passed down to lower-income families.

Third, commercial capital involves professionals such as real estate agents who are engaged in the market distribution of housing. Because they make a profit by charging for their services as coordinators between buyers and sellers, real estate agents tend to encourage turnover in the housing market. Also, as they are a major source of information concerning vacancies, real estate agents can introduce a deliberate bias by channeling households into or away from specific neighborhoods (Palm 1979). In particular, they have a tendency to overrecommend areas in which they list homes. In some situations, real estate agents, through their gatekeeping role, try to maintain the social status of a neighborhood. Perhaps the best example of this phenomenon is the discrimination based upon race and ethnicity (Brown 1972). In other situations, however, real estate agents can facilitate change, as when they stimulate the gentrification process by advising financial institutions to make money available for the purchase and rehabilitation of dilapidated property (Williams 1976).

Fourth, landed capital refers to landowners and landlords. Access to rented housing is considerably influenced by the gatekeeping activities of landlords, although the behavior of individual landlords is often based upon informal personal judgments rather than profit maximization policies, which characterize large corporate landlords (Elliot and McCrone 1975). Unlike home owners, however, landlords are primarily interested in exchange value rather than use value. Nevertheless, only in those situations where all landlords maintain or improve their properties will an individual landlord maximize the returns on his or her investment. For this reason, landlords often try to slightly underinvest relative to other landlords in the neighborhood, thus accelerating the deterioration of the housing stock. In areas experiencing gentrification, however, landlords are more likely to cooperate with each other to protect their mutual interests.

Fifth, various actors within the public sector influence the operation of the housing market. Governmental policies relating to both private- and public-sector housing are generally formulated at the national level but implemented at the local level. As a result, significant regional variation in the implementation of policy often exists (Murie, Niner, and Watson 1976:241). Harvey (1974) suggests that national governments tend to manage the housing sector in order to achieve three major goals: they attempt to maximize economic growth by ensuring an orderly relationship between construction rates and new household formation, they try to achieve economic stability by using the housing sector as a kind of Keynesian regulator, and the provision of housing is managed in such a way as to defuse social discontent.

There have been two major criticisms of the institutional, or managerial, perspective. First, managerialism should be considered a framework for study rather than a coherent theory (Williams 1978). An empirical object, managers, is the central focus of the analysis, rather than any theoretically derived social process. At worst, institutional analysis can degenerate into a mindless empiricism, involving exercises of gathering descriptive data on those individuals who are assumed to occupy important positions (Saunders 1979:168). There is little conceptual basis for the identification and selection of urban managers, and it is exceedingly difficult to assess their interrelationships and relative importance. It is especially difficult to isolate the management role in the private sector from the larger capitalist economic system. For example, real estate agents are both managers and capitalists. The distinction is somewhat easier to make in the public sector, as long as one is willing to accept a substantial degree of economic and political autonomy.

This latter issue, concerning the extent of autonomy in social systems, provides the basis for the second major criticism of managerialism. It has been repeatedly argued that managerialism should be related to more general theories concerning the political economy of cities in a capitalist society. To what extent do managers behave as independent units, and to what extent are they constrained by the overall socioeconomic structure within which they operate? While managers are responsible for the allocation of scarce resources, they are not responsible for creating scarcity in the first place (Bassett and Short 1980:52). It is only possible to interpret, rather than merely describe, the actions of managers by placing them within the larger political economy of which they are a part (Williams 1982). As a result, Marxists have tended to dismiss managerialism as merely diverting attention from more fundamental structural issues.

In this context it is possible to distinguish two stages in the development of the managerial perspective. Initially, Pahl (1969) seemed to suggest that managers could be analyzed as autonomous units; he saw managers as the independent variables in the explanation of any given pattern of resource distribution. In later analyses, however, he viewed managers more as intervening variables, mediating between the pressures of private profit and public welfare and between the central government and local populations (Pahl 1979). This later conceptualization stresses the danger of ascribing too much independent authority to the managers of the system, while at the same time recognizing that the peripheral agents of a centralized state inevitably enjoy a certain amount of discretion in policy implementation. The extent of this autonomy is still unresolved, however, and the kinds of circumstances under which managers might be expected to exercise significant discretion remain unclear. In any event, there is a need to consider the underlying socioeconomic and political structure of society. As a result, the political economy approach has become increasingly popular in recent years.

Political Economy

Woods (1985) suggests that any general theory of migration needs to include at least two major elements: the structural context and the behavioral response. The term *structural context* refers to the economic and material circumstances of a society, including its political and legal framework. Behavior, in this case migration, is conditioned, although not determined, by this structural context. The theoretical importance of such an underlying structure is also suggested by Fielding (1985), who discusses the relationship between migration and the new spatial division of labor. It is in this context, then, that an increasing number of scholars have turned to Marxist theories of political economy, in order to explicitly relate migration patterns to the wider organization of society. Such scholars contend that all social phenomena are inextricably linked to the prevailing mode of production, so that any understanding of contemporary migration patterns in the United States, for example, cannot be divorced from an analysis of the capitalist mode of production.

In particular, migration patterns within cities, as represented by such processes as suburbanization and gentrification, have been interpreted via the theme of capital accumulation. Harvey (1978) articulates this framework by identifying three circuits of capital. The primary circuit of capital is involved in production, and the tendency toward overaccumulation is manifested in a number of ways: the overproduction of commodities relative to consumption rates, a falling rate of profit, and surplus capital. These problems encourage capital to switch to the secondary and tertiary circuits. The secondary circuit involves fixed capital investment and consumption funds, while the tertiary sector comprises investment in research and technology and expenditures on a wide range of social needs, such as education and health, which facilitate the reproduction of labor power. Within the secondary circuit a certain proportion of capital flows into the urban built environment, thus providing the necessary physical infrastructure for production and consumption through the creation of factories, houses, and roads. The flow of capital into the secondary circuit and the associated investment in long-term assets are dictated by the rhythms of capital accumulation in the primary circuit, whereby periodic crises of overaccumulation lead to surpluses of both capital and labor. Investment in the built environment, however, is also related to the physical and economic life expectancy of the building stock. Thus the switch of capital from the primary to the secondary sector is manifested by cycles of building activity, which tend to exhibit a fifteen- to twenty-five-year periodicity.

Suburbanization, according to Walker (1981), is an example of capital switching from the primary to the secondary circuit. The underconsumption problems of the 1930s were at least partly alleviated by massive suburban development, which generated a wide range of investment possibilities in single-family housing and related consumer items such as washing machines, refrigerators, and cars. Governmental intervention actively stimulated this process through Federal Housing Administration mortgage subsidies and the construction of highways. As Castells (1977:388) has observed, the single-family home in the suburbs became the perfect vehicle for maximizing capitalist consumption. This explanation of suburbanization thus reflects the underconsumptionist perspective of Baran and Sweezy (1966), who stress the importance of the suburbs in absorbing economic surplus and emphasize the role of the state in encouraging car ownership and owner-occupied housing.

As might be expected, however, Marxists claim that the suburbanization process contains within it a series of contradictions and can only be a short-term solution to the crises associated with capital accumulation. The political power of the suburbs, built as a response to the underconsumption problems of the 1930s, is now being used to inhibit growth and thus resist the further accumulation of capital in the built environment (Harvey 1975). In other words, after initially being a vehicle for capital accumulation, the suburbs have become a barrier to further accumulation. Redevelopment in the suburbs will not occur until previously invested capital has lived out its economic usefulness. As Harvey (1978) expresses it, capitalist development is continually faced with the problem of preserving the exchange values of past investments in the built environment while at the same time having to destroy the value of those investments to make room for further development and accumulation.

Viewed in this light, inner-city gentrification is merely a continuation of the forces and relations that led to suburbanization. In general, the logic behind uneven development suggests that the development of any area tends to create barriers to further development but that the ensuing underdevelopment then creates opportunities for a new round of development. Thus gentrificaiton involves a particular phase in what Smith (1982) has called the "locational seesaw," through which capital jumps from one place to another and then back again. In other words, capital investment undergoes locational switching as well as sectoral switching. Given these arguments concerning the role of capital in urban restructuring and its associated migration patterns, it is worthwhile to consider in some detail the nature of Marxist theories of political economy.

Marx argued that social science should penetrate the realm of appearances in order to uncover the underlying relations that give rise to those appearances. He suggested that classical economists obscured the distinctions between social appearances and social reality by concentrating on so-called objective laws governing commodity exchange within market economies. In contrast, he attempted to explore the structures of different modes of production by emphasizing the interrelationships between a variety of theoretical entities that are not themselves directly observable. In pursuing the nature of these interrelationships, Marx stressed that no single aspect of reality can be analyzed independent of the social system of which it is a part. His commitment to dialectical analysis, with its concern for the perpetual resolution of opposites in which each resolution generates its own contradiction, made him extremely suspicious of any mode of analysis that failed to relate the part to the whole. Thus Marx never treated any concept as fixed; rather each concept was reinterpreted when juxtaposed with other concepts. In other words, the relationships between the concepts are what really count (Harvey 1982:2). Thus, according to Marx, our insights shift as we successively probe different conceptual relationships; in contrast, the building-block approach of much contemporary social science isolates and scrutinizes individual components of the overall system before making them fixed foundations for further inquiry.

In particular, Marxists argue that social phenomena result from the prevailing mode of production, the way in which societies organize their productive activities. The mode of production is an analytical construct comprising the productive forces (labor, resources, and instruments of labor) and the associated social relations of production. The social relations of production are embodied in class conflict between those controlling the means of production and the laborers. Latent contradictions within any particular mode of production are periodically manifested as crises, and these crises eventually result in a transition from one mode of production to another. Historically, four successive modes of production, with their associated social relations, have been identified: primitive communism, slavery, feudalism, and capitalism. Within the capitalist mode of production, the means of production are controlled by a capitalist class, or bourgeoisie, and carried out by a class of wage earners, or proletariat. The economic structure of a society, as represented by its particular mode of production, provides the basis for a superstructure of social, political, and legal forms.

According to Marx, the need for capital accumulation governs capitalist behavior. This rule, enforced by competition between capitalists, is the hallmark of individual behavior. The extraction of surplus value from labor generates the process of capital accumulation. Much of this capital is recycled into new production, thus expanding the bases of production, as there are limits to conspicuous consumption on the part of capitalists. Only if the proletariat has the purchasing power to consume what is produced, however, will the capitalist be able to realize surplus value in money form. Capitalists must realize their profits in this way in order to keep employing labor and producing.

Marxists argue, however, that the insatiable quest for capital accumulation creates conditions that are inconsistent with the further accumulation of capital and the reproduction of class relations. In other words, the capitalist system is inherently unstable and subject to periodic crises. Three such crises deserve particular attention. First, a basic contradiction exists between the pressure to increase surplus value by maintaining low wages and the need for people to buy products so that the surplus value can be realized. If workers cannot afford new appliances, cars, and homes, an underconsumption, or realization, crisis will occur. Capitalists must pay sufficient wages to ensure that the working class possesses the effective demand needed to reproduce itself, but individual capitalists are forced to compete continually with each other and thus keep wages at a minimum.

Second, a decline in the rate of profit can occur due to the substitution of machinery for labor, thus reducing the rate of surplus value derived from labor and increasing unemployment, which further exacerbates the aforementioned underconsumption crisis. Capitalists tend to substitute capital for labor in order to compete more effectively with their fellow capitalists, so the basic process of technological innovation tends to undermine the stability of the capitalist system. Individual capitalists, acting in their own self-interest under the social relations of capitalist production, generate a technological mix that threatens further accumulation and the reproduction of the capitalist class. In short, individual capitalists necessarily act in a way that destabilizes capitalism (Harvey 1982:188).

Third, these inherent contradictions within the capitalist system lead to various forms of state intervention and associated fiscal crises. Public spending is often needed to cope with the by-products of accumulation, such as urban congestion, pollution, and social tensions. Labor is diverted to sectors which, although they provide employment, do not effect any increase in the production of surplus value. A number of commodities, such as streets, subway systems, and bridges, are directly produced by the state in order to take advantage of various economies of scale. State intervention in providing such large-scale items of collective consumption and various kinds of social services helps to maintain, temporarily at least, the capitalist system. Class struggle is regulated by appeasing labor with employment and economic concessions, while at the same time combating underconsumption crises.

A variety of important criticisms have been leveled at Marxist theory. First, although many varieties of contemporary Marxist discourse exist (Agnew and Duncan 1981), one of the most pervasive criticisms of the Marxist tradition concerns its commitment to some form of economic determinancy. Duncan and Ley (1982), for example, charge that to reduce the range of social experience to the surficial manifestations of some underlying economic structure is to present an excessively impoverished view of the social, cultural, and political realms of life. Some neo-Marxists have attempted to distance themselves from what Gregory (1981) has called "brute economic determinism" by emphasizing the variety of social formations that can be associated with a dominant mode of production. For example, as history has demonstrated, there is the potential for a good deal of cultural, institutional, and political variation under capitalism. Also, Marxists recognize that at any particular moment in history we are likely to find, alongside a dominant mode of production, the remains of previous modes and the beginnings of future modes. Marxists continue to contend, however, that, although a variety of political structures can coexist within a given form of economic structure, it is the economic structure, as represented by the mode of production, that has causal primacy (Wright 1983). In contrast, critics of the Marxist tradition suggest that the developmental tendencies of economic and political structures are autonomous, in the sense that no general principles govern their interconnection (Giddens 1981). In any specific historical situation, either one could be the major force behind social change, but there is no general priority of one over the other.

Second, Marxist analysis can be criticized for its functionalist approach to constructing social theory. Functionalism, a type of holistic explanation, views societies as composed of individual parts that both form and maintain the whole. In other words, various properties of society are explained by their functions within the social totality. Systems analysis is often invoked within this context, as it captures the interrelationships between the various elements of the total system. Harvey (1973:289), for example, espouses a functionalist viewpoint when he suggests that capitalism shapes the elements and relationships within itself in order to reproduce itself as an ongoing system. The Achilles' heel of the functionalist perspective, however, is that it falsely imputes "needs" to social systems. For example, Marxists often explain state policy as a response to the need for capital accumulation or unemployment as a result of the need of capitalism for a reserve army of labor. While functional descriptions may serve a useful purpose in social theory, the functionality of a given institution can only provide a partial explanation of that institution.

Third, Marxism often involves a reification of a priori categories. Reification occurs when mental contructs or abstractions are viewed as substantive phenomena with causal properties. Such constructs are often initially used as mere heuristic devices but later take on more concrete characteristics; hence reification has sometimes been called the fallacy of misplaced concreteness. Marxist social theory has tended to reify such abstract concepts as capitalism, mode of production, the state, and class. For example, the mode of production is seen as a driving force behind the development of social formations, or capitalism is described as maturing. Such statements suggest that these abstract, intellectual concepts, or categorizations, somehow have an independent existence of their own.

Fourth, and related to the problem of reification, Marxism can also be criticized for its dependence on evolutionary thinking. Societies are viewed as evolving through different modes of production, with their associated social relations. Giddens (1981) argues, however, that no empirical evidence exists that the forces of production develop throughout history; thus the mode of production cannot form the basis for a general trajectory of historical development. Moreover, societies do not have transhistorical imperatives to adapt to their material resources. Societies are not organisms, and it is dangerous to view them as evolving in the manner of biological organisms. In the extreme, theories of social evolution are sometimes grounded in teleological arguments, involving the inexorable development toward some kind of adaptively optimal end state. As an alternative to this implied succession of societies in a given sequence of stages, it might be more useful to view social change as involving a set of qualitatively distinct transitions that overlap and have no overall pattern of development.

Fifth, a standard criticism of Marxism is that it represents a class reductionist theory. Most Marxists retain a commitment to constructing an overall theory of historical development which revolves around the genesis and contradictions of class relations. Types of social formations are primarily rooted in the concept of class structure, which is itself based on the concept of mode of production. It is potentially misleading, however, to classify societies primarily by class structure, as societies are characterized by multiple forms of domination and exploitation which cannot be reduced to the single principle of class (Parkin

1979). Indeed, it could be argued that at present the principal form of domination is by the state apparatus over its citizens, as best exemplified by many Marxist states (J. Duncan 1985). Similarly, Giddens (1981:242) argues that the relations between states, ethnic groups, and races all form alternative axes of exploitation. Following from this, Giddens (1981:108) makes an important distinction between class society, in which class is the central structural principle, and class-divided society, in which there are merely classes. Marxists have tended to respond to this argument by accepting that there are various nonclass forms of domination, such as those based on race and gender, but by reemphasizing that class relations most deeply structure society and generate constraints under which individual actors are forced to operate (Wright 1983). Thus, no matter how people conceive their own identities, Marxists continue to assert that one's most basic identity is as a member of a particular class. As a result, it has been argued that Marxism tends to distort contemporary class relations "by underemphasizing the crucial divisions within the working class, by oversimplifying the cleavages between different classes, by inflating class awareness into class consciousness, and by conflating the articulated ideologies of activists with the unarticulated world views of those they claim to represent" (Saunders and Williams 1986:398).

Sixth, within the context of class structure, Marxists have been criticized for their simplistic distinction between the bourgeoisie and the proletariat. One can argue that during the twentieth century there has been a growing interpenetration of the labor and capitalist classes. Workers have begun to join the owning class by purchasing shares in companies and thus deriving a part of their income from profits. It would be unfair to suggest, however, that Marxists have not been at least partially sensitive to the complexity of class structure. Harvey (1982:26–27, 74) notes that Marx began to disaggregate the capitalist class into separate strata: financial capitalists who live entirely off the interest on their money capital, landlords who live off the rent of land, merchant capitalists who circulate commodities, and industrial capitalists who organize the production of surplus value. Moreover, Harvey (1982:450) reminds us that class configurations should not be assumed a priori; rather, they are being constantly reproduced and thus take on particular manifestations at particular points in time and space.

Finally, structural Marxism in particular has tended to generate a passive model of the human being that underestimates the processes by which people change their economic and social environments. Even Harvey (1982:114) concedes that Marx himself tended to subjugate the authenticity of experience to the revelatory power of theory, thus underestimating the subjective dimensions of class struggle. As a result, a number of contemporary Marxists have recently begun to emphasize the role of human agency. Castells (1983), for example, suggests that Marxism has been unable to comprehend urban social movements because of its inability to accommodate the scope for human action in history. By way of criticizing his previous work, Castells admits that the Althusserian form of structural Marxism encourages researchers to interpret social findings in accordance with a preexisting theoretical system. It is this recognition of the complex interplay between structure and agency that suggests the more balanced approach to which we now turn.

Structure and Agency

Social theorists have recently been consumed by the debate concerning the relative importance of social structure and human agency, or what Gregory (1981) refers to as action and structure. In the extreme, society can be viewed as either conditioning all human activity, as in structural determinism, or as the product of unconstrained human action, as in voluntarism. It would be inappropriate, however, to view any social theory as completely embracing either of these two perspectives in their most exaggerated forms. Rather, most social theories are a mixture of both dimensions and are best represented as points along a continuum. Thus, in migration research, care must be taken to consider the interplay between structure and agency, in the sense not only of spatial structure (Clark 1972) but also of the larger social, economic, and political structure of a given society.

Giddens (1979) has proposed the most elaborate theory to date of social structure and human agency, in which social structures are viewed as both the medium and the outcome of the practices which constitute social systems. This theory of structuration is built around a concept of the duality of structure and agency (rather than a dualism), which emphasizes the recursive relationship between individuals and society. Social structure and human agency are combined in such a way that structure is not merely a barrier to action but is actively reproduced by that action. Thus social practices are constituted by social structures and also produce those structures. In other words, structure is created by human action, while at the same time being the medium of that action, with "the accumulation of previous decisions creating the framework within which future decisions are made" (Johnston 1984:483). Thus determinist and voluntarist approaches are dialectically synthesized, and in this way structuration theory provides a possible mode of analysis for transcending the debate about whether the social formation or individual human agency should be the ultimate basis of explanation.

Structuration theory also entails a number of other related postulates, or axioms (Johnston 1983:104–5). First, agency and structure are temporally and spatially specific; societies and the individuals that form societies are uniquely located within a particular configuration of time and space. Structuration is therefore concerned with the connections between structure and agency during specific periods, at specific places. Second, human agency is constrained by social structures; humans produce society, but only as historically located actors, not under conditions of their own choosing. Third, structures are not simply conceptualized as constraints, as they also enable human agency. Thus structure both constrains and enables, while simultaneously being reproduced and transformed by individuals.

This proposed marriage of structure and agency entails certain problems, however (Thrift 1983). First, the notion of determination is not clearly specified, and unless one endorses a conception of the absolute randomness of society, social theory must involve some form of determination, whether it be based on the mode of production, individual behavior, or some more complex combination acknowledging the capacities of a bounded human agency. Second, there is no currently acceptable theory of social action that can be incorporated within the structurationist framework. Such a theory is exceedingly difficult to generate, as the reasons an actor gives for an action are not necessarily the real ones. Third, a theory of structuration must explicitly articulate how social structure is inextricably interwoven with spatial and temporal structure (Giddens 1985). Fourth, as presently conceived, the synthesizing characteristic of structuration theory means that it is somewhat uncomfortably situated on several theoretical interfaces, such as Marxist and Weberian sociology, and is thus open to charges of theoretical eclecticism (Moos and Dear 1986).

Moreover, it is one thing to appreciate the elegance and richness of structuration theory, but quite another to use it in substantive contexts. As yet, only a very limited amount of empirical work has been carried out within the guidelines provided by structuration theory (Gregson 1986). In particular, empirical work is hampered by the need to preserve the recursive nature of the structure-agency duality; it is difficult to know how to cut into the data without emphasizing one side at the expense of the other. A structurationist explanation must attempt to balance structure and agency, without according a priori primacy to either side (Smith 1983; Duncan 1988). In reality, however, attention has been focused on examples of voluntarism and determinism, which are then simply clamped together in a form of a conceptual vise (Archer 1982).

Thus far, perhaps the best application of structuration theory has been provided by Dear and Moos (1986), who explored the ghettoiza-tion of former psychiatric patients in Hamilton, Ontario. Throughout their analysis, they took great care to explicitly focus on the interaction of structure and agency, without resorting to simply welding together two separate investigations. Neither agency nor structure was accorded primary ontological status, and Gidden's (1984:326) advice that the concepts of structuration theory be regarded primarily as sensitizing devices was duly followed. Although a variety of problems remain, such as the designation of "ideal types" in the context of agent and institutional categories, Dear and Moos managed to convey the im-pression that the empirical application of structuration theory can in-deed generate a set of substantive insights that might not otherwise be obtained. The nagging doubt persists, however, that structuration the-ory provides no clear and unambiguous rules of interpretation. Crite-ria for determining the adequacy of a given explanation, or for gener-alizing results, are simply not provided.

Resolution of the structure-agency debate partly entails construct-ing viable theories of the state within capitalist society. Almost all aspects of production and consumption are now profoundly influenced, either directly or indirectly, by state policies at the local, regional, national, and international levels. It is scarcely surprising, therefore, that re-searchers have devoted a great deal of time to constructing viable theo-ries of the state within capitalist society (Johnston 1982a). Definitions of the term *state* vary. Miliband (1969) suggests that the term stands for a number of institutions, including the government, the judiciary, and the police. Harvey (1976), on the other hand, conceptualizes the state as a process for the exercise of power, rather than as a circumscribable entity.

As one might expect, many theories of the state exist (Jessop 1982). Perhaps most simply, the state has been viewed as a supplier of public goods and services and as a mechanism for regulating and facilitating the operation of the market economy. The state can also be seen as taking on the role of arbiter in disputes between different interest groups. Marx himself did not develop any rigorous theory of the cap-italist state, but neo-Marxists have made a number of important contri-butions during the past two decades, ranging from the instrumentalist model, involving the implied conspiracy between the ruling class and the state, through the structuralist perspective, which suggests that the functions of the state are determined by the structure of society itself rather than by a few key people within that society. Clark and Dear (1984:33) make a persuasive argument for a materialist theory of the state, in which the state is viewed as an actor in its own right, while at the same time being embedded in the social relations of capitalism.

These theories are by no means mutually exclusive, however, and there is considerable consensus concerning the general role of the state in capitalist society. The state provides a framework for exchange, while guaranteeing property rights and facilitating social reproduction by providing housing, education, health care, and social services. It regulates competition by various antitrust laws and regulates the employment of labor through legislation on minimum wages and maximum hours of employment. The state also undertakes the production of public goods, such as roads and bridges, that are necessary for capitalist production and exchange but which individual capitalists are unable to provide at a profit. Finally, the state acts as a legitimator of the capitalist mode of production (Johnston 1984). It protects a particular set of production relations by propagating an ideology that emphasizes business enterprise and profit maximization.

Finally, the issue of empirical verification is of critical importance to the structure-agency debate, as well as to contemporary social science in general. Any analysis of migration must be sensitive to the complex relationship between theory and data. No data are independent of a priori conceptual formulations; while observation is neither theory-neutral nor theory-determined, it is certainly theory-laden (Sayer 1984:78). As a result, empirical observations cannot be the sole adjudicator between competing theories, and empirical verification should not be regarded as a peculiarly privileged form of verification (Sheppard 1988). Thus social theory sits uneasily within Karl Popper's system of falsification and refutation, lacking the controlled experimental situations in which to truly test the correspondence between theoretical propositions and empirical measurements (Chouinard, Fincher, and Webber 1984). All research programs involving migration face similar problems in evaluating theory via empirical research, as the relations between postulated causal mechanisms and expected empirical outcomes are always muted or disguised by the presence of uncontrolled external factors.

Despite these problems, however, we should be committed to constructing theories of migration that are empirically grounded. Failure to do so leaves us susceptible to tautological reasoning. Structural Marxists have been particularly criticized in this context. Saunders (1981) argues that they postulate universal tendencies, such as a declining rate of profit, but merely invoke counteracting tendencies, or contingencies, if such a tendency does not occur. Thus structural Marxists claim to identify inderlying mechanisms in society but are suspicious of any attempt to empirically validate these claims, on the grounds that contengent factors may be in operation. At the extreme, this viewpoint implies that because we cannot know the world directly, empirical research has little significance, and in those situations where theoretical concepts and categories are imposed on historical reality, that reality becomes merely illustrative, rather than contributing to the creation of theory. This friction between abstract theorizing and empirical research has been characterized as a tension between the universal and the concrete (Spencer 1977). Most contemporary social scientists are sensitive to this problem and accept the need to explore the intersection between theoretical abstractions and actual historical configurations. Harvey (1983:xiv), for example, notes that Marxist theory should not be regarded as correct and sacrosanct but should be continually modified through a thorough testing against the historical record. He urges Marxists to bridge the gap between the abstract theorists and those wishing to reconstruct the complex historical geographies of actual social formations (Harvey 1982:450).

On the other hand, the inherent problems of intertwining theory and observation should not encourage us to retreat to the atheoretical posture that has characterized so much migration research. Massey's (1985:19) observation that "the unique is back on the agenda" does not represent a call for concentrating on the uniqueness of events but reflects a concern for theoretically informed investigations of specific localities. In this respect, the knife-edge we are attempting to negotiate, between what Johnston (1985:335) has called the generalization trap and the singularity trap, is a fine one. While there are obvious limitations to excessively abstract theorizing, there are equally obvious limitations to narrow, empirical case studies. Theorizing devoid of empirical content should not be replaced by mindless empiricism.

In recent years realism has become an increasingly popular methodological stance for mediating between theory and observation (Sayer 1984, 1985). Such an approach distinguishes between necessary and contingent relations and argues that abstract theory pertains to necessary relations while observed geographic patterns are the product of localized contingent relations that mute and obfuscate the underlying mechanisms. That is, general causes can, through the presence of localized contingencies, produce different outcomes in different places. Thus realism treats laws as tendencies, rather than as empirical regularities, and in so doing emphasizes the need to view theory as conceptualization (Sayer 1984:49). In this context, social scientists are admonished to unpack their so-called chaotic conceptions. For example, Urry (1987) suggests that the occupational characterization of the service sector is problematic, as it contains a wide variety of rather diverse and distinctive activities which deserve to be disentangled.

The realist approach, however, tends to shelter theory from the possibility of empirical disconfirmation, as it insists on distinguishing between so-called real causal mechanisms and mere phenomenal appearances. In this way, causuality can only be determined theoretically, and emprical research is reduced to the role of illustrating theory, as opposed to evaluating or reconstructing that theory. As expressed by Saunders and Williams (1986:395), "the 'necessities' are simply asserted while the catchall category of 'contingency' is used to mop up all the problems." Similarly, within Gidden's (1984) conceptualization of structuration theory, the dialogue between theory and observation also tends to be one-way. While theory is used to sensitize empirical research, there is apparently no place for the interrogation of theory through empirical application (Gregson 1987). We need to be able to move backward and forward between the theoretical and the empirical, such that each activity sheds light on the other.

Thus a position of theoretical pluralism seems justified. In their less extreme forms, different approaches can be informed by each other. Attempts to emphasize the complementarity of different approaches, as expressed here and elsewhere (Johnston 1980, 1982b), however, should not be portrayed as encouraging the search for a single universal theory. Rather, as Dear (1986:295) has stated: "Theoretical analysis in social science does not aim to resolve inter-theory conflicts in favour of one grand theory; instead, it deliberately maintains the creative tension between theories." While preserving this creative tension between different theoretical perspectives, however, we should not underestimate the areas of overlap between them (Sayer 1984:68). In this context, we need to be able to move between structure, institution, and human agency, while at the same time maintaining an appropriate and mutually reinforcing balance between theory and observation. In other words, both macro- and micro-level approaches must be involed in the explanation of migration phenomena.

Macro and Micro Approaches

Many exhortations for theory development have suggested that a synthesis of macro and micro approaches is most likely to provide a unified, yet flexible, theoretical framework for investigating migration

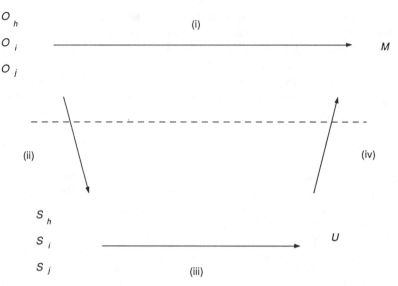

Figure 1.2. A conceptual framework for linking macro- and micro-level approaches to migration.
Source: Cadwallader 1989a:fig. 1.

behavior (Woods 1982:157). In many respects, this line of reasoning parallels the structure-agency debate, with its consideration of the inter-action between large-scale socioeconomic landscapes and individual decision-making. Within this context, the present author has con-structed a theoretical schema that provides an example of how macro- and micro-level work on migration might be most usefully integrated (Cadwallader 1989a). Such a framework can be used to locate a variety of research questions that have previously only been related in a rather ad hoc fashion. In addition, the gaps in our present knowledge and the potential areas of future research can be more easily identified.

The proposed framework contains four major sets of relationships (fig. 1.2). First, the so-called objective variables O_h, O_i, and O_j can be combined in various ways to explain overt migration behavior M. Thus the first link represents the traditional macro, or aggregated approach to modeling migration patterns. Second, the objective variables are transformed, through the individual cognitions of potential migrants, into their subjective counterparts S_h, S_i, and S_j. Third, the subjective variables are combined to form an overall measure of attractiveness U that allows potential migrants to choose between alternative destina-tions. Fourth, subject to certain constraints, the individual utility func-tions are translated into overt behavior. Note that the links below the broken line represent the behavioral perspective, which attempts to shed light on the factors that intervene between the objective variables and migration behavior.

This schema is similar to that used in psychology (Anderson 1974), in which the two major conceptions of an organism are explicated. The top part of the diagram would represent a behaviorist view, in which a set of physical stimuli impinge on the organism to produce an overt response, thus generating a physical law that relates the observable response to the observable stimuli. A more cognitive conception is contained within the lower part of the diagram where unobservables within the organism become a legitimate part of the conceptualization. A psychophysical law is used to describe the ways in which the physical stimuli produce subjective representations within the organism, a psychological law describes how these subjective values are combined to produce an implicit response, and a so-called psychomotor law addresses the relationship between this implicit response and the overt response. Louviere (1982) has commented on the appropriateness of this overall framework as a paradigm for research into spatial behavior in general.

The explication of this framework involves an examination of the following four relationships:

$$M = f(O_h, O_i, O_j) \tag{1.1}$$

$$S_h = X(O_h) \tag{1.2}$$

$$U = \phi(S_h, S_i, S_j) \tag{1.3}$$

$$M = Z(U) \tag{1.4}$$

where M is overt migration behavior; O_h, O_i and O_j are objectively measured attributes of regions or neighborhoods; S_h, S_i, and S_j are their subjectively measured counterparts; and U is the overall attractiveness associated with any region or neighborhood.

Most explorations of equation 1.1 have involved the estimation of single-equation regression models, whereby a set of regional characteristics, such as wage rates and unemployment levels, are used to predict migration rates for various kinds of spatial units, such as states or cities. Distance has tended to play a prominent role in such models, although there is considerable debate about whether a purely "friction-of-distance" effect can ever be satisfactorily isolated (Sheppard 1984). These single-equation models are discussed in Chapter 2, but they are often unsatisfactory, in that they fail to reflect the mutual interaction between the characteristics of regions and their associated migration patterns. For this reason, a simultaneous equation approach, as discussed in Chapter 3, is generally preferable.

Following the lead of psychophysics, the transformation represented by equation 1.2 is usually expressed by using some kind of power function. For example, it is generally agreed that the relationship between cognitive distance and physical distance is best represented by a power function (Baird, Wagner, and Noma 1982) and is thus similar to the psychophysical law relating the strength of an external stimulus to an individual's impression of the subjective intensity of that simulus. This relationship has been shown to hold for a variety of directly perceivable stimuli, such as brightness and loudness, as well as for stimuli that cannot be directly perceived, such as the relatipnship between perceived status and annual income (Stevens 1975). In noting the similarity in the results obtained using both perception and cognitive data, Thorndyke (1981) has suggested an analogy between the perceptual and cognitive processes of distance estimation. In particular, he postulates that subjects perceptually scan a route, or an image of a route, and then estimate the distance according to the time taken to complete that scan.

A growing number of researchers have begun to investigate explicitly the interrelationships between the objectively and subjectively measured attributes of places (Pacione 1982). Knox and MacLaran (1978), in a study based on Dundee, Scotland, assessed the compatibility between objective and subjective indicators of well-being. Although there was some overlap between the objective and subjective indicators, only one-third of the correlations between the two were statistically significant, and one-sixth of the correlations were negative. These results indicate, then, that the relationships between objective and subjective variables are exceedingly complex. The correspondence between objective and subjective measures of the same phenomenon can vary from a very strong relationship to a comparatively weak one, and in the present absence of appropriate transformations, it has been suggested that subjective attributes should be regarded as independent sources of explanation in migration models, not merely as dependent variables of objective attributes (Todd 1982).

Information levels and personality traits are among the factors that have been investigated in order to help disentangle the interrelationships between objective and subjective variables. Using data from Swedish schoolchildren, Gould (1975a) concluded that the configuration of information surfaces could be satisfactorily accounted for by a gravity model formulation. Similar results have also been reported when measurements were made concerning the accuracy of information, rather than just the quantity (Webber, Symanski, and Root 1975). In regard to personality traits, both Sonnenfeld (1976) and Taylor (1979) have suggested that personal dispositions might be useful explanatory variables in the analysis of human spatial behavior. For example, Walmsley's (1982) evidence indicates that introverts and extroverts differ in their residential preferences for different parts of eastern Australia. Apparently introverts prefer inland, temperate, and settled areas, whereas extroverts perfer wilderness areas, costal resorts, and large cities. The author himself notes, however, that the extremely small sample size prevents his drawing any general conclusions.

The integrative function involved in equation 1.3 is especially difficult to disentangle, as one is attempting to algebraically describe the combination rule by which individuals act as if they integrate various items of information in order to evaluate some stimuli. A variety of integrative functions are possible, and the following three are representative:

$$U_{ak} = \sum_{l=1}^{n} S_{alk} \tag{1.5}$$

$$U_{ak} = \sum_{l=1}^{n} S_{alk} W_{lk} \tag{1.6}$$

$$U_{ak} = \prod_{l=1}^{n} S_{alk} \tag{1.7}$$

where U_{ak} is the overall attractiveness of region a for individual k, S_{alk} is the attractiveness rating of region a on attribute l for individual k, and W_{lk} is the relative importance of attribute l for individual k. These equations represents additive, weighted additive, and multiplicative forms, respectively.

Much of the recent experimental work suggests that multiplicative forms, or related algebraic forms, are the dominant integrative function associated with spatial choice, although in the case of residential preferences there is perhaps insufficient evidence to disconfirm additivity (Louviere 1978). Unlike the multiplicative version, the additive and weighted additive formulations are examples of compensatory models, in which low ratings on one attrribute can be compensated for by high ratings on another attribute. In general, additive models perform well whenever the predictor variables are monotonically related to the dependent variable (Dawes and Corrigan 1974).

Finally, equation 1.4 represents the translation of preferences into overt behavior. The often-found disparity between preferences and behavior could simply imply that people are inconsistent in their behavior or that currently available techniques are inappropriate vehicles for eliciting true attitudes (Pipkin 1981). More important, however, a series of constraints are in operation that inhibit the behavioral manifestation of underlying preferences. Such constraints make it exceedingly difficult to isolate underlying preferences by observing overt behavior. Rather, migration patterns are a complex balance of preferences and constraints. Indeed, the observed discrepancies, or residuals, associated with the relationship between preferences and behavior enable us to speculate on the nature and extent of the constraints in any specific situation (Desbarats 1977).

The constraints that operate within the context of migration involve obstacles that produce attitude-discrepant behavior in three major ways: by restricting the opportunity set, by influencing the formation of preferences, or by preventing choice actualization (Desbarats 1983b). These constraints can be either individual or institutional in their origin. For example, at the individual level, a potential migrant's income will obviously restrict where he or she can live, regardless of underlying preferences. Similarly, the location of the individual's workplace is a constraining influence on residential choice (Reitsma and Vergoossen 1988; Long 1988:236). Individuals are also constrained by the amount of information they possess concerning potential destinations, as choice set formation is a function of location. The expected relationship between information levels and migrational search behavior has been well documented (W. A. V. Clark 1982a).

At the instituional level, the urban housing market provides an excellent laboratory for investigating the constraints that are generated by various kinds of institutions. Real estate agents, banks, and savings and loan associations all regulate the flow of information and mortgage money into the housing market. In addition, both national and local governments seek to influence migration patterns as a means of achieving various policy goals (Clark 1983). Such influence is usually indirect, involving policies designed to create a more desirable distribution of population. For example, tax incentives can be used to attract business and industry to less-developed regions. Similarly, the distribution of new highways and defense contracts can also exert an indirect influence on migration patterns. More direct governmental intervention is involved in such projects as the provision of public housing in cities.

The balance between choice and constraints has been most fully explored within the context of ethnic migration and segregation (Jackson and Smith 1981). Social geographers, in particular, have engaged in a prolonged debate concerning the role of voluntary and discriminatory forces in the maintenance of ethnic neighborhoods. It is exceedingly difficult to explain segregation purely as a result of discrimination, but the current focus on a simple dichotomy between choice and constraints is probably inadequate to unravel the complex interplay between social and physical space. It has been suggested that the choice-constraint concept might be more usefully formulated within a Marxist framework, whereby a broader societal analysis would take precedence over the present empirical emphasis (K. Brown 1981).

Returning to the overall framework, the behavioral component of this conceptual schema, as represented by equations 1.2, 1.3, and 1.4, is especially susceptible to a sequential series of analyses. For example, if we have a set of three objectively measured variables, with subjective counterparts, and we are postulating an additive integrative function, then we might expect the following succession of relationships:

$$S_{ahk} = a_1 O_{ahk}^{b_1} \tag{1.8}$$

$$S_{aik} = a_2 O_{aik}^{b_2} \tag{1.9}$$

$$S_{ajk} = a_3 O_{ajk}^{b_3} \tag{1.10}$$

$$U_{ak} = S_{ahk} + S_{aik} + S_{ajk} \tag{1.11}$$

$$M_{ak} = a_4 + b_4 U_{ak} \tag{1.12}$$

where the notation is the same as in equations 1.1–1.7.

It should be noted, however, that a variety of assumptions are associated with this theoretical structure. First, it is assumed that the development of aggregated models relating overt behavior and objectively measured variables might obscure significant intermediate relationships. Second, it is assumed, as in much contemporary choice theory, that potential migrants do not evaluate regions, neighborhoods, or houses per se, but rather their cognitions of the varying levels of attributes associated with those alternatives. Third, it is assumed that the levels of the independent variables which are used to generate an overall evaluation are some function of the observed levels of those same

2

Patterns of Migration

Many of our current ideas about interregional migration stem from the pioneering work of E. G. Ravenstein. More than one hundred years ago, Ravenstein published two influential papers in the *Journal of the Royal Statistical Society*, describing his so-called laws of migration (Ravenstein 1885, 1889). These laws, or perhaps more accurately generalizations, were inductively derived from place-of-birth data published in the British censuses of 1871 and 1881, together with similar data from North America and Europe. Among his more important generalizations were the following: the majority of migrants move only a short distance; migrants do not proceed directly to their ultimate destination, but get there via a series of steps; each migration stream tends to generate a compensating counterstream; and the major causes of migration are economic. These simple statements about migration flows have generated a remarkable amount of empirical research, and many of Ravenstein's hypotheses have since been confirmed (Grigg 1977).

More recently, Lee (1966) modified Ravenstein's ideas to create a framework for migration involving factors associated with the area of origin, factors associated with the area of destination, intervening obstacles, and personal factors. Positive and negative signs were used to indicate the attractive and unattractive features, respectively, associated with each origin and destination. For example, high unemployment levels at the origin would constitute a push factor, while high wage rates at the destination would constitute a pull factor. Between each potential origin and destination, however, there are various obstacles to overcome, the most omnipresent of which is distance. Finally, a variety of personal factors, such as age and level of education, influence how the characteristics of the origins, destinations, and intervening obstacles are perceived. Thus, the positive and negative characteristics of regions and their associated push and pull forces are differentially defined by different subgroups of prospective migrants. Like Ravenstein's assertions, Lee's conceptualization has generated a massive quantity of empirical work, and the relative importance of push and pull factors continues to provide a framework for much contemporary research (Dorigo and Tobler 1983).

Spatial Patterns

Many scholars have since substantiated Ravenstein's generalization that migration behavior is affected by distance (Morrill 1963; Stillwell 1991). More specifically, the so-called friction-of-distance effect has frequently been observed; this means that the number of migrants from any given region decreases with increasing distance. The form of this relationship between the amount of migration and distance from the origin has usually been described by a power function. The power function, in this particular context, can be expressed as follows:

$$M = aD^{-b} \qquad\qquad (2.1)$$

where M is migration, D is distance, and a and b are empirically derived constants. The negative b coefficient indicates that migration is an inverse function of distance.

For example, in a now-classic study, Hagerstrand (1957) used a power function to investigate the migration pattern to and from the village of Asby, in central Sweden. He measured migration by the relative density of migrations per unit area, while measuring distances from the midpoints of successive distance bands around the village. Hagerstrand concluded that migration is indeed an inverse function of distance and that the relationship is curvilinear. Moreover, the temporal decline in the value of the b coefficient indicated that Asby's migration field was expanding. In general, empirical estimates of such migration-distance elasticities have suggested a range from –0.5 to –1.5 (Shaw 1975:83).

Some researchers have suggested that the negative exponential function is more appropriate for representing the relationship between migration and distance (Haynes 1974). Such a function would be expressed as follows:

$$M = ae^{-bD} \qquad (2.2)$$

where the notation is the same as in equation 2.1, and e is the base of natural logarithms. Regardless of the precise functional form, however, the weight of evidence indicates that the role of distance has decreased over time. For example, Clayton (1977a) found that the contribution of distance to the total explained variation in interstate migration in the United States declined progressively between 1935 and 1970. There is considerable doubt, however, about whether the individual effect of distance can ever be satisfactorily isolated. It has been argued that distance-decay parameters reflect a complex combination of spatial structure, involving the size and configuration of origins and destinations in a spatial system and intrinsic interaction behavior, thus precluding any simple interpretation of such parameters (Fotheringham 1981, 1991).

In a causal sense, distance is merely being used as a surrogate for other, less easily measured variables. In particular, the fact that migration decreases with increasing distance has been attributed to the notion that distance serves as a proxy for the psychic costs of movement (Greenwood 1975). In some situations, however, distance might reflect information flows or the uncertainty about employment and income prospects in other regions. Given this range of interpretations applied to the causal role of distance, it is not surprising that distance has been measured in a variety of ways. Mileage, time, and cost distance are all appropriate under different circumstances, and researchers have also attempted to use the concept of cognitive distance in migration models (Madden 1978).

Cognitive distance refers to an individual's estimate of the distance between pairs of places. Unlike perceived distance, which has attracted the attention of psychologists for a number of years (Baird 1970), cognitive distance concerns those physical distances that are too large to be perceived in a single glance. It is assumed, therefore, that people can think about distances in the abstract, without actually seeing them. Thus our cognitions include not only information gathered from direct experience, as in perceived distance, but also information gathered from various other sources, such as road maps. In this way people can estimate the distances to places they may never have actually visited.

As mentioned in Chapter 1, the relationship between cognitive and physical distance is usually expressed by a power function, thus suggesting that physical distances can be easily transformed into their cognitive counterparts when being used in migration models. A power function suggests that short distances are overestimated, while longer distances tend to be underestimated, although the point of changeover in this relationship obviously varies with spatial scale. Somewhere between six and seven miles has been put forward as the breakpoint for London, and only about three miles for Dundee, Scotland (Pocock and Hudson 1978:53). Researchers have advanced a variety of reasons to explain the discrepancies between cognitive and physical distances, although the empirical evidence for them has often been less than impressive. Direction, familiarity, and length of residence are some of the variables that have been invoked within this context (Cadwallader 1976). In addition, MacEachren (1980) has suggested that greater attention should be focused on the cognition of travel time.

A variety of methodological and conceptual problems prevent any simple, universal transformation from physical to cognitive distance (Ewing 1981). In particular, individual distance estimates tend to be somewhat unstable across different methodologies. That is, the distance estimates provided by an individual subject are sometimes affected by the way in which he or she was asked to provide those estimates. Moreover, distance estimates are sometimes both intransitive and noncommutative, which suggests that people do not possess mental representations of the physical world that have the mathematical properties of a metric space (Cadwallader 1979b). In other words, any internalized representation of the physical world appears to be highly complex.

Ravenstein's pioneering research on migration is also responsible for the more recent interest in stepwise, or chain, migration. Ravenstein (1885, 1889) suggested that cities grew by attracting migrants from the surrounding area and that those migrants were then replaced by others from even remoter regions. It can thus be argued that the historically important rural to urban migration flows are actually composed of a series of discrete steps. That is, people first move from rural areas to small towns, then from small towns to larger cities, and so on. Such a sequence might occur as a result of information flows, whereby new opportunties present themselves as a migrant moves upward through the urban hierarchy. These new opportunities might also be accompanied by changing aspiration levels.

Due to inadequate data, Ravenstein was unable to empirically investigate the magnitude of stepwise migration, but Riddell and Harvey (1972) have since presented some informative evidence from Sierra Leone. The urban hierarchy was defined as a three-tiered system, with the capital city of Freetown as the highest level, the twelve towns containing district headquarters as the middle tier, and the rural areas as the lowest level. When comparing the actual migration flows with an idealized stepwise pattern, they found support for the hypothesis in some parts of the country, but certainly not in all. In particular, certain situations seemed to inhibit the explicit manifestation of chain migration. First, some rural areas were too close to Freetown for the inter-mediate-sized towns to exert any significant drawing power. Second, the pattern broke down in those situations where a strong attractive force existed outside the urban heirarchy, such as the diamond fields in Kono. Third, the structure of the transportation network also influ-enced the migration flows, thus isolating some of the intermediate cen-ters. In general, however, Riddell and Harvey concluded that at least some parts of the country exhibited evidence of a stepwise migration process. In a similar vein, Keown (1971) also presented evidence of stepwise migration in New Zealand.

Using data from Guatemala, Thomas and Catau (1974) further elab-orated the role of distance in this process. More specifically, they sug-gested that a direct relationship exists between the magnitude of step-wise migration and distance from the largest city. As distance from the largest city increases, so too does the probability that a rural migrant will move to a secondary center rather than to the largest city. On the other hand, a rural migrant living near the largest city is much more likely to skip the local secondary center and move directly to the largest city. Due to improvements in communications and transportation tech-nology, one might expect this weakening of the hierarchical effect to be increasingly prevalent in the future. It is thus not surprising that most of the empirical research on stepwise migration has been conducted in less-developed countries.

Besides stepwise flows, a significant amount of return migration can also be observed at the interregional level (Long 1988:136; Rogers and Belanger 1990). Return migration describes the movement of peo-ple to regions where they have previously lived, and approximately 25 percent of all migrants in the United States can be designated as re-turnees (DaVanzo and Morrison 1981). In particular, return migration has often reversed the direction of traditional migration streams. For example, the net outflow of black migrants from the South is now ex-ceeded by a counterstream, two-thirds of which represents returnees (Cromartie and Stack 1989; Long and Hansen 1975; McHugh 1987). Ravenstein (1885, 1889) had mentioned the notion of such counter-streams, but it is unclear whether he was referring to returnees or merely to flows of migrants moving in the opposite direction to the dominant stream.

Despite its widespread occurrence, however, return migration has been a rather neglected phenomenon (King 1978). The main reason for this comparative neglect is that the data requirements for the analysis of return migration are particularly severe (Alexander 1983). Data on migration are usually only available on a discontinuous time scale, and many moves go unregistered in conventional statistics that measure migration by comparing an individual's residential location at two points in time. As always, the level of temporal resolution influences the quality of observed data, and this is especially true for return migration, as such moves often occur quite soon after a previous move. Besides these data problems, research on return migration has also been hampered by the lack of an appropriate conceptual framework. The challenge is to formulate an approach that can account for migration sequences where the emphasis is on a series of moves rather than on an individual event (Dierx 1988b).

DaVanzo and Morrison (1981) have made some progress toward this goal by specifying a framework that highlights the role of location-specific capital and imperfect information. Location-specific capital comprises all the factors that tie a person or household to a specific place. These factors include concrete assets plus more intangible variables such as job seniority, an established clientele, personal knowledge of the area, community ties, and friendship networks. Such considerations suggest that a migrant will favor a previous area of residence as a potential destination, due to the location-specific capital there. In addition, the propensity to return will decrease with increasing length of absence, since location-specific capital tends to depreciate over time. Consistent with this latter proposition, DaVanzo and Morrison found that family heads are most prone to return within a year and that the probability of moving back decreases thereafter.

The notion of imperfect information suggests that a move can sometimes turn out to have been an unwise decision, thus generating a category of discouraged migrants whose employment or income expectations did not materialize (Bell and Kirwan 1979). These unfulfilled expectations may be the result of imperfect information, leading to an overly optimistic assessment of the labor market conditions at the destination. A return move might then be the most appropriate corrective action, as the migrant would not want to repeat the mistake. Support for this line of reasoning is provided by two kinds of empirical evidence (DaVanzo and Morrison 1981). First, the unemployed are especially prone to make return moves, particularly when the migration interval is short. Second, the less-educated segments of the population, who tend to possess only fragmented information about national employment opportunities, are also more likely to return to familiar surroundings.

Finally, it has been argued that return migrants can have significant consequences for regional growth and development (King 1986:18–27). First, returning migrants sometimes have sources of accumulated capital, which are then invested in new enterprises and thus generate further employment and capital in the region. Second, returning migrants often possess newly acquired labor skills and innovative entrepreneurial attitudes. On the other hand, evidence also suggests that return migrants do not nessarily assume positions of social or psychological leadership (Townsend 1980). Rather, the locals who have stayed within the region often tend to take on positions of industrial and political responsibility.

Migration Fields

Migration fields represent a useful way of summarizing different kinds of migration flows; a migration field refers to the overall pattern of flows associated with a particular place (Roseman and McHugh 1982). An in-migration field is thus a functional, or nodal, region that delineates the origins of immigrants to an area, while an out-migration field characterizes the destinations of emigrants from that area. Roseman (1977) has empirically investigated the notion of urban migration fields in the United States, and figure 2.1 shows the migration fields associated with Cleveland for 1955–60 and 1965–70. The in-migration maps indicate those State Economic Areas (SEAs), both urban and rural, which contributed more than a specified number of migrants to Cleveland during a particular time period. For example, 1 percent of the total in-migration to Cleveland was chosen as the threshold for 1955–60, thus providing a spatial distribution of the 145,931 migrants who were in Cleveland in 1960 but not in 1955. Conversely, the out-migration fields are defined as those SEAs which received more than a specified number of migrants from Cleveland during a particular time period. These maps illustrate the relative stability of migration patterns over time, although some changes are evident. For example, Los Angeles is part of Cleveland's in-migration field during the period 1965–70 but does not appear on the 1955–60 map.

Roseman (1977) argued that migration fields reveal certain systematic spatial patterns. For in-migration, he identified hinterland, interurban, and channelized components. Hinterland migration refers to the fact that cities tend to attract migrants from the surrounding rural areas. For example, in the case of Cleveland, the rural SEAs in northern Ohio and northwestern Pennsylvania contribute a significant number

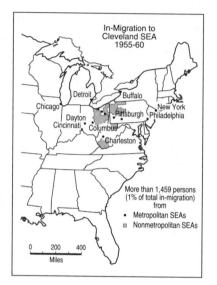

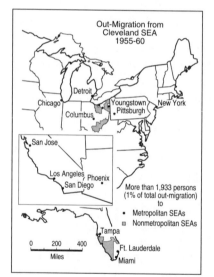

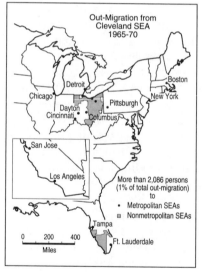

Figure 2.1. In- and out-migration fields of the Cleveland, Ohio, SEA, 1955–1960 and 1965–1970.
Source: Roseman 1977:fig. 6.

of migrants. Such hinterland migration is partly due to the information about job opportunities provided by local newspapers and television stations. Prospective migrants also augment this information during trips to the city for shopping and entertainment purposes. In general, the areal size of the hinterland component depends upon the location of other large cities. On the East Coast, where cities are closely spaced, the hinterland migration areas are characteristically small. Farther west, however, where major cities are not so clustered, the hinterland areas are appreciably larger.

The interurban, or hierarchical, component of in-migration fields reflects the attraction of migrants from other metropolitan areas. In the case of Cleveland, most of the nearby cities are represented, regardless of size. At greater distances, however, only the largest cities, such as Boston, New York, Philadelphia, and Los Angeles, are included. This type of migration is again related to information flows, which tend to be highly structured by the urban hierarchy. The television markets associated with major cities are often national in scope, whereas the market areas associated with smaller cities are much more localized. Thus the areal dissemination of information concerning job opportunities and life-styles is closely related to position in the urban hierarchy.

Finally, channelized migration refers to the tendency for a city to attract migrants from one or two rural areas outside its immediate hinterland. For example, Cleveland exhibits a channelized flow from southern West Virginia that appears in both 1955–60 and 1965–70. Such flows are shaped by interpersonal communication, rather than by the mass media. In this respect, family ties and friendship networks are particularly important. A social system connecting two widely separated places can develop, thus stimulating a continuous flow of migrants that becomes entrenched over time. Roseman (1971) has shown that channelized flows are particularly characteristic of migration from the rural South, and most large cities in the Midwest and Northeast have such connections (fig. 2.2). More specifically, the Midwest cities, such as Rockford, St. Louis, Kalamazoo, Muncie, and Youngstown, tend to draw from Arkansas, Mississippi, Alabama, and Tennessee, while the East Coast cities draw more from the Carolinas. There are also channelized flows elsewhere, however, such as from North Dakota to Seattle, and Montana to Minneapolis–St. Paul.

Three systematic components also characterize out-migration fields: hinterland, interurban, and amenity, or recreation-related, migration. In this case the hinterland migration represents those migrants leaving a city for the surrounding rural area. Such migrants often prefer the life-styles associated with smaller towns or rural areas but choose to

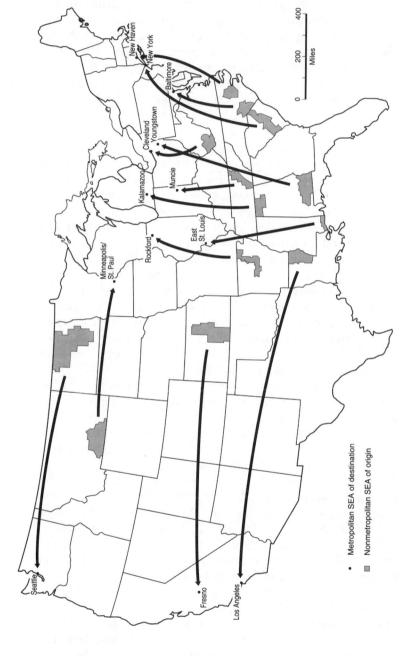

Figure 2.2. An example of channelized flows in the United States.
Source: Roseman 1977:fig. 7.

- Metropolitan SEA of destination
- Nonmetropolitan SEA of origin

48

remain fairly close to the metropolitan area in which they grew up or spent most of their working lives. A number of migrants, for example, have left Cleveland for the nonmetropolitan areas in northern Ohio.

The interurban component of out-migration is also similar to its in-migration counterpart and thus emphasizes the symmetry exhibited by migration fields. The amenity or recreation component, however, is more specific to the out-migration fields of urban areas in the Midwest and Northeast, as it often represents flows of retirees to Arizona, California, and Florida. The out-migration fields for Cleveland suggest the attractiveness of such cities as Los Angeles, San Diego, Phoenix, Tampa, and Fort Lauderdale, plus certain rural areas in southern Florida.

Migration fields can be represented more formally, and abstractly, by using such concepts as vector flows (Tobler 1978) and linkage analysis (Slater 1984). In particular, the technique known as primary linkage analysis can be used to identify individual migration fields (Haggett, Cliff, and Frey 1977:485–90). Consider figure 2.3, which depicts a hypothetical flow matrix for ten different regions. The values in the cells of the matrix indicate the number of migrants moving betwen various pairs of regions during a particular time period. For example, 14 people moved from region 2 to region 3, and 12 people moved from region 3 to region 2. The hierarchical order of a region is measured by the total number of people moving to that region, so region 7, with 207 migrants, is the first region, region 3 is the second region, and so on.

The hierarchical structure of the various regions is determined by the largest outflow to a higher-order region. For regions 1, 3, and 7, the largest outflow is to a low-order region, so these three regions form the terminal points of the graph. The remaining seven regions are then assigned, either directly or indirectly, to one of these terminals. For example, the largest outflow from region 2 is to region 1, thus an arrow connects those two regions. Similarly, the largest outflow from region 8 is to region 5, and the largest outflow from region 5 is to region 3. The resulting graph identifies three distinct subgraphs, or migration fields.

Clayton (1977a,b) has used linkage analysis to explore interstate migration flows in the United States for the periods 1935–40, 1949–50, 1955–60, and 1965–70 (fig. 2.4). The number of terminal nodes identified for each of these time periods is six, eight, four, and four, respectively. Those identified for the last two periods—California, Florida, New York, and Virginia—are also present in both earlier periods. This reduction in the number of terminal nodes reflects the increasing concentration around a few major destinations. In general, then, the structure of the migration system contains two major components. First, a series of local linkages connects small clusters of contiguous states,

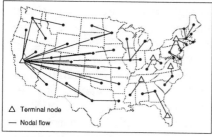

Nodal analysis results, 1935-1940

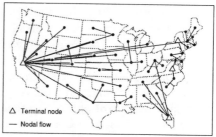

Nodal analysis results, 1955-1960

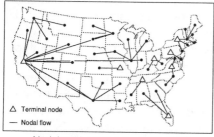

Nodal analysis results, 1949-1950

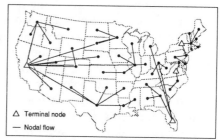

Nodal analysis results, 1965-1970

Figure 2.4. Linkage analysis for interstate migration in the United States. *Source:* Clayton 1977a:figs. 1–4.

spatial system that comprises places, the attributes of those places, and the interactions among them. While groups of places with similar characteristics form uniform regions, functional regions are based on similar patterns of interaction. The essential postulate of general field theory is that these two types of regions are isomorphic; there is a mutual equilibrium in structure and behavior. Any change in the characteristics of places will change the pattern of migration, and vice versa.

Such a theory, concerning the interdependencies between migration behavior and regional characteristics, can be operationalized through the multivariate technique of canonical correlation analysis. Canonical correlation analysis involves articulating the interrelationships between two groups of variables, in this case the regional characteristics and the migration patterns. The two sets of variables are transformed into orthogonal canonical vectors, such that the correlations between certain variables of the two sets are maximized. The canonical weights express the degree of association between the original variables and the canonical vectors, while the canonical correlation expresses the degree of association between the two sets of variables for each canonical vector.

Schwind (1975) has used general field theory and the associated technique of canonical analysis to explore interstate migration in the United States. The migration data covered the period 1955–60, and the attribute data consisted of thirty-one variables describing the demographic, economic, social, and climatic characteristics of the individual states. Nine migration fields were extracted by the canonical technique, and eight of them were significant. Four of the fields reflected relatively closed migration systems, with strongly symmetrical, or reciprocal, origin-destination patterns. The remaining fields were more open, with asymmetrical origin-destination patterns. For example, California received large numbers of migrants from the Midwest, while its own out-migrants were more oriented toward Oregon and Washington. Thus climate was particularly associated with asymmetrical patterns, while industrial labor force characteristics tended to be associated with reciprocal movements.

In general, however, using canonical correlation analysis involves certain problems. In particular, canonical analysis would appear to be a useful tool only where the investigator has little a priori theoretical knowledge about the system at hand. Even in situations where it is used as a primarily exploratory technique, various difficulties are often encountered. First, it is sometimes extremely difficult to substantively interpret the canonical vectors, as the importance of those vectors is determined not by how well they account for the variation within the two sets of variables but by how well they account for the relationships between the two sets. Second, the canonical weights cannot be interpreted like regression coefficients, as they show the degree to which the variables and canonical vectors are related but not how they are related. For this latter reason, it is often more appropriate to explore the complex interrelationships betwen the characteristics of regions and the migration flows between those regions using various kinds of structural equation models. Such models are the major topic of Chapter 3.

The Determinants of Migration

Many variables are either directly or indirectly linked to migration (Cebula 1979; Liaw 1990; Shaw 1985). Notions of equilibrium derived from neoclassical economics suggest that in any situation characterized by income differentials, labor will tend to migrate from low- to high-income areas (Clark and Gertler 1983; Tabuchi 1988). As a result of this movement, the supply of labor is increased at the destination and decreased at the origin, so that over time, due to supply and demand considerations, income levels will tend to equalize throughout the system. Such an argument assumes, of course, that there are no major barriers to mobility and that people desire to maximize income. It is noteworthy, however, that a number of studies have suggested that destination income has a greater influence on migration flows than does origin income (Shaw 1985:144). This relationship is partly conditioned by cost-of-living differentials, as there is empirical evidence that variations in the cost of living have a significant impact on migration patterns (Cebula 1980a; Renas and Kumar 1981). Finally, when considering the relevance of the income variable, it should be remembered that only wage earners will respond to interregional differences. This variable would presumably have less impact in predicting the migration flows of the retired sector of the population. Also, it would seem that short-distance moves would be less reflective of income differentials than would long-distance moves.

Employment opportunities are also related to migration patterns (Odland 1988b; Barff 1989, 1990). Theoretically, the greater unemployment is in a region, the greater the rate of out-migration. Conversely, in-migration should be negatively related to unemployment levels. Some studies, however, have indicated that employment levels, especially in origin regions, do not account for much of the variation in migration rates (Shaw 1985:145). One reason for this finding can be found in the use of aggregated data, as the unemployed constitute a relatively small proportion of the total population. High unemployment rates are likely to be of less significance to those individuals who already have jobs. Using micro-level data, DaVanzo (1978) has been able to substantiate this argument by showing that the unemployed are more likely to move than the employed. Indeed, Herzog and Schlottmann (1984) provide evidence that the premove unemployment rate of migrants is as much as three times that of nonmigrants. In sum, high unemployment rates tend to encourage the out-migration of those who are unemployed but exert little influence on the majority of the population.

The probability of obtaining employment elsewhere is often the key issue when one considers the influence of unemployment rates. The calculation of such probabilities requires information on the number of job vacancies and the number of people seeking those jobs. Data on job vacancies are generally not available, and using unemployment levels as a measure of expected job competition entails a number of problems (Isserman 1985). First, unemployment rates ignore those workers who are not actively seeking jobs but who would quickly do so if jobs became more widely available. Second, unemployment rates do not take into account the aging of the labor force in different regions and thus do not reflect potential openings due to retirement. As a result, various surrogates for the probability of gaining employment have been used. For example, Fields (1979) calculated the ratio of new hirings to unemployment rates, while Plaut (1981) used the ratio of vacancies to unemployment.

In a similar vein, the employment profile of a region tends to be related to the net migration of that region. In particular, growth in the secondary and tertiary sectors of an economy, rather than in agricultural employment, has been found to be positively related to levels of in-migration (Gober-Meyers 1978c). Evidence about the relationship between migration and urbanization is less clear, however. Until recently migrants have had a strong tendency to move from nonmetropolitan to metropolitan areas of the United States. Since at least 1970, however, a reversal of this trend has occurred, and the growth rates for nonmetropolitan areas have exceeded those of metropolitan areas (Greenwood 1981:91).

Researchers have suggested a variety of reasons to explain this migration turnaround (Chalmers and Greenwood 1977; Fuguitt 1985; Kontuly and Bierens 1990; Wilson 1987). First, the economies of scale that characterized the process of urban growth have often turned into diseconomies, and the social costs of urban disamenities have begun to exceed urban-rural wage differentials. Second, an increasingly affluent retirement-age population has been moving in large numbers to small retirement communities in Florida and the Southwest. Third, the increased demand for domestic energy sources, especially coal, has induced growth in rural regions. Fourth, the decreasing importance of manufacturing employment has led to the declining attraction of urban areas.

Education is generally found to be positively related to in-migration (Shaw 1985:147). At the aggregate level, a number of studies have succeeded in showing that educational differentials account for differential migration rates between places (Cebula 1979:66). In particular, the well educated are much more likely to make long-distance moves than are their more poorly educated counterparts (Schwartz 1973), although there is less of a distinction for short-distance moves. In other words, the correlation between education and migration appears to become stronger as the migration distance increases. This differential is due to the fact that the better educated are dealing with a labor market that is national rather than local in scale, and they also have better information concerning job opportunities.

The propensity of labor force members to migrate tends to decrease with increasing age (Nakosteen and Zimmer 1980), as older people have a shorter expected working life over which to realize the advantages of migration. Moreover, family ties and job security are also likely to be more important for older people, thus further decreasing their incentive to migrate. As a result, adults in their early twenties have the highest migration rates, and migration decreases monotonically beyond that age (Rogers 1979). On the other hand, the event of retirement, usually between the ages of sixty-five and seventy-five, often precipitates a long-distance move, especially toward a more congenial climate. So, although migration rates generally decrease with increasing age, there is often a slight upturn in rates for those approaching retirement age.

The provision of local governmental services also has an impact on migration patterns (Cebula 1980b; Harkman 1989). Pack (1973) found that high welfare payments act as a strong attraction, especially to nonwhites, as welfare is an important source of income for many families. Subsequent studies of migration to Standard Metropolitan Statistical Areas (SMSAs) have tended to support Pack's findings (Cebula 1974). As Curran (1977) demonstrates, however, the direction of causality between migration and welfare can run both ways; this suggests that both migration and welfare should be treated as endogenous variables in a system of simultaneous equations. Migration is also influenced by local govermental expenditure on services such as education, but as with welfare payments, a reciprocal relationship exists between expenditure and migration (Liu 1977). Moreover, one can also expect local governmental expenditures and local taxes to be simultaneously determined, the level of one depending upon the level of the other (Loehman and Emerson 1985).

Quality of life and amenity variables have become increasingly common ingredients of migration models (Cushing 1987a; Knapp and Graves 1989). For example, Liu (1975) included such variables as crime rates, recreational acres per capita, and library books per capita. In the context of metropolitan migration, Porell (1982) used principal components analysis to reduce individual quality of life variables into a smaller number of underlying components, representing climate, natural recreational amenities, social amenities, crime, air pollution, and health. When comparing the quality of life variables with their more traditional economic counterparts, Porell found that neither set of variables seemed important as determinants of out-migration. On the other hand, both quality of life and economic factors were significant determinants of in-migration, thus reinforcing Lowry's (1966) statements concerning the relative importance of push and pull forces. In this context, it is quite likely that economic determinants become more important than quality of life considerations in eras of national economic stagnation and high unemployment (Clark 1983:52).

A number of recent migration studies have used climatic variables as indicators of quality of life. Most of these studies use some kind of temperature measurement (Ballard and Clark 1981), although a wide variety of indices have been constructed (Cushing 1987b). For example, Kau and Sirmans (1979) measured the absolute deviation of the mean yearly temperature from sixty-five degrees Fahrenheit, while Alperovich Bergsman, and Ehemann (1977) defined temperature by examining the absolute deviation of the mean January temperature from sixty-five degrees Fahrenheit and the absolute deviation of the mean July temperature from sixty-five degrees Fahrenheit. After testing a variety of climatic indicators in the context of net migration into SMSAs, Renas and Kumar (1983) concluded that people generally prefer areas which have moderate climates, rather than extremely hot or cold climates.

Climatic variables have most often been invoked within what Graves (1980) has termed the amenity-oriented equilibrium approach to explaining migration. In this approach, a city is envisioned as supplying a particular climatic bundle. For equilibrium, or spatial indifference, to obtain, attractive climatic bundles can be traded off against less-attractive economic attributes. That is, it can be argued that income and unemployment differences across cities do not reflect real utility differentials, but rather the compensation required for differences in location-fixed goods, such as climate. Thus, one would not necessarily expect income differences to generate migration, since those differences might merely reflect compensation for climatic differences. On the other hand, rational individuals might use migration to trade off income for increased quality of life consumption. If such a long-run equilibrium between economic and quality of life bundles is to be accepted as plausible, however, it must be accepted that the present system is in a state of significant disequilibrium. Several cities, such as San Francisco and Atlanta, presently offer favorable economic incentives in addition to an attractive quality of life, while other cities, such as Buffalo and Syracuse, offer neither (Porell 1982). Recent evidence suggests that such variables as jobs and wages are considerably more important than location-specific amenities in explaining metropolitan migration rates of employed individuals (Greenwood and Hunt 1989).

Finally, a variety of studies have argued that migration is a cause of economic change as well as a reaction to it (Vanderkamp 1989). In particular, a number of regional development theorists have suggested that migration contributes to increased inequality in regional per-capita income (Hirschman 1958; Myrdal 1957). The major contributor to this increased inequality is the fact that migrants do not typically represent the population in general, and so the high-income regions that gain in population as a result of migration also experience a favorable change in their population composition. In general, Greenwood's (1973) empirical evidence supports the notion that migration tends to increase rather than decrease regional economic differences. In particular contexts, however, migration may have a variety of effects on local income levels (Clark 1983:55). For example, out-migration could reduce labor supply and thus increase wages, or alternatively, the loss of high-wage earners might decrease average wages in the short run.

Migration also influences unemployment levels, and contrary to expectations, out-migration can worsen rather than improve the unemployment problems in depressed areas (Parr 1966). Unemployed persons take with them a certain level of expenditure when they migrate, thus decreasing the purchasing power, and ultimately the level of employment, in the region. Indeed, Vanderkamp (1970), using the Maritime region of Canada as his data base, has suggested that for every five unemployed persons leaving the region, two previously employed persons became unemployed. Similarly, looking at the destination region, Olvey (1972) found immigration and employment growth to be self-reinforcing processes. Irrespective of the detailed manifestations in particular regions at particular points in time, evidence thus clearly indicates that migration rates are both a cause and an effect of income and unemployment variables (Chalmers and Greenwood 1985).

These interrelationships suggest that the overall relationship between migration and capital can be quite complex (Clark 1983:86–100). In general, however, it can be argued that labor migration should lag behind the movement of capital. That is, capital can react faster than labor to the changing map of economic opportunities. Researchers need to take such leads and lags into account when modeling the empirical interrelationships between labor and capital. In the short run the movement of capital can initiate migration, but in the long run capital and migration might well readjust to each other as part of the larger macroeconomic system. The empirical evidence on this issue, at the level of interstate labor movements, indicates that indeed lags do occur between migration and capital. In particular, Clark and Gertler (1983) suggest that most states experience one- to two-year lags. Only in very rare instances does prior migration initiate a spatial flow of capital.

Such empirical evidence tends to compromise the neoclassical economic viewpoint that migration and capital growth are initiated separately, but in reaction to similar macroeconomic variables. Rather, capital often determines migration because of its ownership of the means of production and its right to initiate and terminate employment. This uneven distribution of power in employment relationships, although partly mitigated by unionization, casts some doubt on the assumptions of free will and independence that characterize neoclassical conceptions of labor migration. Indeed, it can be argued that in those situations where a firm has the luxury of choosing from a wide variety of potential locations, the firm will locate in order to use a relatively vulnerable labor force. That is, two sets of variables will come to dominate the process of locational choice: labor costs and the degree of local worker organization (Walker and Storper 1981).

Discriminant Analysis

One way to empirically assess which variables play a role in determining migration behavior is to use the statistical technique of discriminant analysis (Klecka 1980). Discriminant analysis, for example, can be used to distinguish between groups of cities or regions that differ in migration rates. For this purpose a set of discriminating variables are chosen that measure characteristics on which the groups are expected to differ. These variables are then weighted and linearly combined in order to form a series of discriminant functions, such that the differences between the groups are maximized. The maximum number of functions which can be derived is one less than the number of original groups, or equal to the number of discriminating variables if there are more groups than variables. In practice, however, it is often possible to obtain a satisfactory solution by using fewer than the maximum number of functions, similar to extracting factors in factor analysis. In other words, it is assumed that the location of the groups in the m-dimensional variable space can be captured by a few basic composites of those m variables.

Several statistics are available to measure the success of the discriminant functions. The eigenvalue associated with a particular discriminant function reflects the relative importance of that function, as the sum of the eigenvalues is a measure of the total variance existing in the discriminating variables. By expressing an individual eigenvalue as a percentage of the sum of the eigenvalues, one can determine the percentage of the total variance accounted for by each discriminant function. The discriminant functions are derived in order of importance, and the procedure can be stopped when the eigenvalues become too small.

The canonical correlation is a measure of association between a single discriminant function and the dummy variables which define group membership and thus reflects the function's ability to discriminate among the groups. In other words, the canonical correlation indicates how closely the discriminant function and the groups are related. The discriminant functions can be interpreted by analyzing the standardized discriminant function coefficients. If the sign is ignored, the size of one of these coefficients indicates the relative contribution of the associated variable to the discriminant function. That is, as in multiple regression analysis or factor analysis, the coefficients identify the variables which contribute most to the differentiation along each function.

The present author (Cadwallader 1991) used discriminant analysis to explore the pattern of net migration rates for cities in the United States. Until relatively recently most U.S. cities were experiencing above-average population growth. During the 1970s, however, a new trend emerged, and the term *counterurbanization* was coined to represent a period of absolute decline or relatively slow growth. For example, of the twenty-five largest metropolitan areas, only Pittsburgh lost population between 1960 and 1970, whereas since then many more have experienced absolute declines (Burns 1982). These changes are themselves part of a more general redistribution of population from the highly industrialized states in the Northeast to the southernmost tier of states within the South and West. Despite the profound implications of such population shifts for making efficient and equitable decisions concerning the direction of future capital investments or subsidies, remarkably little is known about the actual process of urban growth and decline (Miron 1979). Indeed, opinions differ markedly concerning even the degree of instability in the rate of population change (Borchert 1983; Gaile and Hanink 1985).

The present author used the largest sixty-five metropolitan statistical areas in 1970 to document net migration rates for the period 1965–70, while using sixty-four for the period 1975–80. The reason for this discrepancy is that for the period 1975–80 the Census Bureau merged Dallas and Fort Worth. The net migration rate was determined by subtracting the number of out-migrants from the number of in-migrants and dividing by the population at the end of the time period. For both time periods a substantial number of cities experienced negative net migration rates (table 2.1) More specifically, 45 percent of the cities had negative net migration rates for 1965–70, while 66 percent had negative migration rates for 1975–80. In all, 77 percent of the cities experienced a

Table 2.1. Net migration rates for 1965–1970 and 1975–1980

City	1965–70	1975–80	City	1965–70	1975–80
Akron	-.11	-.85	Milwaukee	-.58	-.82
Albany	.07	-.53	Minneapolis	.29	-.24
Allentown	.21	.07	Nashville	.08	.87
Anaheim	4.33	.47	Newark	-.67	-1.34
Atlanta	1.45	.92	New Orleans	-.51	-.21
Baltimore	-.04	-.27	New York	-.98	-1.58
Birmingham	-.45	.09	Norfolk	.25	-.06
Boston	-.34	-.86	Oklahoma City	.16	.58
Buffalo	-.63	-1.29	Omaha	-.39	-.90
Chicago	-.64	-1.14	Paterson	-.39	-1.25
Cincinnati	-.21	-.64	Philadelphia	-.09	-.61
Cleveland	-.53	-1.28	Phoenix	2.10	3.56
Columbus	.11	-.38	Pittsburgh	-.60	-.74
Dallas	1.70	1.32	Portland	1.08	1.33
Dayton	.09	-.80	Providence	.41	-.36
Denver	1.21	1.09	Richmond	.60	.70
Detroit	-.41	-1.02	Rochester	.33	-.81
Fort Lauderdale	4.16	3.97	Sacramento	.06	1.18
Fort Worth	2.03	—	St. Louis	-.27	-.69
Gary	-.65	-.94	Salt Lake City	-.33	.79
Grand Rapids	.12	.12	San Antonio	.50	.18
Greensboro	.09	.35	San Bernardino	1.57	3.46
Hartford	.77	-.71	San Diego	2.32	1.69
Honolulu	.72	-.97	San Francisco	-.01	-.73
Houston	1.68	2.11	San Jose	2.33	-.27
Indianapolis	-.05	-.32	Seattle	1.77	1.12
Jacksonville	-.13	-.09	Springfield	.06	-.66
Jersey City	-1.44	-1.49	Syracuse	-.07	-.69
Kansas City	-.13	-.47	Tampa	2.44	3.16
Los Angeles	-.56	-1.27	Toledo	.02	-.44
Louisville	-.06	-.78	Washington	1.00	-1.03
Memphis	.18	-.27	Youngstown	-.15	-1.01
Miami	.78	-.29			

Source: Cadwallader 1991: table 1.
Note: For the period 1975–80 the Census Bureau merged the Dallas and Fort Worth data.

decline in net migration rates between the two time periods. Those cities that exhibited migration gains between the two periods were all located outside of the heavily industrialized northeast and midwest regions of the country.

Table 2.2 indicates the mean characteristics of growing and declining cities for the two time periods. The data were calibrated for 1960 and 1970, as one would expect net migration rates to respond to the characteristics associated with some previous time period. The average

Table 2.2. Mean characteristics of growing and declining cities

	1965–70		1975–80	
	Growing (N = 36)	Declining (N = 29)	Growing (N = 22)	Declining (N = 42)
Income per capita	1,875	2,051	3,269	3,436
Unemployment rate	4.61	5.01	4.34	4.04
Percentage employed in manufacturing	24.57	32.18	21.91	28.15
Median housing value	12,777	14,124	17,168	20,200
Property tax per capita	102	122	185	231
Local governmental tax per capita	117	139	224	278
Local governmental spending per capita	279	274	581	625
Educational spending per capita	103	99	230	237
Crime rate per 100,000 population	1,323	1,259	3,462	3,284
Climatic attractiveness	592.34	595.17	607.59	594.50

Source: Cadwallader 1991: table 2.

income levels were higher for the declining cities, while unemployment rates were higher for the growing cities in 1975–80. In all cases, however, the differences were relatively minor. A far more substantial difference between growing and declining cities was evident in the data for manufacturing employment, with the declining cities being more heavily oriented toward manufacturing activitiy. Similarly, housing costs and various kinds of local taxes were uniformly higher for the declining cities. By contrast, local governmental expenditures were very similar for the two groups of cities, with the growing cities having slightly higher rates for the first period but slightly lower rates for the second period. Finally, values for the climatic attractiveness index were fairly even, while crime rates were slightly higher for the growing cities. Climatic attractiveness was measured by a combination of variables involving temperature, heating- and cooling-degree days, freezing days, zero-degree days, and ninety-degree days, while crime rates were calibrated for seven categories of personal and property crimes.

In general, the relationships between net migration and various other variables were as expected (table 2.3). Statistically significant negative relationships were found for percentage employed in manufacturing, the median value of owner-occupied housing units, per-capita property tax rates, and per-capita general tax rates, while positive relationships were found for educational expenditures per capita and climatic attractiveness. Somewhat surprisingly, however, net migration was negatively related to per-capita income and positively related to crime rates. Unemployment and general spending were not associated with net migration for either of the time periods.

The first discriminant analysis, based on the net migration rates for

Table 2.3. Correlation coefficients between net
migration rate and other variables

	1965–70	1975–80
Income	–.11	–.22*
Unemployment	–.07	.10
Manufacturing	–.41**	–.45**
Housing costs	–.08	–.31**
Property tax	–.09	–.27*
General tax	–.07	–.31**
General spending	.14	–.08
Education spending	.38**	.02
Crime	.21*	.22*
Climate	.24*	.05

Source: Cadwallader 1991: table 3.
Note: ** indicates significant at .01; * indicates
significant at .05.

1965–70, used two groups of cities (table 2.4). In order to highlight the
differences between growing and declining cities, two subgroups of
extreme cases were chosen. The declining group included all cities with
more extreme negative migration rates than –.25, while the growing
group contained all cities with positive migration rates greater than
.50. This categorization created a growing group of nineteen cities and
a declining group of eighteen cities. As there were two groups, only
one discriminant function was extracted. This function, however, had a
canonical correlation of .80 and successfully classified 95 percent of the

Table 2.4. Two-group discriminant analysis for 1965–1970

	Standardized coefficients	Means	
		Growing (N = 19)	Declining (N = 18)
Income	–.42	1,979	2,118
Unemployment	.23	4.56	4.96
Manufacturing	1.23	19.64	32.71
Housing costs	.35	13,437	15,056
Property tax	–1.20	105	132
General tax	1.48	122	149
General spending	.55	280	281
Education spending	–.87	107	96
Crime	.29	1,508	1,306
Climate	–.48	620.63	586.83

Canonical correlation = 0.80; cases classified correctly = 95%.
Source: Cadwallader 1991: table 4.

Table 2.5. Two-group discriminant analysis for 1975–1980

	Standardized coefficients	Means Growing (N = 22)	Declining (N = 20)
Income	.06	3,269	3,577
Unemployment	.33	4.34	4.03
Manufacturing	.85	21.91	31.06
Housing costs	.41	17,168	22,400
Property tax	−.80	185	257
General tax	2.23	224	306
General spending	.01	581	650
Education spending	−1.26	230	238
Crime	.03	3,462	3,296
Climate	−.81	607.59	601.75

Canonical correlation = 0.82; cases classified correctly = 90%.
Source: Cadwallader 1991: table 5.

cases. That is, the discriminant function was able to correctly identify 95 percent of the cases as members of the group to which they actually belonged. The standardized coefficients indicated that manufacturing and taxes contributed most to the discriminating function, while spending on education made a somewhat less-important contribution to the discrimination process. These results were confirmed by comparing the variable means for each group, which showed that the percentage employed in manufacturing, property taxes, and general taxes were all higher for the declining group.

A similar analysis was undertaken for the 1975–80 data (table 2.5). In this case the declining group consisted of cities with negative migration rates greater than −.75, while the growing group contained all those cities with positive migration rates. The results were equally encouraging, as the discriminant function had a canonical correlation of .82 and successfully classified 90 percent of the cities. The standardized coefficients displayed a pattern similar to those for the previous time period, in that manufacturing, taxes, and spending on education were again the important variables. This time, however, the general tax variable was nearly twice as important as any of the other variables, and climatic attractiveness also emerged as an important variable. An examination of the respective group means shows that the percentage employed in manufacturing and tax rates were still considerably higher for the declining cities, while climatic attractiveness was greater for the growing cities.

A three-group discriminant analysis was then undertaken for both time periods, with the additional third group containing those cities

Table 2.6. Three-group discriminant analysis

| | Standardized Coefficients | | | |
	1965–70		1975–80	
Income	−.04	.25	−.17	1.23
Unemployment	.29	.09	.08	.37
Manufacturing	1.01	−.61	.93	.12
Housing costs	.29	.43	.54	.07
Property tax	−.18	.69	−.93	.97
General tax	.49	.11	2.02	−2.15
General spending	.75	−.59	.26	.90
Education spending	−1.08	−.18	−1.12	−.59
Crime	.35	.37	.20	.17
Climate	−.53	−.05	−.68	−.01
Percentage variance accounted for	66.26	33.74	96.77	3.23
Canonical correlation	.68	.56	.76	.21
Cases classified correctly	70%		55%	

Source: Cadwallader 1991: table 6.

not included in the previous two-group analysis (table 2.6). As there were now three groups, two discriminant functions could be extracted. In general, however, the discriminant functions were less successful here than in the two-group analysis. For the 1965–70 data the canonical correlations were .68 and .56, while 70 percent of the cases were correctly classified. The first function accounted for 66 percent of the total variance, while the remaining variance was associated with the second function. The analysis for 1975–80 was even less successful, as the second canonical correlation was only .21, and only 55 percent of the cases were correctly assigned by the model. Furthermore, the first function accounted for nearly 97 percent of the total variance, leaving an insignificant role for the second function. As in the two-group analysis, however, the standardized coefficients emphasized the importance of the manufacturing, tax, and educational spending variables for both time periods. In general, then, the two- and three-group discriminant analyses suggested that manufacturing activity, local tax rates, and spending on education were particularly important discriminators between growing and declining areas.

Single-Equation Regression Models

Regression models can also be used to help sort out the relative importance of the variables that influence migration. One of the most enduring single-equation regression models is the gravity model, whereby the amount of migration betwen any two regions is expected to be directly proportional to the product of their populations and inversely proportional to the distance between them (Haynes and Fotheringham 1984). In symbolic form it is usually represented as follows:

$$M_{ij} = a \frac{P_i^{b_1} P_j^{b_2}}{D_{ij}^{b_3}} \tag{2.3}$$

where M_{ij} is the amount of migration between regions i and j; P_i and P_j are the populations of regions i and j; D_{ij} is the distance between regions i and j; and a, b_1, b_2, and b_3 are constants that reflect the relative weightings of the constituent variables. If the variables are expressed in logarithmic form, multiple regression analysis can be used to estimate the coefficients:

$$\log M_{ij} = \log a + b_1 \log P_i + b_2 \log P_j - b_3 \log D_{ij} \tag{2.4}$$

where the notation is the same as in equation 2.3.

Flowerdew and Salt (1979) used the gravity model to explore the migration flows between a set of 126 Standard Metropolitan Labor Areas in Great Britain. Fitting a gravity model of the form described in equation 2.4, they derived a multiple coefficient of determination of .527, thus implying that over 50 percent of the variation in migration flows could be statistically accounted for by the gravity model formulation. All the coefficients were significantly different from zero and had very low standard errors. As expected, the coefficients associated with both population variables were positive, while the coefficient associated with the distance variable was negative. Similar results were also obtained by Clayton (1977a), who used the logarithmic form of the gravity model to explain interstate migration flows in the United States. The multiple coefficient of determination varied from .586 for the 1935–40 data to .739 for the 1965–70 data. In all cases the population coefficients were positive, while the distance coefficients were negative.

Although it can be demonstrated that the gravity model is a useful predictor of aggregate migration behavior, scholars have often argued that such an approach cannot articulate an explanation of that behavior as it relates to the underlying decision-making process. Although efforts have been made to erect a theoretical foundation for the gravity model, especially within the contexts of utility theory (Sheppard 1978) and entropy maximizing concepts (Wilson 1971), in many ways the model is little more than a crude physical analogy of the individual choice strategy. It is obviously naive to presume that people choose migration destinations on the basis of a simple psychological trade-off between size and distance. In other words, the gravity model can be regarded as a kind of black box which provides useful information about aggregate migration behavior for reasons which are not altogether clear for individual migrants.

Although it can be criticized for its rather weak theoretical base, the gravity model at least demonstrates how the notion of push and pull factors might be profitably operationalized. In particular, rather than simply using population as a measure of regional attractiveness, the gravity model offers the possibility of substituting a variety of other variables into the equation. For example, Lowry (1966) used, along with distance, number of persons in nonagricultural employment, manufacturing wage rates, and unemployment. Rogers (1967) calibrated a modified form of Lowry's model using interregional migration flows in California. The model took the following form:

$$M_{ij} = a \left(\frac{LF_i LF_j}{D_{ij}} \cdot \frac{U_i}{U_j} \cdot \frac{WS_j}{WS_i} \right) \qquad (2.5)$$

where M_{ij} is the number of migrants going from i to j; LF_i and LF_j are the labor force eligibles at i and j; D_{ij} is the shortest highway mileage distance between the major county seats at i and j; U_i and U_j are the civilian unemployment rates at i and j; and WS_i and WS_j are the per-capita wages and salaries at i and j.

Equation 2.5 can be log-transformed for the purposes of estimation via least-squares regression analysis. It thus takes the following form:

$$\log M_{ij} = \log a + b_1 \log LF_i + b_2 \log LF_j - b_3 \log D_{ij} + \\ b_4 \log U_i - b_5 \log U_j - b_6 \log WS_i + b_7 \log WS_j \qquad (2.6)$$

where the notation is the same as in equation 2.5. When this so-called Lowry-Rogers model was applied to migration flows between metropolitan areas in California, the multiple coefficient of determination was .92 (table 2.7), although only four of the regression coefficients were significantly different from zero at the .1 probability level. In particular, distance and size of the labor force were the most important variables. Unemployment level at the destination was also significant, but it had a positive rather than a negative relationship.

In recent years a wide variety of single-equation multiple regres-

Table 2.7. Regression statistics for the
Lowry-Rogers model

Variable	Coefficient	Partial correlation coefficient
Constant	−10.8427	
$\log LF_i$	.88427*	.84628
$\log LF_j$	.74402*	.80071
$\log D_{ij}$	−.73903*	−.82692
$\log U_j$	1.15472*	.46413
$\log WS_j$	.66320	.20751
$\log WS_i$	−.56814	−.17879
$\log U_i$	−.26044	−.11737
		$R^2 = .92306$

Source: Rogers 1967: table 2.
Note: * indicates significance at the
.1 percent level.

sion models have been fit to migration data, using the kinds of variables described in the above section "The Determinants of Migration" (Barber and Milne 1988; Burnley 1988; Flowerdew and Amrhein 1989; Owen and Green 1989). For example, Renas and Kumar (1983) estimated a number of models involving net migration rates for Standard Metropolitan Statistical Areas in the United States. One of their models took the following form:

$$M_i = a + b_1 I_i + b_2 IC_i + b_3 C_i + b_4 CC_i + b_5 U_i + b_6 E_i + b_7 WT_i + b_8 ST_i \qquad (2.7)$$

where M_i is the net number of migrants into SMSA i between 1960 and 1970 expressed as a percentage of the 1960 population, I_i is the median family income in SMSA i in 1969, IC_i is the annual rate of change of median family income in SMSA i between 1959 and 1969 expressed as a percentage, C_i is a measure of the cost of living in SMSA i in 1969, CC_i is the annual rate of change in the cost of living in SMSA i expressed as a percentage, U_i is the unemployment rate in SMSA i in 1960, E_i is the median school years completed in 1960 for the population aged twenty-five years old and over in SMSA i, WT_i is the absolute deviation of the mean January temperature from sixty-five degrees Fahrenheit for SMSA i, and ST_i is the absolute deviation of the mean July temperature from sixty-five degrees Fahrenheit for SMSA i.

Table 2.8. Regression statistics for the
Renas and Kumar model of net
migration rates for SMSAs in the
United States

	Coefficients
Constant	28.436
Income	.001
Change in income	4.862*
Cost of living	−.007*
Change in cost of living	2.256
Unemployment	−2.757*
Education	2.741*
Winter temperature	−.467*
Summer temperature	−.716*
	$R^2 = .69$

Source: Renas and Kumar 1983: table 1.
(S. Renas and R. Kumar, "Climatic condi-
tions and migration: An economic inquiry,"
Annals of Regional Science, Vol. 17, 1983.)
Note: * indicates significant difference from
zero at the .05 probability level.

The multiple coefficient of determination for this model was .69,
and six of the coefficients were significantly different from zero at the
.05 probability level (table 2.8). These six coefficients also had the expected signs. Net migration was negatively related to cost of living,
unemployment, and the two temperature variables. On the other hand,
there was a positive relationship between net migration and level of
education, and between net migration and change in income. In this
latter context it is interesting to note that absolute income level was not
significantly related to migration. One of the weaknesses of this model,
however, is that some of the explanatory variables were measured for
1960 while others were measured for 1969.

McHugh (1988) provided a second example of a single-equation
regression model. In this case the dependent variable of interest was a
measure of interstate migration among blacks in the United States. The
following model was tested:

$$M_{ij} = a + b_1P_i + b_2P_j + b_3PB_i + b_4PB_j + b_5D_{ij} + b_6I_i + b_7I_j + b_8M_i + b_9M_j + b_{10}W_i + b_{11}W_j \qquad (2.8)$$

where M_{ij} is the number of blacks five years of age and older residing in
state j in 1980 and in state i in 1975; P_i is the population of state i in 1985;
P_j is the population of state j in 1975; PB_i is the percentage of the population that is black in state i in 1975; PB_j is the percentage of the popula-

Table 2.9. Regression statistics for the McHugh model of interstate migration among blacks in the United States

	Beta coefficients
Population i	.326**
Population j	.308**
Percentage black i	.259**
Percentage black j	.168**
Distance ij	−.247**
Black per-capita income i	.062**
Black per-capita income j	.091**
Blacks in armed forces i	.127**
Blacks in armed forces j	.222**
Welfare i	−.037*
Welfare j	−.068**
	$R^2 = .777$

Source: McHugh 1988: table 3. (K. McHugh, "Determinants of Black interstate migration, 1965–70 and 1975–80," *Annals of Regional Science,* Vol. 22, 1988.)
Note: * indicates significant difference from zero at the .05 probability level; ** indicates significant difference from zero at the .001 probability level.

tion that is black in state j in 1975; D_{ij} is the distance in highway miles between the principal city of black population in state i and the principal city of black population in state j; I_i is the per-capita income for blacks in state i in 1979; I_j is the per-capita income for blacks in state j in 1979; M_i is the number of blacks in the armed forces in state i in 1980; M_j is the number of blacks in the armed forces in state j in 1980; W_i is the average monthly payment for Aid to Families with Dependent Children in state i in 1978; and W_j is the average monthly payment for Aid to Families with Dependent Children in state j in 1978.

Estimates for the model were generated via least-squares regression analysis, using a double logarithmic specification. Data involved migration flows between the contiguous forty-eight states, plus the District of Columbia, providing 2,352 individual migration flows in all. The multiple coefficient of determination for this particular model was .777, and all but one of the beta coefficients was significantly different from zero at the .001 level, while that for W_i was significantly different from zero at the .05 level (table 2.9). As expected, all four population variables had significant positive relationships with black migration, while the distance variable displayed the traditional negative relationship. The variables related to the military appeared to be quite important determinants of black migration, but income and welfare levels seemed to play only minor roles.

As one might imagine, the explanatory variables in such models are often interrelated, thus posing problems of multicollinearity in estimating the regression coefficients by ordinary least-squares analysis. Consequently, Riddell (1970) has suggested that the set of explanatory variables might first be subjected to principal components analysis, thus generating a smaller number of orthogonal components that reflect the underlying similarities of the original variables. These components, as measured by the component scores, are then used in the regression equation, permitting a more realistic interpretation of the coefficients. Rodgers (1970) used this strategy when looking at the relationship between migration and industrial development in southern Italy. A principal component representing "socioeconomic health" proved to be a good predictor of out-migration between 1952 and 1968.

In addition to isolating the important variables to be included in such single-equation regression models, researchers have also focused attention on identifying the most appropriate functional form. The two most popular specifications involve the linear formulation, in which migration is assumed to be a linear function of the explanatory variables, and the log-linear formulation, in which all the variables are logarithmically transformed. The log-linear formulation has been especially common, as it generally provides a higher coefficient of determination, and the elasticity of migration with respect to an explanatory variable can be obtained directly from the estimated coefficients. A variety of other functional forms, such as semi-log, reciprocal, or log-reciprocal, can also be utilized (Goss and Chang 1983).

Most recently the polytomous logistic model, as developed by McFadden (1973), has become a popular vehicle for modeling migration (Shaw 1985:184). Here it is assumed that the migration decision involves choosing among a finite number of mutually exclusive potential destinations. The utility of a particular destination, and thus its probability of being chosen, depends upon both the attributes of the destination and the attributes of the individual making the decision. The dependent variable can be represented as the ratio of the probability of moving to destination j and the probability of staying in origin i. Estimating the effects of destination and personal characteristics involves using log transformations to produce a log-linear model.

Even when an appropriate functional form is identified, however, single-equation migration models are often inadequate. First, their use precludes the possibility of establishing causal links between the explanatory variables themselves, and thus they disregard indirect effects. Second, they do not allow for any kind of feedback effect, or reciprocal causation, between the constituent variables. These more complex interrelationships can be explored by using structural equation models, including both path analysis and systems of simultaneous equations. In chapter 3 we will turn our attention to the formulation of such multiequation models. First, however, it is useful to explore how migration models can incorporate a dynamic component in order to reflect temporal change.

Dynamic Approaches

During recent years scholars have increasingly tried to construct migration models that reflect the dynamic nature of migration streams (Odland and Bailey 1990; Plane 1987; Plane and Rogerson 1986; Rogerson 1990; Weidlich and Haag 1988). For example, temporal change has been formally analyzed using Markov chain models (Joseph 1975; Hirst 1976). Migration transition probability matrices can be constructed to describe the probability of moving from one region to another during some specified time period. Clark (1986), for example, reported a transition probability matrix in which the values represented the probability of moving to some other region in the United States, based on data for the period 1975–80. Thus, there was a .0153 probability that an individual living in the South in 1975 had moved to the North Central region by 1980 (table 2.10). As one would expect, the highest values were along the diagonal, indicating the probabilities of people remaining in their regions of origin.

Although Markov models are attractive, in that the transition probabilities reflect both the relationships between regions and the stochastic nature of migration decisions, they are limited by a number of rather restrictive assumptions. First, the transition probabilities are assumed to be temporally stable. Second, the population is assumed to be

Table 2.10. Transition probabilities for regional population shifts in the United States

	1975				
	Northeast	North Central	South	West	Total
Northeast	.9358	.0064	.0097	.0069	.2188
North Central	.0098	.9380	.0153	.0165	.2629
South	.0381	.0332	.9592	.0274	.3310
West	.0163	.0224	.0159	.9492	.1873
Total	.2273	.2695	.3215	.1817	1.0000

Source: Clark 1986: table 3.6d. (Clark, W.A.V., *Human Migration*, p. 63, copyright © 1986 by Sage Publications, Inc. Reprinted by permission of Sage Publications, Inc.)

homogeneous, and this implies that everyone obeys the same transition matrix. Third, the Markov property suggests that the probability of migrating between two areas is solely dependent upon current location, not upon previous behavior. More recently researchers have attempted to construct models of change that relax the assumption of stationary transition matrices by explicitly incorporating heterogeneous populations and changing preferences (Huff and Clark 1978b).

Perhaps the most impressive use of the Markov approach has been in multiregional demographic analysis (Rees 1983; Rogers and Willekens 1986), which is characterized by the demographer's concern for precise measurements on disaggregated populations. A multiregional life table requires information concerning the probability of individuals surviving to certain ages, measures of fertility, and estimates of mobility. Such data allows one to address the issues of how individuals born in one region will redistribute themselves across other regions and at what stage in the life cycle such movement is most likely to occur. In this way changing patterns of population distribution can be related to differential growth rates across regions over time. Increasingly, however, multiregional demography has begun to introduce socioeconomic factors that can be used to explain the values taken by the model parameters. As a result, the lack of behavioral content in Markov models indicates that they can be profitably combined with a regression-based approach, which explicitly incorporates a set of explanatory variables (Rogerson 1984).

An alternative approach for capturing the dynamics of migration flows is also available in the form of various time-series techniques (Chatfield 1984). For example, one can develop moving average models and autoregressive models. In the moving average model the value of an individual variable at a particular point in time is generated by the weighted average of a finite number of previous and current random disturbances, or shocks. By contrast, in an autoregressive model the current observation is generated by a weighted average of past observations, together with a random disturbance in the current period. Mixed autoregressive–moving average models can be developed for stationary time series, and certain types of nonstationary time series can be differenced in order to produce a stationary time series, thus allowing the development of a general integrated autoregressive–moving average model. Within the context of migration, this autoregressive integrated moving average process, known as ARIMA, suggests that the amount of migration from one time period to the next is a complex function of previous migration plus current and previous random disturbances.

The implications of these time-series models for migration have only just begun to be explored. Markovian models of interregional migration are essentially autoregressive. Similarly, demographic forecasting models that specify the determinants of population change by accounting for births, deaths, and migration (Rees and Wilson 1977) are also autoregressive and assume the random disturbance term to be negligible. Most geographic processes are stochastic rather than completely deterministic, however, as a variety of unknown variables, or an exogenously generated random element, may affect the dependent variable. Consequently, when a variable like migration is treated in dynamic terms, one is observing an underlying stochastic process that can be treated as some form of ARIMA model.

G. L. Clark (1982a) has investigated gross migration flows using ARIMA models and suggests that both autoregressive and moving average processes are at work. In particular, Markovian, or autoregressive, models are apparently inappropriate for many rapidly growing regions. Such regions contain a sizable moving average component, implying that in-migration is a volatile process, more influenced by exogenous and rapid shocks than by previous patterns of in-migration. In contrast, average and decelerating growth areas seem better approximated by autoregressive models. Future efforts along these lines are likely to incorporate spatial autocorrelation by using space-time autocorrelation functions. The prior assignment of weights reflecting the effects of contiguous interregional migration flows, however, remains problematic. The usual assignment of weights according to distance-decay principles might be unwise, as regions are not necessarily highly integrated with their immediate neighbors, at least in the context of migration (G. L. Clark 1982b).

Distributed lag models allow the incorporation of temporal information in the explanatory variables (Dhrymes 1971). In this case migration acts as the dependent variable, while some explanatory variable, such as unemployment level, is measured over a series of prior time periods. The equation can then be specified as follows:

$$Y_t = a + b_0 X_t + b_1 X_{t-1} + b_2 X_{t-2} + b_3 X_{t-3} + e \qquad (2.9)$$

where Y_t is a measure of migration at time period t, X_t is a measure of unemployment at time period t, X_{t-1} is unemployment in the previous time period, and so on. The use of such lagged variables allows one to take into account the fact that the relationships between variables such as unemployment and migration are not always instantaneous and often involve time lags.

Bearing in mind the usual assumptions of the multiple regression model, one can use ordinary least-squares procedures to estimate the coefficients, at least in principle. In practice, however, certain problems associated with the distributed lag model tend to preclude the direct application of ordinary least-squares analysis (Katz 1982:181). First, the estimation of an equation with a large number of lagged explanatory variables will be compromised by multicollinearity, leading to imprecise parameter estimates. Second, a lengthy lag structure will require the estimation of a large number of parameters, often severely reducing the degrees of freedom. Third, the creation of lagged variables reduces the number of observations, which are often in short supply in time-series models.

Some of these difficulties can be resolved if one is prepared to make some a priori specifications concerning the form of the distributed lag and thus impose some restrictions on the lag weights. For example, in the Koyck geometric lag model (Koyck 1954), the weights associated with the lagged explanatory variables are all positive and decline geometrically with time. Such a condition reduces the number of parameters to be estimated; although the weights never become zero, beyond a certain time the effects of the explanatory variable are negligible. While the geometric lag model can be quite useful, it is somewhat limited by the fact that it postulates a declining set of lag weights. A more general formulation is provided by the Almon polynomial distributed lag model (Almon 1965), which merely assumes that the lag weights will follow certain patterns and that these patterns can be approximated by fitting polynomial functions. Often a third- or fourth-degree polynomial will be sufficient, although higher-order polynomials can be specified when sufficient data are available (Pindyck and Rubinfeld 1976:218).

Where the data allow, Fourier analysis and spectral analysis can be used to describe fairly complex temporal changes (Rayner 1971). Fourier analysis involves modeling a time series by fitting sine and cosine functions. A cosine series represents a regular wave with a specific length from crest to crest. Sine waves can be added to allow for the fact that the series may not begin at the top of a crest. Spectral analysis can be viewed as an extension of Fourier series analysis, in that it does not use exact wavelengths but instead involves frequency bands of specified width; thus it is more appropriate for the kind of fluctuations encountered in migration flows, which are seldom exactly periodic. Cross-spectral analysis can be employed when one is interested in the relationships between two or more time series.

Event history analysis represents a particular type of dynamic approach that allows one to model the interrelationships between specific life course events, such as leaving school, marriage, or divorce, and migration. In general, an event is some qualitative change that occurs at a particular point in time, rather than a gradual change in some quantitative variable (Davies 1991). Thus the occurrence of an event implies a relatively sharp disjunction between what precedes and what follows, and an event history is a longitudinal record of when events happen to a sample of individuals (Allison 1984). There is no single method of event history analysis, but rather a variety of related techniques developed in such disparate disciplines as sociology, biostatistics, and engineering. Whereas biologists and engineers have tended to emphasize methods for single, nonrepeatable events, such as death, sociologists have tended to emphasize repeated events, such as job change. All three traditions, however, have focused on regression-type models where the occurrence of an event depends upon some linear function of explanatory variables. Sandefur and Scott (1981), using a method of event history analysis described by Tuma, Hannan, and Groeneveld (1979), were able to show that the traditional inverse relationship between age and migration is primarily due to the effects of family life cycle and career variables.

Dynamic data on mobility, however, are often much more readily available for discrete time intervals, as in panel studies, than for the continuous time mobility histories employed in event history analysis. Panel data involves successive waves of interviews, using a particular sample of individuals or households (Sandefur, Tuma, and Kephart 1991). Panel surveys became especially popular during the late 1970s as a means of monitoring the effectiveness of federally funded social experiments, but only more recently has information on geographic mobility been available from such sources (Dahmann 1986). Great care should be taken when utilizing panel data, however, as different experimental designs concerning the number and spacing of waves can lead to different substantive conclusions (Sandefur and Tuma 1987). For example, monitoring the mobility of individuals during a single short interval can generate different interpretations than monitoring the same group of individuals during a single long interval. Furthermore, measuring explanatory variables at the end of a particular time period can be misleading, especially if those variables are likely to change over time due to migration. Finally, panel studies suffer what has been called the "initial condition problem" (Davies and Pickles 1985). That is, data from panel studies interrupt the process of interest at some intermediate point, rather than starting at the beginning.

3

Structural Equation
Models of Migration

Structural equation models provide a powerful approach for examining the structure of relationships among a set of variables. Such models include causal models, path analysis, and systems of simultaneous equations (Cadwallader 1986b). These models are stochastic and are composed of exogenous and endogenous sets of variables. Each equation represents a causal link, rather than a mere empirical association, and each of these links generates a hypothesis that can be tested by estimating the magnitude of the relationship (Dwyer 1983). In general, structural equation models involve the analysis of nonexperimental data, whereby statistical procedures are substituted for the conventional experimental controls that can be utilized under laboratory conditions. The notion of a system is also relevant, as the models usually consist of several equations that interact together.

The use of the word *cause* in the term *causal modeling* is not unproblematic, however. Bunge (1959) suggests that one of the central characteristics of the scientist's conception of causality is the notion of producing. That is, if X is a cause of Y, then a change in X should produce a change in Y, not simply that a change in X is always followed by a change in Y, or that a change in X is always associated with a change in Y. This idea of producing a change is similar to the concept of forcing as applied to an external stimulus that generates changes in a physical system. Unfortunately, however, a fundamental objection to the idea that causes involve a producing or forcing phenomenon is that such phenomena cannot be directly observed. We have only indirect evidence concerning covariation and temporal sequence.

Perhaps a more productive way to capture the nature of causal terminology is to focus on the ingredients of causality. As Kenny (1979:3) notes, at least three conditions must hold for a scientist to claim that X causes Y. First, a temporal sequence should be involved, as the idea of causality implies a process that takes place over time. For X to cause Y, X must precede Y in some kind of temporal sequence. An effect cannot precede its cause. Second, causality implies the presence of a functional relationship between cause and effect. Cause and effect are operationalized as variables, and these two variables should not behave independently of each other. That is, a known value of one variable for any particular observation should provide information about the value of the other variable for that same observation. Furthermore, we determine whether the relationship could be explained by chance, and a variety of statistical procedures can help us infer whether a sample relationship indicates a relationship within the population.

The third condition is more difficult to detect empirically: the relationship should be nonspurious. That is, there should not be a third variable Z that causes both X and Y such that the relationship between X and Y disappears when Z is controlled for. A difficulty here is that controlling for Z might mask the fact that Z is really an intervening variable, in that X might cause Z and Z might cause Y. In either event, controlling for Z will make the relationship between X and Y vanish, but while a spurious variable explains away a causal relationship, an intervening variable helps to elaborate the causal argument. Distinguishing between spurious and intervening variables is not always easy in an empirical context, and the so-called third or excluded variable problem provides a major difficulty for causal analysts.

In practical terms, it is probably best not to attach any elaborate philosophical meaning to the use of the word *cause* in causal modeling, and the term *system modeling* might be an equally appropriate label. No specific definition of the word *cause* need by implied, as it merely corresponds to a hypothesized, unobserved process that represents the mechanisms embodied in a system of equations. As such, it is perhaps most useful to think of structural equation models simply as formal representations of the ideas that we have about a particular phenomenon. In this sense, we will not be in danger of losing sight of the fact that causality is merely a preconceived idea that we use to interpret our experience of phenomena.

What distinguishes structural equation models from conventional regression analysis is the focus upon unmixed, autonomous, and invariant structural parameters. Regression parameters tend to be mixtures of the structural parameters, and if one structural parameter changes, all the regression coefficients may alter (Goldberger 1973). The issue of invariance relates to the comparison of parameters across different populations and is associated with discussions concerning the appropriateness of using standardized parameters in structural equation models. In certain situations, comparing standardized parameters can be misleading, since they involve inseparable combinations of more fundamental parameters. For this reason, Duncan (1975:65) has argued that the multiple correlation coefficient should not be interpreted as a structural parameter.

The development of structural equation models has involved the convergence of a number of originally disparate research traditions. Econometrics has a rich tradition of interest in simultaneous equation models, involving nonrecursive relationships among a set of variables that contain negligible measurement error (Goldberger 1972). Psychometrics, on the other hand, has been primarily responsible for the concept of latent, or unmeasured, variables and has encouraged the areas of inquiry known as factor analysis and reliability theory (Bentler 1980). Wright (1934), in his work in biometrics, first suggested the overlap of these approaches by considering simultaneous equation models, sometimes involving latent variables, in the context of path analysis. Path analysis subsequently became an important part of the structural equation models literature in sociology (Bielby and Hauser 1977). Indeed, the integrative role of sociologists proved to be pivotal, as path analysis encouraged economists to recognize that identification can be attained in the presence of measurement error and psychologists to recognize that identification can be attained in the presence of simultaneous relationships (Goldberger 1973). Finally, the psychometrician Jöreskog (1982) probably deserves the major credit for developing the so-called LISREL model, which represents a flexible method for dealing with extremely complex models, especially those including latent variables.

In the present chapter causal models and path analysis are first introduced, and then two path models of interregional migration are described. Simultaneous equation models, involving two-way causation, are then examined, again followed by two examples from the migration literature. Finally, the issue of urban growth and migration is discussed from the perspective of a simultaneous equation approach. Consideration of structural equation models with latent variables is postponed until Chapter 5.

Causal Models and Path Analysis

Simon's (1985) work on the problem of spurious correlation and Bla-lock's later extension of these ideas (Pringle 1980) stimulated much of the original work in causal modeling. This approach can be illustrated by the simple three-variable recursive model presented in figure 3.1.

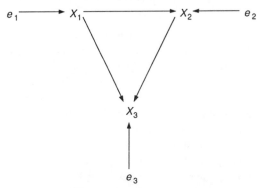

Figure 3.1. A three-variable recursive model.
Source: Cadwallader 1986b:fig. 1.

All the arrows indicate one-way causality, and X_1 is an exogenous variable, determined by forces outside the system, while X_2 and X_3 are endogenous variables, as their values are at least partly determined by variables within the system itself. This causal structure can be mathematically described by the following three equations:

$$X_1 = e_1 \tag{3.1}$$

$$X_2 = b_{21} X_1 + e_2 \tag{3.2}$$

$$X_3 = b_{31.2} X_1 + b_{32.1} X_2 + e_3 \tag{3.3}$$

Note that the a terms can be omitted by simply assuming that each variable is measured in standardized form, thus ensuring that the least-squares line passes through the origin and that the a terms, or intercepts, are therefore zero.

In general, any kind of causal structure can be described by an appropriate set of equations. For example, the four-variable recursive model represented by figure 3.2(a) can be expressed as follows:

$$X_1 = e_1 \tag{3.4}$$

$$X_2 = b_{21} X_1 + e_2 \tag{3.5}$$

$$X_3 = b_{31.2} X_1 + b_{32.1} X_2 + e_3 \tag{3.6}$$

$$X_4 = b_{41.23} X_1 + b_{42.13} X_2 + b_{43.12} X_3 + e_4 \tag{3.7}$$

The empirical adequacy of this causal structure is best understood by successively removing individual causal arrows from figure 3.2a (Blalock 1964:66). If the arrow between X_1 and X_3 is eliminated (fig. 3.2b), it means that X_1 only has an indirect effect on X_3 via X_2. In other words, we are really saying that $r_{31.2}$ equals zero, meaning that when the intervening variable X_2 is controlled for, the partial correlation between X_1 and X_3 should be approximately zero. Also, if $r_{31.2}$ equals zero, then the associated standardized regression coefficient $b_{31.2}$ equals zero and thus disappears from equation 3.6.

If we next omit the arrow linking X_1 and X_4 (fig. 3.2c), we are saying that X_1 will only influence X_4 via X_2 and X_3. We are therefore predicting that $r_{41.23}$ equals zero and that the associated standardized regression coefficient $b_{41.23}$ will disappear from equation 3.7.

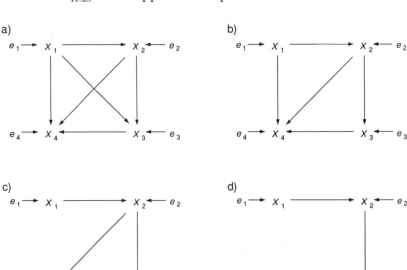

Figure 3.2. Examples of four-variable recursive models.
Source: Based on Blalock 1964:figs. 3–6.

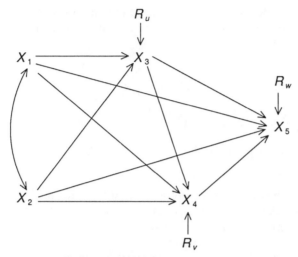

Figure 3.3. A path diagram.
Source: Based on Duncan 1966:fig. 1.

Finally, if the arrow linking X_2 and X_4 is removed (fig. 3.2d), we are hypothesizing that X_2 only influences X_4 via X_3, thus creating a simple causal chain going from X_1 to X_2 to X_3 to X_4. If this hypothesis is true, then $r_{42.13}$ equals zero and $b_{42.13}$ equals zero.

Path analysis represents a straightforward extension of this causal modeling framework, as it involves estimating the magnitude of the linkages between variables, rather than merely focusing upon their presence or absence. In addition, path analysis allows one to distinguish between the direct and indirect effects between variables and to decompose the correlation between any two variables into a sum of simple and compound paths. Some of these compound paths involve theoretically meaningful indirect effects, while others may represent noncausal components of association. Note that path analysis includes information provided by the previously described causal modeling technique, in that a nonexistent link is implied by a zero path coefficient.

Consider the path diagram represented by figure 3.3. One-way arrows lead from each determining variable to each dependent variable, and two-headed arrows indicate unanalyzed correlations between variables that are not causally dependent upon other variables in the system. Such two-headed arrows are drawn curved, rather than straight, to distinguish them from true causal links. The numerical values placed on the diagrams are the path coefficients, or in the case of the two-headed arrows, simply the zero-order correlation coefficients.

If each of the variables is measured in standardized form, then the causal structure in figure 3.3 can be represented by the following structural equations:

$$X_3 = P_{31}X_1 + P_{32}X_2 + P_{3u}R_u \tag{3.8}$$

$$X_4 = P_{41}X_1 + P_{42}X_2 + P_{43}X_3 + P_{4v}R_v \tag{3.9}$$

$$X_5 = P_{51}X_1 + P_{52}X_2 + P_{53}X_3 + P_{54}X_4 + P_{5w}R_w \tag{3.10}$$

where the P terms are path coefficients, and R_u, R_v, and R_w refer to the residual, or disturbance, terms. As can be seen from the diagram, these residual terms are uncorrelated with any of the immediate determinants of the variable to which they pertain and are also uncorrelated with each other. In this context, the path diagram supplies important information about the causal system that is not directly discernible from the structural equations themselves (Duncan 1966).

In this simple recursive situation the path coefficients can be estimated from ordinary least-squares regression analysis, as they represent standardized regression coefficients. Thus, for example, P_{32} equals $b_{32.1}$, and P_{31} equals $b_{31.2}$. Similarly, P_{42} equals $b_{42.13}$, and P_{43} equals $b_{43.12}$. Unlike the notation for partial regression and correlation coefficients, the notation for path coefficients does not identify the other variables influencing the particular endogenous variable under consideration. The path coefficient associated with the residual term is simply the square root of the unexplained variation in the dependent variable, since standardized variables have a variance of one.

One way to decompose the correlation coefficients between the constituent variables is to use the following expression:

$$r_{ij} = P_{iq}r_{jq} \tag{3.11}$$

where i and j denote two variables in the system, and the index q runs over all variables from which paths lead directly to X_i, or, in other words, those variables having a direct impact on X_i. This expression is the basic theorem of path analysis and states that the correlation between any two variables can be decomposed into the sum of simple and compound paths, where a compound path is equal to the product of the simple paths comprising it.

Using this formula in the context of figure 3.3, it can be seen that

$$r_{53} = P_{53} + P_{51}P_{31} + P_{51}r_{12}P_{32} + P_{52}P_{32} + P_{52}r_{12}P_{31} +$$
$$P_{54}P_{41}P_{31} + P_{54}P_{41}r_{12}P_{32} + P_{54}P_{42}P_{32} +$$
$$P_{54}P_{42}r_{12}P_{31} + P_{54}P_{43} \qquad (3.12)$$

This expression can be most easily obtained by referring to the path diagram and reading back from variable i, then forward to variable j. When doing so, three instructions should be observed. First, no path can pass through the same variable more than once. Second, no path can go back along an arrow having started forward on a different arrow. Third, a path can go in either direction along a two-headed arrow, but only one such two-headed arrow can be used in any single path.

In this way correlations can be decomposed into four components of association (Alwin and Hauser 1981). As can be seen from figure 3.4, these components involve a direct effect, an indirect effect due to some intervening variable, an effect due to associated causes (or some un-analyzed correlation), and an effect due to common causes (or spurious causation).

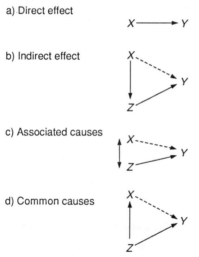

a) Direct effect

b) Indirect effect

c) Associated causes

d) Common causes

Figure 3.4. The components of association between X and Y.
Source: Cadwallader 1986b:fig. 4.

Two simple three-variable models can be used to describe these various components of association. Looking at figure 3.5a, we can decompose three different correlations. First,

$$r_{12} = P_{21} \qquad (3.13)$$

Structural Equation Models

a)

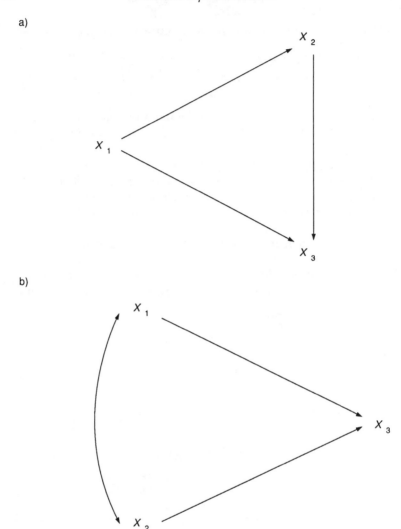

b)

Figure 3.5. Two three-variable models that illustrate the four components of association. *Source:* Cadwallader 1986b:fig. 5.

which means that the entire correlation between X_1 and X_2 is attributable to the direct effect P_{21}. Second,

$$r_{13} = P_{31} + P_{32}P_{21} \tag{3.14}$$

which means that the correlation between X_1 and X_3 is generated by the direct effect P_{31} and the indirect effect $P_{32}P_{21}$. Third,

$$r_{23} = P_{32} + P_{31}P_{21} \qquad (3.15)$$

which means that the correlation between X_2 and X_3 is generated by the direct effect P_{32} plus correlation due to a common cause, $P_{31}P_{21}$.

Figure 3.5b illustrates the idea of associated causes. In this case,

$$r_{13} = P_{31} + P_{32}r_{12} \qquad (3.16)$$

where P_{31} is the direct effect and $P_{32}r_{12}$ represents that part of the correlation due to associated causes, or correlation with another cause. It should be noted that figure 3.5b represents a single-equation regression model, where the correlation between the exogenous variables is indicated by the double-headed arrow. Such models correctly represent the direct effects of the two exogenous variables but supply no information about how any indirect effects are generated, as the causal structure of the relationship between the exogenous variables is unknown. In this sense, a major goal of theory construction should be to generate models that will make some of the exogenous variables endogenous (Duncan 1975:43).

Of particular importance in this discussion is the distinction between total association and total effect. The total association between two variables is the sum of the four components of association noted above and is given by the zero-order correlation coefficient. The total effect, on the other hand, is the sum of the direct and indirect effects, where the indirect effects are transmitted by variables which intervene between the cause and effect of interest. Most important, one cannot usually calculate the indirect effect by simply subtracting the direct effect from the zero-order correlation coefficient.

Path Models of Migration

Path analysis is thus a useful way to analyze the interrelationships between a set of explanatory variables and migration, as it allows one to estimate the magnitude of the linkages between variables, which then provide information about the underlying causal processes. In the first example to be described (Cadwallader 1985b), the causal model is recursive, since there are no feedback effects between variables. As a result, ordinary least-squares regression techniques can be used to obtain the path coefficients, although all the normal regression assumptions should be met. In particular, we are forced to assume that the disturbance terms in the structural equations are independent of the causal variables in those same equations (Duncan 1975:5).

The term *path coefficient,* as originally used by Wright (1934), referred to the standardized regression coefficient, or beta coefficient. As Wright (1985) himself later pointed out, however, the standardized and unstandardized coefficients should be seen as complementary, since they provide different kinds of information. In the context of migration models, when comparing models for different subgroups or parts of the country, it seems advisable to use unstandardized estimates, since they will be unaffected by the different variances in the same variable that might occur for different subgroups or regions. On the other hand, if one wishes to compare the relative importance of variables within a particular subgroup or regional context, as in the present instance, then the standardized coefficient is the more appropriate, as it adjusts for the different measurement scales associated with the different variables.

The causal model to be analyzed via path analysis is represented by the following set of structural equations:

$$X_4 = b_{41}X_1 + b_{42}X_2 + b_{43}X_3 + e_4 \tag{3.17}$$

$$X_5 = b_{51}X_1 + b_{52}X_2 + b_{53}X_3 + b_{54}X_4 + e_5 \tag{3.18}$$

$$X_6 = b_{61}X_1 + b_{62}X_2 + b_{63}X_3 + b_{64}X_4 + b_{65}X_5 + e_6 \tag{3.19}$$

where X_1 is the percentage of the civilian labor force employed in agriculture, forestry, and fisheries; X_2 is the percentage of the population living in urban settlements; X_3 is the median number of school years completed by all adults aged twenty-five years and over; X_4 is the percentage of males sixteen years and over in the civilian labor force who are unemployed; X_5 is median income; X_6 is net migration; b_{41}–b_{65} are the path coefficients; and e_4, e_5, and e_6 are the disturbance terms, or residual path coefficients.

The data to calibrate this model were collected for all forty-two State Economic Areas in the Upper Midwest (Michigan, Minnesota, and Wisconsin). State Economic Areas were chosen as the basic units of analysis because they have greater internal homogeneity, in socioeconomic characteristics, than do either states or counties. The data for all the variables were obtained from the *State Economic Area Reports.* In particular, the major variable of interest, net migration, was measured by subtracting the amount of out-migration from the amount of in-migration and dividing by the population, using the migration flow data in the *State Economic Area Reports,* for each State Economic Area. This particular measure of migration was used as the central variable in

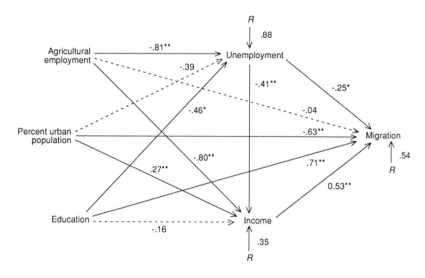

Figure 3.6. The path coefficients for migration in the Upper Midwest, 1955–1960.
Source: Cadwallader 1985b:fig. 1.
Note: ** indicates path coefficients that are significant at .05; * indicates path coefficients that are significant at .10; hashed lines indicate path coefficients that are not significant at .10. R refers to the residual path coefficient.

the analysis because it conveniently combines information concerning both in- and out-migration flows, although it should be noted that there is no such individual as a "net migrant" (Rogers 1990). In other circumstances, where the focus is on distinguishing between the causal factors involved in generating out-migration as opposed to in-migration, more disaggregated measures of migration flows are desirable. Net migration was obtained for two time periods, 1955–60 and 1965–70, in order to explore any temporal variation.

The standardized regression coefficients associated with the structural equations represent the path coefficients (figs. 3.6 and 3.7), and the path coefficient associated with the disturbance term, incorporating the combined effect of all unspecified variables, is the square root of the unexplained variation in the dependent variable under consideration. For comparative purposes, statistical significance is reported both at the .10 and .05 levels, although it should be remembered that the significance level per se says nothing about the strength of the relationship but merely indicates the amount of risk associated with assuming that the relationship exists.

The constituent path coefficients can be conveniently discussed by

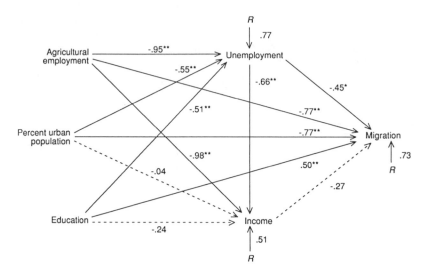

Figure 3.7. The path coefficients for migration in the Upper Midwest, 1965–1970.
Source: Cadwallader 1985b:fig. 2.
Note: ** indicates path coefficients that are significant at .05; * indicates path coefficients that are significant at .10; hashed lines indicate path coefficients that are not significant at .10. R refers to the residual path coefficient.

distinguishing between the effects of the exogenous and endogenous variables on migration. Focusing first on the direct influence of the three exogenous variables—agricultural employment, the percentage urban population, and education—we can see that the percentage urban population is negatively related to net migration in both 1955–60 and 1965–70. Similarly, education is positively related to net migration in both time periods, which indicates that higher educational levels are related to higher levels of migration-induced regional growth. The behavior of the agricultural employment variable is less systematic, however, as it is negatively associated with migration in 1965–70 but not significantly related in 1955–60.

Second, with respect to the endogenous variables, unemployment is negatively related to migration in both time periods, which implies that high levels of unemployment are not associated with large net influxes of migrants. As expected, income levels are positively associated with net migration in 1955–60. This relationship is negative in 1965–70, however, although it is not significantly different from zero at the .10 level.

Overall, the pattern of statistically significant path coefficients is remarkably similar for the two time periods. The only differences are that the percentage urban population is not significantly related to unemployment in 1955–60 or income in 1965–70, agricultural employment is not significantly related to migration in 1955–60, and income is not significantly related to migration in 1965–70. It is somewhat of a surprise that education is not significantly related to income in either of the two time periods, although it should be remembered that the percentage urban population, agricultural employment, and unemployment were all being controlled for.

The total effect of each causally prior variable on the succeeding variables can be readily partitioned into direct and indirect components. The direct effect is represented by the path coefficient linking two variables, whereas the indirect effect is calculated by multiplying the path coefficients associated with the intervening variables. For example, besides the direct path between agricultural employment and migration, there are three indirect paths, one via unemployment, a second via unemployment and income, and a third via income. As previously noted, the total effect between any two variables in a recursive model is not necessarily the same as the correlation coefficient between those two variables, as the latter term can also include association due to the correlation between predetermined variables and spurious association caused by joint dependence on a prior variable, as well as direct and indirect effects (Alwin and Hauser 1981; Finney 1972).

In the present instance, many of the indirect effects run counter to the direct effect and thus reduce the total effect (table 3.1). For example, the large negative direct effect of the percentage urban population on migration is partially offset, in both 1955–60 and 1965–70, by positive indirect effects. Similarly, the negative direct effect of agricultural employment in 1965–70 is partially offset by a positive indirect effect, although in 1955–60 both the direct and indirect effects of this variable on net migration are only marginal. In contrast, the positive direct effect of education is compounded in both time periods by the indirect effects via unemployment and income. It is thus important, in any migration context, to be able to disentangle these different kinds of influences.

Todd (1981) provides a second example of a path model of migration. He used path analysis to investigate the different kinds of push factors that induce rural out-migration from southern Manitoba and was thus concerned with the characteristics of origins rather than destinations. In particular, he postulated that average family income would influence both the level of community satisfaction and the rate of rural

Table 3.1. The effects of each variable on migration in the Upper Midwest

	Direct effect	Indirect effect	Total effect
1955–60			
Agricultural employment	-.04	-.04	-.08
Percentage urban population	-.63	.32	-.31
Education	.71	.14	.85
Unemployment	-.25	-.22	-.47
Income	.53	—	.53
1965–70			
Agricultural employment	-.77	.52	-.25
Percentage urban population	-.77	.16	-.61
Education	.50	.20	.70
Unemployment	-.45	.18	-.27
Income	-.27	—	-.27

Source: Cadwallader 1985b: table 1.

out-migration and that rural out-migration would also be dependent upon community satisfaction (fig. 3.8). In other words, income would have a direct effect on migration and also an indirect effect via community satisfaction, where the latter variable represents the level of satisfaction expressed by rural dwellers concerning the availability of social facilities in their local service centers. Income should be positively related to satisfaction and negatively related to out-migration, while community satisfaction should also be negatively related to out-migration.

A series of exogenous variables were then added to the model. For example, family income was expected to depend upon such variables

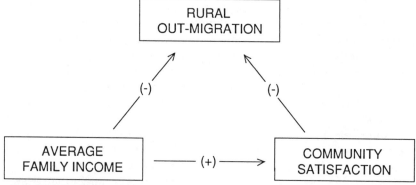

Figure 3.8. The recursive relationships among the endogenous variables for rural out-migration in Southern Manitoba.
Source: Todd 1981:fig. 1.

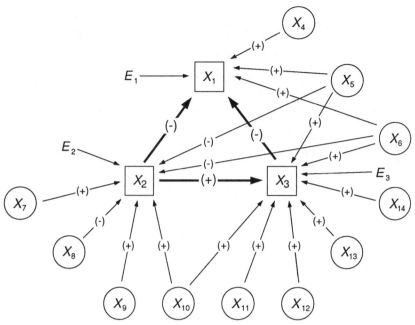

Figure 3.9. The predicted recursive path system for rural out-migration in Southern Manitoba.
Source: Todd 1981:fig. 2.

as the proportion of the labor force engaged in manufacturing and the proportion of the rural population with high school or university education. Similarly, community satisfaction was expected to be dependent upon such variables as proportion of the work force classed as public administration and defense, and the average number of rooms per house. Finally, rural out-migration was expected to be related to average family size, distance to regional centers, and distance to Winnipeg. These predicted relationships are summarized in figure 3.9.

The associated structural equations are as follows:

$$X_1 = -b_{1.2}X_2 - b_{1.3}X_3 + b_{1.4}X_4 + b_{1.5}X_5 + b_{1.6}X_6 + e_1 \tag{3.20}$$

$$X_2 = -b_{2.5}X_5 - b_{2.6}X_6 + b_{2.7}X_7 - b_{2.8}X_8 + b_{2.9}X_9 + b_{2.10}X_{10} + b_{2.11}X_{11} + e_2 \tag{3.21}$$

$$X_3 = b_{3.2}X_2 + b_{3.5}X_5 + b_{3.6}X_6 + b_{3.10}X_{10} + b_{3.12}X_{12} + b_{3.13}X_{13} + b_{3.14}X_{14} + e_3 \tag{3.22}$$

Table 3.2. Regression estimates associated with the recursive path system for rural out-migration in Southern Manitoba

	X_1	X_2	X_3
X_2	-.196**		-.214**
	(2.146)		(1.790)
X_3	-.069		
	(.803)		
X_4	.046		
	(.521)		
X_5	.230**	-.088***	.235**
	(2.333)	(2.421)	(2.082)
X_6	.404***	-.047**	.058
	(4.004)	(1.171)	(.481)
X_7		-.080**	
		(2.268)	
X_8		-.107***	
		(3.176)	
X_9		.042	
		(1.160)	
X_{10}		.101***	.004
		(2.443)	(.033)
X_{11}		-1.033***	
		(26.207)	
X_{12}			.126
			(1.032)
X_{13}			.011
			(.100)
X_{14}			.084
			(.700)
R^2	.249	.910	.096
F	7.165***	152.545***	1.598
d	1.894	1.683	1.798

t-values are in parentheses.
  *$\alpha = .10$
 **$\alpha = .05$
***$\alpha = .01$
Source: Todd 1981: table 2.

where X_1 is ratio of net out-migration, 1971–76, to rural population, 1971; X_2 is average family income, 1971; X_3 is community satisfaction, 1971; X_4 is average family size, 1971; X_5 is distance to regional centers; X_6 is distance to Winnipeg; X_7 is a measure of farm sales; X_8 is percentage of population of Ukrainian origin, 1971; X_9 is percentage of labor force in manufacturing; X_{10} is a measure of education; X_{11} is population, 1971; X_{12} is percentage of population denoted as Mennonite, 1971;

X_{13} is percentage of labor force in public administration and defense, 1971; X_{14} is average number of rooms per house, 1971; b_{ij} is the path coefficient; and e is the disturbance term or residual path coefficient. Data to calibrate the model were drawn from 114 census subdivisions in the agricultural portion of southern Manitoba.

The equations were estimated using ordinary least-squares regression analysis, and the results are reported in table 3.2. The overall goodness-of-fit for each equation, as represented by the coefficient of multiple determination, is rather disappointing for community satisfaction and out-migration, but quite encouraging for family income. More specifically, three of the five explanatory variables are significant for equation 3.20, all but one are significant for equation 3.21, while only two out of seven are significant for equation 3.22. With respect to the original hypothesized relationships between out-migration, family income, and community satisfaction, it should be noted that, as predicted, out-migration is inversely related to both family income and community satisfaction, although the latter relationship is not statistically significant. On the other hand, the relationship between income and community satisfaction is unexpectedly negative, indicating that higher average income promotes community dissatisfaction, perhaps due to increasing aspiration levels. In any event, as a result of the rather large residual path coefficients associated with equations 3.20 and 3.22, the original path model was modified, and the possibility of feedback effects was entertained (Todd 1981). The inclusion of such feedback effects, which are likely to occur in many migration contexts, involves the specification of simultaneous equation systems.

Simultaneous Equation Models

An introduction to causal models in general was provided earlier in this chapter, but the issue of nonrecursive models involving two-way causation was not explicitly examined (Todd 1979). The causal structure depicted in figure 3.10a represents a nonrecursive model, as there is a feedback relationship between variables X_1 and X_3. This causal structure can be expressed by the following equations:

$$X_1 = a + b_3X_3 + e_1 \tag{3.23}$$

$$X_2 = a + b_1X_1 + e_2 \tag{3.24}$$

$$X_3 = a + b_1X_1 + b_2X_2 + e_3 \tag{3.25}$$

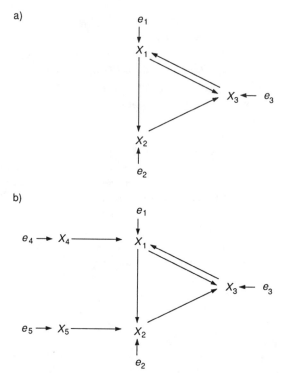

Figure 3.10. Causal models with reciprocal relationships.
Source: Cadwallader 1986b:fig. 6.

Note that there is one equation for each variable, as the values for each variable are at least partly determined by the other variables within the causal system. Each equation also contains an error term, summarizing the effects of those variables that are not explicitly included within the causal system.

Three major issues are involved when one is dealing with a simultaneous equation model: specification, identification, and estimation. Misspecification, or specification error, involves what might be more simply called "using the wrong model" (Duncan 1975:101). Specification error includes the omission of relevant variables in the model and the misspecification of the correct form of the equations. In the latter context, equations 3.23, 3.24, and 3.25 assume that the relationships between the variables are both linear and additive. A linear relationship implies that a unit change in X_2 has the same effect on X_1, whatever the value of X_2, while an additive relationship implies that a unit change in X_2 has the same effect on X_1, whatever the values of the other variables in the equation (Macdonald 1977:84).

The general linear model can, however, be adapted to handle many kinds of nonlinearity, such as logarithmic relationships, polynomials, or exponentials (Stolzenberg 1979). Similarly, some nonadditive relationships, such as those found in multiplicative models, can also be explored within the framework of the general linear model. For example, consider the following equation:

$$X_1 = a + b_2X_2 + b_3X_3 + b_4X_4 \tag{3.26}$$

where X_4 is the product of X_2 and X_3. This equation can be estimated by creating a variable equal to the product of X_2 and X_3 and then simply using least-squares regression analysis. If b_4, the coefficient for the multiplicative term, is significantly different from zero, then there is evidence that the effects of X_2 and X_3 on X_1 are nonadditive. Extreme caution is urged, however, when substantively interpreting the estimated regression coefficients, due to the correlations between the individual X's and the product term (Althauser 1971). Methods have been developed for calculating total, direct, and indirect effects in nonlinear and nonadditive multiequation models (Stolzenberg 1979).

In order for the unknown coefficients in equations 3.23, 3.24, and 3.25 to be estimated, the model should be appropriately identified. The issue of identification is a rather complex one, involving the relation ship between the number of equations and the number of unknowns (Fisher 1966). A necessary, although not sufficient, condition for the identifiability of an individual equation within a given linear model is that the number of variables excluded from that equation should be at least equal to the number of equations, or, in other words, endogenous variables, minus one. Thus, if there are k equations, then at least $k - 1$ of the coefficients must be set equal to zero. If precisely $k - 1$ are set equal to zero, the equation is exactly identified, while if more than $k - 1$ are set equal to zero, the equation is overidentified (Namboodiri, Carter, and Blalock 1975:503). In those situations where the parameters cannot be identified in any given equation and so the equation is underidentified, exogenous variables, or lagged endogenous variables, must be added to the system (Fisher 1985).

Put another way, a model is overidentified when the moments of the observable variables provide more information than is necessary to determine the structural parameters. The resulting restrictions on the observable moments can be utilized in at least two ways. First, if it is assumed that the model is correct, then the restrictions can be used to obtain more efficient estimates of the unknown parameters. Second, if one is unwilling to assume that the model is correct, then the restrictions can be used to test the model. For example, if one or more equations are overidentified, the excess of empirical information over the number of unknowns can be used to make predictions that will not be satisfied unless the data conform to the model (Namboodiri, Carter, and Blalock 1975:517). In other words, the supposedly zero parameters can be reinserted into the model to make all the equations exactly identified, and then the empirical estimates of those coefficients should be close to zero. Note that a just-identified model is not really testable and that in overidentified models the restrictions, or null hypotheses, are tested, rather than the model itself, which represents the maintained hypotheses (Goldberger 1973).

With respect to the causal model represented in figure 3.10a, all three equations—3.23, 3.24, and 3.25—are underidentified, as none of them omit as many as two variables. By adding two exogenous variables, X_4 and X_5, to the causal system (fig. 3.10b), however, we obtain the following equations:

$$X_1 = a + b_3X_3 + b_4X_4 + e_1 \tag{3.27}$$

$$X_2 = a + b_1X_1 + b_5X_5 + e_2 \tag{3.28}$$

$$X_3 = a + b_1X_1 + b_2X_2 + e_3 \tag{3.29}$$

Note that two of the five variables are omitted from each of the equations, leaving them all exactly identified.

There are a variety of ways in which the structural parameters contained within simultaneous equation models can be estimated. Ordinary least squares should not be used as an estimation procedure when dealing with nonrecursive systems, as the disturbance, or error, terms in each equation will ordinarily be correlated with the independent variables in that equation, thus leading to biased estimates (J. Johnston 1972:376). For example, in equations 3.27 and 3.29, e_1 influences X_1, which in turn influences X_3. Therefore, e_1 is not independent of X_3.

In nonrecursive systems containing exactly identified equations, as in the present example, either indirect least squares or two-stage least squares can be used to estimate the structural coefficients. The two-stage least-squares estimator appears to be satisfactory as regards both bias and mean-squared error and is fairly insensitive to specification errors (Intriligator 1978:385, 419). As the name implies, this technique involves a two-stage procedure for estimating the structural coefficients (James and Singh 1978). First, the reduced form equations are generated by regressing each of the endogenous variables on the predetermined variables. Second, the structural coefficients are estimated by inserting the predicted values for the endogenous variables, obtained from the reduced-form equations, on the right-hand side of the structural equations. Thus, two-stage least squares involves purifying the endogenous variables that appear in the equation to be estimated in such a way that they become uncorrelated with the disturbance term in that equation (Namboodiri, Carter, and Blalock 1975:514).

More specifically, in the context of equations 3.27, 3.28, and 3.29, we have two exogenous variables, X_4 and X_5, and three endogenous variables, X_1, X_2, and X_3, thus producing the following three reduced-form equations:

$$\hat{X}_1 = a + b_4 X_4 + b_5 X_5 \tag{3.30}$$

$$\hat{X}_2 = a + b_4 X_4 + b_5 X_5 \tag{3.31}$$

$$\hat{X}_3 = a + b_4 X_4 + b_5 X_5 \tag{3.32}$$

where $\hat{X}_1$, $\hat{X}_2$, and $\hat{X}_3$ are predicted values of X_1, X_2, and X_3, respectively, based upon the use of ordinary least-squares analysis. These predicted values are then substituted into the right-hand side of the original simultaneous equations 3.27, 3.28, and 3.29, giving the following equations:

$$X_1 = a + b_3 \hat{X}_3 + b_4 X_4 + e_1 \tag{3.33}$$

$$X_2 = a + b_1 \hat{X}_1 + b_5 X_5 + e_2 \tag{3.34}$$

$$X_3 = a + b_1 \hat{X}_1 + b_2 \hat{X}_2 + e_3 \tag{3.35}$$

These three equations are then estimated using ordinary least-squares analysis. Thus two-stage least-squares analysis essentially involves two separate applications of ordinary least-squares analysis.

Two-stage least-squares analysis and the previously mentioned indirect least-squares analysis are both examples of the limited information approach to estimating systems of simultaneous equations. Limited information methods estimate one equation at a time and utilize neither the restrictions imposed in other equations nor the parameter estimates of other equations (Hanushek and Jackson 1977:277). By contrast, full information methods, such as three-stage least squares and full information maximum likelihood, estimate the entire system of equations simultaneously and thus utilize information concerning the specification of all the equations. The full information methods are ideal when the model is correctly specified and the variables are correctly measured, but they are extremely sensitive to both specification error and measurement error (Intriligator 1978:420). This sensitivity should not be surprising, because, as the equations are all estimated simultaneously, an error in one equation, or one variable, will be propagated throughout the entire system. On the other hand, the limited information approach, because it only estimates one equation at a time, restricts a specification error to the equation in which it occurs and restricts any measurement error in a particular variable to those equations containing that variable.

The structural equation models that have been discussed here are static in nature, although more dynamic models can be incorporated into this methodological framework in a variety of ways. For example, a dynamic model can be generated by treating lagged endogenous variables as though they were exogenous, thus creating a form of difference equation (Blalock 1969:80). Such a strategy encourages the interpretation of reality as a series of stimulus and response interactions in which definite time lags occur, although collecting appropriate data can often be a difficult task, as the time lags must be identified a priori. If change occurs more or less continuously over time, rather than in the discrete intervals implied by difference equations, then differential equations should be used. Such differential equation models can be estimated using time-series data, and the importance of maximum likelihood estimation methods have been particularly stressed (Doreian and Hummon 1977).

Both recursive and reciprocal relationships can be effectively combined within a block-recursive model. In such models the variables are divided into various blocks, with the relationships between the blocks being recursive, although those within any individual block can be reciprocal (Fisher 1966). This kind of approach is especially useful for suggesting appropriate subdivisions within the overall research design and for explicating the relationships among various submodels (Blalock 1969).

Finally, evaluating structural equation models is not an unproblematic exercise. As a variety of different models can yield correct predictions, we are unable to establish any given model as the single correct one. That is, we are forced to proceed by eliminating unsatisfactory models, rather than by confirming a particular model as the only correct one. In those situations where two models are composed of different variables, it would be inappropriate to assume that one of them must be wrong.

The traditional criterion for evaluating a regression equation is the coefficient of determination, but there are a number of ways to increase this coefficient that involve no real causal insight. For example, aggregated data often yield higher coefficients of determination than individual-level data, but one should be wary of the ecological fallacy. Causal inferences drawn from aggregated data refer to the aggregated units and cannot necessarily be ascribed to the individuals within those units. Although maximizing the coefficient of determination should never be the ultimate goal of causal modeling, some correlation is necessary for causal analysis.

Overidentification is very helpful for model evaluation. When overidentification occurs, it should be possible to find an overidentifying restriction, and one can then determine whether that overidentifying restriction is satisfied by the data. For example, if a zero path coefficient is predicted by the model, then one can check to see if the data support that assertion. If the path coefficient is significantly different from zero, then the model contains a specification error. The model can be empirically rescued by adding the appropriate parameter, but such a strategy betrays the theoretical integrity of the model. If we continue to modify a model by simply adding causal arrows, we will soon reach a situation where the model very easily satisfies the data. Unfortunately, however, there will tend to be a corresponding increase in the number of alternative models that also fit the data. It should also be noted that if an overidentifying restriction fails, it is not always easy to pinpoint exactly where the specification error lies. A variety of specifications might be incorrect, so not meeting a restriction might not be sufficient to locate the specification error (Kenny 1979:260).

Traditional tests of significance that certain path coefficients are zero tend to be less useful when the sample size is extremely large. In this case there is a tendency to always reject the model as being at least slightly incompatible with the data. Also, even if the model were perfectly correct, a large sample would often generate sufficient measurement error to reject most null hypotheses concerning zero path coefficients. In this respect, tests of significance associated with individual paths must be augmented with information concerning the pattern of departures from zero. For example, most of the departures from zero might involve a single variable, perhaps implying measurement error in that variable. Alternatively, the problem might result from specification error, involving the omission of relevant variables or failure to take into account nonlinearity and nonadditivity.

A useful distinction within the context of evaluating structural models is that between convergent and discriminant validity. The terms were originally used to explore the validity of constructs (Campbell and Fiske 1959). Convergent validity implies that a model can be replicated across different samples, measurement procedures, and estimation methods. On the other hand, discriminant validity suggests that a model should imply very different interpretations than the alternative competing models. In particular, the pattern of zero path coefficients and overidentifying restrictions should be sufficiently distinctive for empirical observations to adjudicate between competing models.

In using observational data to test the predictions of any given model, we are far removed from the experimental ideal. It is thus useful to consider the differences between experimental and nonexperimental designs. In particular, Dwyer (1983:16) identifies three general classes of model testing strategy: cross-sectional, longitudinal, and experimental, where these three strategies are ordered in ascending internal validity. That is, the experiment can most definitively demonstrate a causal link, whereas nonrandomized cross-sectional designs are often the least definitive.

Cross-sectional designs are different from the other designs in two important ways. The observations are made at a single point in time, and no attempt is made to manipulate the observations along any of the measured dimensions. The inferential power of cross-sectional studies can be improved, however, by utilizing statistical rather than experimental controls, although the use of such statistical controls is most meaningful when all the variables relevant to a causal model have been identified and tested. In addition, of course, the empirical results of statistical controlling procedures are only reliable in those situations where the chosen indicators really measure the hypothetical constructs of interest. Nevertheless, cross-sectional designs provide a flexible methodology for exploring patterns of covariation among sets of variables, and the insights gained from such exploration can later be further elaborated using the often more costly designs associated with longitudinal and experimental studies.

Nonrandomized longitudinal designs involve either panel or time-series designs. In a panel design, the same sample of subjects is observed at more than one point in time, although the prohibitive cost of conducting large-scale panel studies usually means that there are not more than two or three waves. By contrast, a time-series analysis involves observing individuals, or spatial units, over an extended period of time. Such an analysis can help to uncover the direction and sequence of causal connections that might underlie a set of cross-sectional correlations.

The true randomized experiment is ideal in the sense that it provides the best opportunity for identifying spurious relationships. The presence in the real world of certain agents that produce changes in the states of systems is paralleled in the laboratory by the manipulations of the experimenter, who acts as just such an agent. Randomization provides a means of methodologically controlling, through research design, what cannot be controlled either physically or statistically. By appropriate manipulations, the experimenter attempts to partial out the separate effects of several explanatory variables that simultaneously influence some dependent variable. Individual subjects, or cases, are randomly assigned to treatments, thus ruling out self-selection and reducing the number of confounding variables.

In practice, however, one can never be certain that some variable, other than the one being intentionally manipulated, has not been inadvertently changed. That is, it is impossible to be sure that all confounding variables have been eliminated through the process of randomization. In this respect, the uncertainty about unmeasured third variables that arises in cross-sectional studies is often exchanged for the problem of irrelevant mediation that occurs in experimental studies. In addition, many causal models in the social sciences, including those concerned with migration, are not suited to experimental testing. For example, we are obviously forced to assess the effects of such variables as social class, family characteristics, and unemployment in a nonexperimental context.

Thus far we have focused on the problem of internal validity. That is, to what extent can it be demonstrated that an observed set of associations between two or more variables implies an underlying set of causal connections? Of equal importance, however, is the issue of external validity. To what degree can the conclusions generated by a particular study be generalized beyond the specific domain, or sampled population, associated with that study? There is often a trade-off between experimental and nonexperimental research strategies. Randomized experiments tend to minimize internal validity, but the costs involved with randomization and the manipulation of relevant variables often result in the use of rather small and restricted samples. By contrast, observational designs, although more problematic for internal validity, are generally able to utilize larger and more theoretically interesting samples.

In sum, although we should readily admit that causal laws can never be empirically demonstrated, even in an experimental context, it seems reasonable to maintain that the development of causal models is a useful heuristic device. In this sense causal relations take on the role of working assumptions, rather than empirically verifiable statements about the system of interest. Causal models provide a highly useful theoretical tool, even though their implications are only indirectly testable. It would be extremely difficult for many social scientists to go about their daily work without clinging to the metaphysical assumption that something similar to causal relations are embedded within social systems. But most social scientists would also accept that such causal relations can at best be only indirectly apprehended, irrespective of whether the research design is experimental or nonexperimental in nature.

Simultaneous Equation Models of Migration

In this section we will consider two major examples of how simultaneous equation models have been used to study migration. Before doing so, however, we should recall two pioneer studies in this field. First, Okun (1968) used a simultaneous equation model to assess the influence of interstate migration on income inequality among the states. He concluded that interstate migration tends to reinforce interstate differences in service income per capita, with migrants flowing from states with low service income per capital to those with high service income per capital. Second, Olvey (1972) also used a simultaneous equation approach, involving five structural equations, one each for growth in manufacturing employment, growth in service employment, gross in-migration from the same or contiguous states, gross in-migration from noncontiguous states, and gross out-migration. The full model consisted of five equations and three identities, and three-stage least-squares analysis was used to estimate the structural coefficients. Olvey's results suggest a strong three-way interaction between in-migration, out-migration, and employment growth, with the simultaneous nature of these relationships justifying the use of a multiequation approach.

The present author (Cadwallader 1985b) continued this line of research by calibrating a simultaneous equation model of net migration in the Upper Midwest, using the same data as for the previously described path model. The particular model that was estimated is shown in figure 3.11 and can be represented by the following structural equations, which indicate the expected relationships:

$$X_6 = a - b_{64}X_4 - b_{65}X_5 - b_{62}X_2 + e_6 \qquad (3.36)$$

$$X_4 = a - b_{46}X_6 - b_{45}X_5 - b_{41}X_1 + e_4 \qquad (3.37)$$

$$X_5 = a - b_{56}X_6 - b_{54}X_4 + b_{53}X_3 + e_5 \qquad (3.38)$$

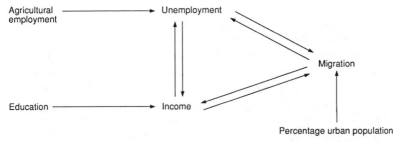

Figure 3.11. A simultaneous equation model for migration in the Upper Midwest. *Source:* Cadwallader 1985b:fig. 3.

where X_1 is the percentage of the civilian labor force employed in agriculture, forestry, and fisheries; X_2 is the percentage of the population living in urban settlements; X_3 is the median number of school years completed by all adults aged twenty-five years and over; X_4 is the percentage of males sixteen years and over in the civilian labor force who are unemployed; X_5 is median income; X_6 is net migration; a is a constant; the b terms are estimated coefficients; and e_4, e_5, and e_6 are the disturbance terms.

Note that reciprocal links are postulated between migration, unemployment, and income. These three variables are thus treated as endogenous variables, whereas agricultural employment, the percentage urban population, and education are treated as predetermined variables. The endogenous variables are to be explained by the theory or model, whereas the predetermined variables are treated as given and are used to provide explanatory power to the model. In general, the predetermined variables can either be lagged values of the endogenous variables or exogenous variables, which are lagged or nonlagged variables that are considered to be separate causes of the endogenous variables. In the present situation the predetermined variables consist entirely of nonlagged exogenous variables.

In particular, the following relationships are postulated. First, with respect to equation 3.36, it is expected that net migration will be negatively related to unemployment, in that areas experiencing relatively high unemployment are likely to experience relatively heavy out-migration (Greenwood 1981:158). On the other hand, net migration should be positively related to median income, as one would expect migrants to move out of relatively low-income areas and into relatively high-income areas. Also, based on the results of the previously reported path analysis, we might expect migration to be negatively related to the percentage of the population living in urban settlements.

Second, with respect to equation 3.37, unemployment should be negatively related to net migration, as the in-migration of labor will increase the demand for local goods and services, thus increasing employment (Greenwood 1981:150). In addition, Borts and Stein (1964) suggest that migration to a region tends to induce investment in that region, which further increases the demand for labor. The relationship between unemployment and income should be negative, with the highest levels of unemployment being associated with low-income regions, and given the results of the path analysis, the relationship between unemployment and the percentage employed in agriculture should also be negative.

Third, with respect to equation 3.38, it is expected that median income will be negatively related to net migration, as out-migration will tend to increase wage levels for those remaining, whereas in-migration will tend to decrease them (Greenwood 1981:150). The relationship between income and unemployment is expected to be negative, with regions experiencing high unemployment levels tending also to be low-income regions. Finally, a positive relationship is expected between income and level of education. This relationship is specified as running from education to income and not vice versa, because the time lags involved in the relationship between income change and education change are likely to be greater than those between education change and income change, since the educational effects of income growth tend to accrue to the offspring (Greenwood 1981:161).

With the use of two-stage least-squares analysis, the estimated coefficients in the structural equations are largely as expected for both 1955–60 and 1965–70 (table 3.3). The signs of the coefficients in the migration equation are as predicted, with net migration being negatively related to unemployment and the percentage urban population and positively related to income. The coefficients for the unemployment and the percentage urban population variables, however, are not significantly different from zero at the .10 probability level. Other migration studies have also found insignificant coefficients with respect to the unemployment variable (Greenwood 1981:174). It has been suggested that when explaining migration, variables relating to job turnover are more relevant than unemployment rates, since potential migrants tend to be more concerned about the rate at which hiring for new jobs is taking place (Fields 1976).

The coefficients in the unemployment equation for both 1955–60 and 1965–70 are exactly as predicted, except that for 1965–70 the net migration variable is not statistically significant at the .10 probability level. All the other coefficients are significantly different from zero at

Table 3.3. The estimated structural equations for migration in the Upper Midwest

Variable	Structural equation
1955–60	
Migration	$= -33.699 - 3.281X_4 + .016X_5{}^* - .503X_2$
	$(22.431)\ (2.640)\quad (.011)\quad\ (.398)$
Unemployment	$= 25.640 - .255X_6{}^{**} - .003X_5{}^{**} - .307X_1{}^{**}$
	$(5.723)\ (.105)\quad\ \ (.001)\quad\ \ (.072)$
Income	$= -21,665.00\ \ - 466.168X_6 + 310.508X_4 + 2,342.500X_3{}^*$
	$(18,410.700)\ (460.947)\quad (369.514)\quad (1,657.840)$
1965–70	
Migration	$= -29.604 - 1.701X_4 + .007X_5{}^* - .338X_2$
	$(20.875)\ (2.208)\quad\ (.005)\quad\ (.263)$
Unemployment	$= 32.290 - .190X_6 - .003X_5{}^{**} - .487X_1{}^{**}$
	$(9.914)\ (.226)\quad\ (.001)\quad\ \ (.178)$
Income	$= -38,284.000 - 442.335X_6{}^* + 546.931X_4 + 3,656.560X_3{}^{**}$
	$(18,908.200)\ (306.229)\quad (434.288)\quad (1,472.710)$

Source: Cadwallader 1985b: table 2.
Note: * indicates significant at .10; ** indicates significant at .05.

the .05 probability level. Agricultural employment and income are negatively related to unemployment in both time periods, and migration also has a significant negative relationship in 1955–60. This latter finding indicates that high rates of net migration tend to be associated with low levels of unemployment.

Finally, the income equation contains the expected relationships with respect to net migration and education. That is, income is negatively related to net migration, since out-migration tends to increase wage levels for those remaining, and vice versa, whereas a positive relationship exists between income and level of education. The only exception to this general pattern is that the effect of net migration is statistically insignificant in 1955–60. Rather surprisingly, however, income is positively related to unemployment for both time periods, although the coefficients are not significantly different from zero.

Of particular interest, of course, are the estimated parameters for the postulated reciprocal relationships between unemployment, income, and migration. There do not appear to be exceptionally strong feedback relationships between unemployment and migration, although migration was a statistically significant determinant of unemployment in 1955–60. Similarly, income is a statistically significant determinant of unemployment, but unemployment seems to have far less effect on income. Finally, at least for 1965–70, income and net migration are reciprocally related, as income is a statistically significant determinant of migration and migration is also a statistically significant determinant of income. More specifically, high-income levels attract migrants, but as net migration increases, income levels decrease. These last results are very similar to those found in Dahlberg and Holmlund's (1978) study of the interaction between migration, income, and employment in Sweden, where income and migration had the strongest reciprocal effects.

A second example of a simultaneous equation model of migration is provided by Gober-Meyers (1978b). She investigated the relationship between interstate migration and economic growth, with net migration, per-capita income growth, and an index of migrant selectivity acting as the endogenous variables. Various aspects of regional attractiveness were represented by the exogenous variables, including growth in nonagricultural employment, unemployment, fertility, ecucation, climate, and population density. The data used to estimate the model were collected for the period 1965–70, and migrants were defined as those individuals who were twenty years old or over in 1965 whose 1965 and 1970 states of residence did not match.

The model consisted of the following set of equations:

$$Y_{1i} = a_1 + a_2 Y_{2i} + a_3 Y_{3i} + a_4 X_{1i} \tag{3.39}$$

$$Y_{2i} = b_1 + b_2 Y_{1i} + b_3 X_{1i} + b_4 X_{2i} + b_5 X_{4i} + b_6 X_{5i} \\ + b_7 X_{6i} \tag{3.40}$$

$$Y_{3i} = c_1 + c_2 Y_{1i} + c_3 X_{1i} + c_4 X_{2i} + c_5 X_{3i} + c_6 X_{5i} + \\ c_7 X_{6i} \tag{3.41}$$

where Y_{1i} is growth in per-capita income from 1965 to 1970 in state i; Y_{2i} is the rate of net migration from 1965 to 1970 in state i; Y_{3i} are the net benefits that accrue to state i as a result of changes in the age, sex, race, and education composition caused by interstate migration between 1965 and 1970; X_{1i} is the growth in nonagricultural employment from 1965 to 1970 in state i; X_{2i} is the average annual unemployment rate in state i for the period 1965–70; X_{3i} is a measure of education for state i; X_{4i} is the crude birth rate in 1950 in state i; X_{5i} is the population density in state i in 1965; and X_{6i} is a climatic variable measuring the mean January temperature in the capital or largest city of state i.

All the Y's represent endogenous variables, while the X's are exogenously determined. In particular, net migration, migration benefits, and per-capita income growth are mutually interdependent, and the exogenous varibles were chosen on the basis of their hypothesized relationships with these three endogenous variables. The most complex

Table 3.4. The estimated structural equations for migration in the United States

$Y_1 = .4214 + .0000047\ Y_3$	$R^2 = .12$
$\quad\quad (F = 6.2)$	
$Y_2 = -.0575 + .2996X_1 + (-.000012)X_5$	$R^2 = .55$
$\quad\quad (F = 18.7) \quad (F = 11.4)$	
$Y_3 = -1,454.37 + 7,454.22X_1$	$R^2 = .25$
$\quad\quad (F = 9.4)$	

Source: Gober-Meyers 1978b: table 1. (P. Gober-Meyers, "Interstate migration and growth: A simultaneous equations approach," *Environment and Planning A,* Vol. 10, 1978.)

Note: All the regression coefficients included in the table were significantly different from zero at a .95 percent level of confidence. None of the excluded variables had coefficients that were statistically significant at this level. Multiple regression coefficients (R^2) are associated with the ordinary least-squares estimates of the structural equations. Second-stage coefficients are not meaningful; that is, it is not possible to interpret an R^2 as indicating the proportion of the variation in the dependent variable explained by the independent variables.

variable is migration benefits, which is an index that captures the over-all impact of interstate migration on the population composition of each state, as measured across age, sex, race, and education. In order to obtain a large positive score for this variable, the in-migrants to the state should have greater income-earning potential than the out-mi-grants, and the number of in-migrants should be large relative to the number of nonmigrants.

Equations 3.39, 3.40, and 3.41 were estimated using two-stage least-squares analysis, and the results are reported in table 3.4. Only those variables with significant relationships at the .05 level are included. In the per-capita income growth equation, the migration benefit coeffi-cient was significantly different from zero and in the expected positive direction. The migration benefit variable was not dependent upon in-come growth, however, thus casting doubt on their hypothesized mutual interdependence. Both net migration and migration benefits were posi-tively related to growth in nonagricultural employment, but among the other indicators of regional attractiveness only population density had a significant impact. The negative coefficient for net migration and population density should not be interpreted as a movement away from urbanized areas, as population density and the percentage urbanized were not perfectly correlated. Rather, the results indicate a net out-migration from the most densely populated areas, such as the North-east, and do not preclude in-migration to many cities in the Southwest which are located in less densely settled states.

Urban Growth and Migration

Simultaneous equation models can also be used to explore the phenomenon of urban growth and decline. The traditional approach to urban change suggests that growth or decline is exogenously determined (Frey and Speare 1988). In particular, the export base concept implies that increased demand in the export, or basic, sector of a city's economy will lead to increased employment and purchasing power. If this increased purchasing power is spent on goods and services produced within the city, then multiplier effects are set in motion that will generate further growth. Besides increased demand for goods and services, other exogenous causes of urban growth are associated with the location of natural resources and product markets. Similarly, growth in a city's hinterland, or surrounding rural population, will also induce growth in the city itself.

An alternative viewpoint argues that urban growth or decline is primarily controlled by a set of endogenous mechanisms. First, it has long been suggested that a strong relationship exists between size and growth (Robson 1973). Larger cities are thought to possess a comparative advantage due to their greater industrial mix, political power, and fixed capital investment. Second, large cities tend to provide a favorable environment for starting new firms and industries, as the necessary services, skilled labor, and factory space are readily available. Once the new industry matures, however, and the production process becomes more routine, the so-called incubator hypothesis implies that parts of the industry will filter down to smaller, less industrially sophisticated settlements (Nicholson, Brinkley, and Evans 1981). Third, urban growth is also related to various kinds of agglomeration economies, once again providing larger cities with a comparative advantage. Such economies of scale, however, can often become diseconomies of scale, generating pollution, traffic congestion, exorbitant service costs, and longer commuting distances.

Finally, a very different perspective on urban and regional growth is provided by neo-Marxist theories of uneven development, in which regional growth and decline are considered to be an inevitable manifestation of the inherent crises and instability of capitalism. Indeed, some scholars see uneven development as not only an inevitable consequence of capitalism but also as a necessary prerequisite for the self-expansion of capital and capital accumulation (Bradbury 1985). Capital accumulation within a region depends upon the rate of profit of the firms located there, and such accumulation cannot occur at an even pace in both space and time (Browett 1984). Rather, capital tends to accumulate in some places as opposed to and at the expense of others.

Behind this pattern of uneven development lies the logic of what Smith (1984:148) has called the "see-saw" movement of capital. Capital moves to where the rate of profit is highest, but the development process itself leads to a decrease in this higher rate of profit. Economic development tends to decrease unemployment, increase wages, and strengthen labor unions, thus lowering the rate of profit and removing the original incentive for development. On the other hand, the lack of capital in underdeveloped regions leads to high unemployment, low wages, and reduced levels of worker organization, precisely those conditions that made an area attractive to capital and susceptible to rapid development. As a result, capital tends to move back and forth, or seesaw, between developed and underdeveloped areas.

A major problem with the above explanations of urban growth, however, is that they fail to include an explicit role for migration. Early efforts to investigate the relationship between migration and urban growth generally involved the previously described single-equation regression model approach (Lowry 1966; Rogers 1967). More recently, however, a simultaneous equation framework has become increasingly popular for exploring this relationship. For example, Greenwood (1981) estimated a model containing fourteen equations when analyzing rates of in-migration and out-migration for large cities in the United States. Besides the various measures of migration, the endogenous variables included the rate of income growth and the rate of employment growth. Using three-stage least-squares estimates, Greenwood found that the endogenous variables were significantly interrelated. Similarly, Izraeli and Lin (1984) have used Standard Metropolitan Statistical Area (SMSA) data to calibrate a simultaneous equation model that examines the effects of real earnings on met migration and employment growth.

Two examples of simultaneous equation models of urban growth and migration will be described here. Greenwood (1973) estimated such a model for the one hundred largest SMSAs in the continental United States in 1960. The migration data referred to civilian labor force (CLF) movements during the period 1955–60, and the use of separate migration variables allowed for differences in the explanations of in- and out-migration. The remaining endogenous variables involved income growth, employment growth, unemployment growth, change in the CLF, and natural increase in the CLF. Overall, the model contained seven equations: five structural equations and two identities. The model was specified as follows:

$$OM = f_1(IM, \Delta INC, \Delta EMP, \Delta UNEMP, INC50,$$
$$UNR50, CLF50, EDU50, AGE60, e_1) \qquad (3.42)$$

$$IM = f_2(OM, \Delta INC, \Delta EMP, \Delta UNEMP,$$
$$INC50, UNR50, CLF50, e_2) \tag{3.43}$$

$$\Delta INC = f_3(OM, IM, \Delta EDU, \Delta GOVT,$$
$$DEW, DNS, e_3) \tag{3.44}$$

$$\Delta EMP = f_4(OM, IM, NATINC, INC50, \Delta EDU,$$
$$\Delta GOVT, DEW, DNS, e_4) \tag{3.45}$$

$$\Delta UNEMP = f_5(OM, IM, NATINC, DEW, DNS, e_5) \tag{3.46}$$

$$\Delta CLF \equiv \Delta EMP + \Delta UNEMP \tag{3.47}$$

$$NATINC \equiv \Delta CLF + OM - IM \tag{3.48}$$

where OM is out-migration; IM is in-migration; ΔINC is change in income: ΔEMP is change in employment; $\Delta UNEMP$ is change in unemployment; ΔCLF is change in the size of the civilian labor force; NATINC is natural increase in the CLF; INC50 is median income in 1950; UNR50 is the unemployment rate in 1950; CLF50 is the size of the civilian labor force in 1950; EDU50 is a measure of education for 1950; AGE60 is the median age of the population in 1960; ΔEDU is the change in level of education; $\Delta GOVT$ is the change in local governmental expenditure; DEW is an East-West dummy variable, where SMSAs of the Mountain and Pacific census regions equal one and all other SMSAs equal zero; DNS is a North-South dummy variable, where each SMSA south of a line drawn across the northern borders of North Carolina, Tennessee, Arkansas, and so on, equals one and all other SMSAs equal zero; and e terms represent error. Note that, beside the migration variables, all variables involving change refer to changes that occurred during the period 1955–60.

The model was estimated using three-stage least squares, and the results are presented in table 3.5. Although the coefficient of multiple determination should not be given its usual interpretation in equations estimated by three-stage least squares, the ordinary least-squares R's are provided in order to give an approximate indication of the percentage of explained variation. With respect to the migration equations, income change has the expected negative relationship with out-migration and positive relationship with in-migration. By contrast, although the income level in 1950 also displays the expected relationships, the magnitudes of the coefficients are less, and income level is only statistically significant in the out-migration equation. Employment growth

Table 3.5. The estimated structural equations for urban growth and
migration in the United States

Independent variables	Equation for				
	OM	IM	ΔINC	ΔEMP	ΔUNEMP
OM b:		.318	−.023	−.224	−.399
t:		(3.290)	(1.090)	(3.229)	(3.192)
IM	.139		.043	.232	.192
	(.880)		(2.220)	(3.945)	(1.965)
ΔINC	−1.247	2.166			
	(1.614)	(2.147)			
ΔEMP	.165	2.843			
	(.303)	(7.491)			
ΔUNEMP	.476	−.598			
	(1.225)	(1.250)			
NATINC				−.011	.047
				(.624)	(1.689)
INC50	−.545	.212		−.065	
	(3.112)	(1.043)		(.345)	
UNR50	.339	−.439			
	(1.876)	(1.983)			
CLF50	.791	−.546			
	(5.525)	(5.477)			
EDU50	1.288				
	(3.474)				
AGE60	−1.212				
	(5.201)				
ΔEDU			.462	−.715	
			(3.364)	(1.464)	
ΔGOVT			.033	.071	
			(.834)	(.588)	
DEW			.045	.129	−.104
			(2.669)	(2.513)	(1.125)
DNS			−.003	.172	.172
			(.212)	(3.005)	(2.305)
Constant	6.431	−3.427	.117	.689	2.064
	(5.059)	(2.191)	(1.177)	(.513)	(3.490)
OLS R^2	.96	.93	.46	.72	.20

Logarithmic regression coefficients (b) and *t*-ratios (t).

Source: Greenwood 1973: table 1. (M. Greenwood, "Urban economic growth and migration: Their interaction," *Environment and Planning,* Vol. 5, 1973.)

is obviously an important inducement to in-migration, but change in
unemployment is not a significant variable in either equation. The unemployment rate variable behaves as expected, while the education
and age variables suggest that increased education levels encourage
out-migration and increased age levels discourage out-migration. Fi-

nally, there is the often-noted relationship between in- and out-migration, indicating that those cities experiencing heavy out-migration also tend to experience heavy in-migration.

In the remaining structural equations, in-migration has a positive and significant relationship with income growth, as does change in education. The coefficients associated with the dummy variables suggest that, while other factors were controlled for, income growth was no greater in the South than in the North, but the West did exhibit greater growth than the East. In the employment change equation, both out-migration and in-migration have the expected signs, although the negative relationship with change in education is both unexpected and statistically significant. The regional dummy variables indicate that employment growth was greater in the West than in the East and greater in the South than in the North. Finally, in the unemployment change equation, out-migration tends to relieve unemployment, while in-migration tends to exacerbate it.

The present author (Cadwallader 1991) has also constructed a simultaneous equation model involving migration rates for cities. Net migration, property tax, and spending on education are treated as endogenous variables, while income, housing costs, manufacturing, climate and crime are exogenously determined. As there are three endogenous variables, the model contains the following three equations:

$$X_2 = a_2 + b_{21}X_1 + b_{23}X_3 + b_{24}X_4 + e_2 \tag{3.49}$$

$$X_3 = a_3 + b_{31}X_1 + b_{32}X_2 + b_{35}X_5 + e_3 \tag{3.50}$$

$$X_1 = a_1 + b_{12}X_2 + b_{13}X_3 + b_{16}X_6 + b_{17}X_7 + b_{18}X_8 + e_1 \tag{3.51}$$

where X_1 is net migration; X_2 is local governmental spending on education per capita; X_3 is local governmental property tax per capita; X_4 is median income; X_5 is median housing value; X_6 is the percentage of the population employed in manufacturing; X_7 is a measure of climatic attractiveness; X_8 is the crime rate per one hundred thousand population; a_1, a_2, and a_3 are the intercepts; the b terms are regression coefficients; and e_1, e_2, and e_3 are error terms. The data used to estimate these models, for both 1965–70 and 1975–80, are described in Chapter 2.

Property taxes and spending on education are postulated to be reciprocally related, as local government's taxing and spending decisions are simultaneously determined (Loehman and Emerson 1985). As described earlier, a necessary, although not sufficient, condition for

Table 3.6. The estimated structural equations associated with migration rates for U.S. cities

1965–70

Education spending $= 40.64 + 8.25X_1 + .27X_3 + .01X_4$
$\qquad\qquad\qquad\quad (17.22) \quad (10.58) \quad (.44) \quad (.03)$

Property tax $\quad= -53.79 - 23.90X_1{}^{**} + 1.33X_2{}^{**} + .29X_5{}^*$
$\qquad\qquad\qquad (38.80) \quad (7.65) \qquad\quad (.42) \qquad\quad (.16)$

Net migration $\quad= .82 + .01X_2 - .01X_3 - .04X_6{}^* + .001X_7 + .0002X_8$
$\qquad\qquad\quad (1.53) \quad (.03) \quad (.01) \quad (.02) \qquad (.002) \qquad (.0003)$

1975–80

Education spending $= -68.48 + 12.76X_1 + .02X_3 + .09X_4$
$\qquad\qquad\qquad\quad (243.33) \quad (20.64) \quad (0.94) \quad (0.13)$

Property tax $\quad= -117.75 - 22.25X_1{}^* + .99X_2{}^{**} + .52X_5{}^{**}$
$\qquad\qquad\qquad (46.62) \quad (10.09) \quad (.19) \qquad\quad (.16)$

Net migration $\quad= -1.43 + .02X_2{}^{**} - .02X_3{}^{**} - .03X_6 + .002X_7 + .0001X_8$
$\qquad\qquad\quad (1.63) \quad (.01) \qquad (.01) \qquad (.02) \quad (.001) \quad (.0002)$

Source: Cadwallader 1991: table 7.
Note: ** indicates significant at .01; * indicates significant at .05.

the identifiability of a structural equation within a given linear model is that at least $k - 1$ of the variables should be excluded from that equation, where k is the number of structural equations. In this case, therefore, at least two variables should be excluded from each equation. Consequently, the educational spending and property tax equations are overidentified, while the migration equation is exactly identified. Note that the structure of the model remained the same for both time periods, in order to facilitate comparison.

The two-stage least-squares estimates for equations 3.49, 3.50, and 3.51 and the associated standard errors reveal a fairly similar pattern across both time periods (table 3.6). In neither case are the relationships for the educational spending equation significant, but for the property tax equation all the coefficients are significantly different from zero at the .05 probability level, and four of them are significant at the .01 probability level. Moreover, the directions of the relationships are as expected. Property taxes are negatively associated with net migration but positively related to educational spending and housing value.

Finally, the net migration equation performs considerably better for the 1975–80 data than for the 1965–70 data. For the earlier time period only the manufacturing variable has a significant coefficient. By contrast, for the later time period, all the variables except crime rate have a significant coefficient at the .10 probability level, and two of them are significant at the .01 probability level. Again, the directions of the relationships are as expected, given the previous analyses, as net migration is positively related to spending on education and climatic attractiveness but negatively related to property taxes and percentage employed in manufacturing.

4

Behavioral Approaches to Migration

A preliminary step toward formulating a more behaviorally oriented approach to migration involves the investment in human capital theory of migration (Dierx 1988a; Islam and Choudhury 1990; Odland 1988a). Human capital theory in general, developed during the early 1960s, involves the idea that people invest in themselves for the sake of future returns. In particular, they may acquire additional education, they may purchase health care, or they may migrate in the hope of obtaining better job opportunities and financial rewards (Milne 1991). As originally conceived by Schultz (1963), Becker (1964), and others, the human capital approach was characterized by methodological individualism, that is, by the view that all social behavior should be traced back to its roots in individual behavior. Thus proponents of this approach have been able to demonstrate that a wide range of social phenomena can be attributed to individual decisions involving the postponement of present gains for the expectation of future gains.

Sjaastad (1962) largely began the tradition of treating migration as an investment. Individuals are assumed to migrate when the real income available at a given destination exceeds the real income available at the origin by more than the costs of moving. A move from i to j is assumed to depend on the income differential between regions i and j, less the costs of migrating from i to j. More formally, this relationship can be expressed as follows (DaVanzo 1981:93):

$$PV_{ij} = \sum_{t=1}^{T} \frac{U_j^t - U_i^t - C_{ij}^t}{(1+r)^t} > 0 \text{ for at least one area } (j \neq i) \quad (4.1)$$

where PV_{ij} is the present value of the net gain of moving from i to j, U_j^t is the expected utility in region i or j at the time t, j is a potential destination, i is an origin, r is the discount rate $(0 \leq r \leq 1)$, T is the expected length of remaining lifetime, and C_{ij}^t is the cost incurred in time period t of moving from i to j. Net real income gains are divided by the discount factor $(1 + r)^t$ to adjust for the fact that individuals attach less value to some future occurrence than to the same occurrence today.

Thus migration locates a worker in a region where his or her earning power is increased. For example, Weiss and Williamson (1972) were able to show that the income of blacks who migrated from the South to the North was higher than that of black nonmigrants. Indeed, lifetime migrants from the South who have been in the North for more than five years tend to have higher earnings than similar individuals at either the origin or the destination (Yezer and Thurston 1976). With the increasing number of two-worker families it is beneficial to view migration as a family investment in human capital and thus focus on net family gain rather than net individual gain (Mincer 1978). Within this context, Sandell (1977) found that two-worker families tend to migrate less than those with only one worker.

Migration is regarded as an investment because the benefits can only accrue over a period of time, and as the investment is in the individual or family it represents an investment in human capital. A cost-benefit framework is utilized, which can include both financial and nonfinancial factors. For example, the costs of migrating from i to j might involve opportunity costs, expressing the loss of wages due to moving and searching for work, and psychic costs, representing the psychological trauma of uprooting the household. More recent versions of the human capital theory have emphasized the notion of expected income differentials (Harris and Todaro 1970), thus arguing that migrants attempt to maximize expected utility. Speare (1971) warns, however, that although the cost-benefit framework provides a reasonable representation of the factors involved in the migration process, researchers should not imply that potential migrants actually calculate the expected costs and benefits. Many migrants will only have a rather vague idea concerning expected earning potential, and moving costs can often only be approximately estimated.

Despite its widespread use in studying labor migration, the human capital approach has not been immune from criticism (Blaug 1976). In particular, most empirical calibrations of the theory have used simple logit or probit transformations in which the decision to move is viewed dichotomously. Also, recent empirical evidence suggests that only comparatively small monetary rewards are obtained from the investment in migration. Most studies reporting positive returns to migration involve lifetime migrants, those individuals living in a different place from their place of birth. In such cases, however, increased education and training might be responsible for the higher incomes, rather than any specific return associated with the move itself.

Grant and Vanderkamp (1980) report that it is difficult to identify a positive relationship between migration and income within the first five years following the move. Furthermore, their data suggest that the payoffs of migration decline with increasing income. Individuals with the lowest initial incomes seem to receive the greatest returns from moving, although this finding might be partly due to the fact that those low-income individuals who had disappointing experiences, and thus moved again, were more likely to be excluded from their particular sample. In general, then, these results suggest that nonmonetary rewards, such as quality of life considerations, are also important determinants of migration in the short run. Indeed, Shaw (1985:170) suggests that the role of such nonmonetary rewards will be especially significant in relatively rich countries like the United States and Canada, where migration might be undertaken as a consumption item rather than as an economic necessity.

Expansions of the human capital theory of migration have included not only expected income differentials but also amenity differentials and the anticipated benefits from local governmental services (Cebula 1980b). Many have suggested that migrants will move to regions that best satisfy their preferences for public goods, and Kleiner and McWilliams (1977) argue that nonwhites, in particular, are attracted to states with high levels of welfare benefits. A search theoretic framework can also be used to strengthen human capital theory, with due consideration being given to the flows of job information and aspects of job competition (Pickles and Rogerson 1984).

Although the investment in human capital models of migration are formulated based on individual utility maximization, they are frequently estimated using aggregate data that refer to average income and unemployment levels in the origin and destination regions. A more explicitly micro-level approach involves the concept of place utility, which summarizes an intended migrant's attitude toward a potential destination (Wolpert 1965). Thus place utility represents the overall attractiveness of a particular place for a particular individual, as evaluated across a set of characteristics. An individual's place utility matrix contains attributes as the rows and places as the columns, with the overall utility associated with any place being a weighted sum of the values in a column. Individual variations will occur due to the differential weighting of attributes and different levels of information about places. More specifically, the ranking of attributes will reflect the individual's stage in the life cycle, while information levels appear to be a function of size and distance variables (Cadwallader 1978).

Lieber (1978) has attempted to uncover the attributes of places which influence their associated utility values by using the grid-sorting technique of personal construct theory and the semantic differential technique. The grid-sorting technique allows subjects to directly identify the relevant attributes of stimuli, in this case places, that are being compared. By contrast, the semantic differential technique involves presenting the subjects with a set of stimuli which they are required to evaluate across a series of scales consisting of bipolar adjectives. Some form of factor analysis is then used to uncover the underlying dimensions, or cognitive categories. Using these methods, Lieber found that four major variables best characterize the evaluative features of potential destinations: proximity to a major city, proximity to fresh-air recreational opportunities, proximity to close relatives, and general economic conditions.

Mental Maps and Migration

A growing number of researchers have begun to explore ways of using the subjective evaluation of alternatives as a theoretical framework for constructing migration models. Much of the work in this area was originally inspired by Gould's pioneering investigations of mental maps (Gould and White 1986), in which he explored the perceived residential desirability of different regions within the United States. If the residential desirability of each state, as rated by a group of subjects, is imagined to be measured on a scale ranging from zero to one hundred, then these values can be used to construct a residential preference surface. Isolines connect the points of equal value, thus creating a surface that reflects the hills and valleys of desirability for a particular group of people. For example, figure 4.1 shows the residential desirability surface for a group of subjects located in California. Widely spaced isolines mean that the perceived residential desirability changes quite slowly, while closely spaced isolines indicate more dramatic changes in the preference surface.

Similar maps have also been constructed for individual cities, and

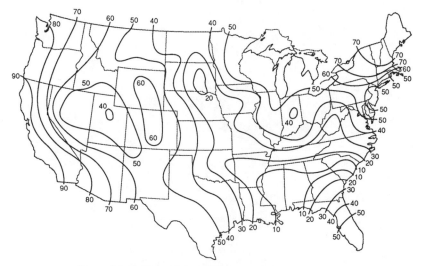

Figure 4.1. Residential desirability surface from California.
Source: Abler, Adams, and Gould 1971:fig. 13.31.

they have implications for the issue of neighborhood revitalization
(Day and Walmsley 1981). Clark and Cadwallader (1973b) analyzed a
series of residential preference maps of Los Angeles. The sample consisted of 1,024 persons spread throughout the metropolitan area. Each
subject was shown a map of Los Angeles which included the freeway
system and the Santa Monica Mountains. In addition, approximately
180 neighborhoods were indicated by name on the map, although their
boundaries were not provided. After looking at the map, each subject
was asked to do the following: "Taking your family income into consideration, please show me on this map the three neighborhoods where
you would most like to live, starting with the one you would like to live
in most." The income constraint was used so that people would not
automatically choose such obviously attractive, but realistically unattainable, communities as Beverly Hills, Bel Air, or Palos Verdes.

The first-choice preferences of the subjects are shown in figure 4.2.
The neighborhoods are mapped and shaded according to the number
of times they were chosen by the 1,024 subjects, so that the most heavily shaded areas represent communities that were chosen by the greatest number of people. A minimum of six subjects was used as the cutoff
point for the highest-preference category, as this was the number of
choices that each community would receive if all were perceived as
equally attractive. The preference map contains four distinct regions of
highly preferred neighborhoods. First, a ridge extends from Santa

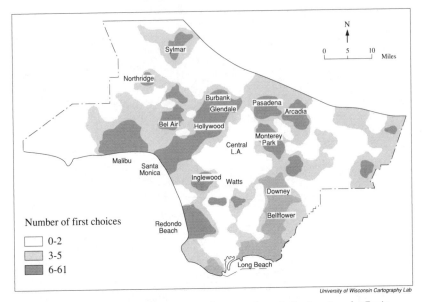

Figure 4.2. First-choice preferences of sample respondents in the Los Angeles Basin.
Source: Clark and Cadwallader 1973b:fig. 3.

Monica in the west to Hollywood in the east, reflecting the physically
attractive nature of this area and its relatively good access to the ocean
and mountains. Second, the beach communities, such as Malibu and
Redondo Beach, are also highly preferred. Third, a highly preferred
region in the eastern portion of the Los Angeles basin includes such
communities as Arcadia and Pasadena, where Arcadia represents newer
housing opportunities and Pasadena represents a long-established residential community. Finally, the belt of highly preferred communities
from Long Beach to Downey reflects the residential preferences of
lower-income whites, blacks, and Mexican Americans.

Efforts have since been made to measure the degree of association
between such mental maps and migration flows. Lloyd (1976) argued
that although it has been suggested for some time that spatial behavior
is at least partly a function of an individual's cognitions of his or her
alternatives, no attempt has been made to explicitly examine the linkages among cognition, preference, and behavior. With this thought in
mind, he identified three abstract spaces that could be used to analyze
interstate migration flows. First, an n-dimensional cognitive space contains information concerning the cognized characteristics of places.
The axes represent the underlying cognitive structure of the attributes
associated with those places, and so the cognized characteristics of any

particular place are defined by its location within that space. Second, an *n*-dimensional preference space contains axes which represent the underlying preference structure and define the degree to which a particular place is preferred. Third, an *n*-dimensional behavior space, such as that associated with interstate migration, involves axes that represent the underlying structure of actual behavior.

Within this conceptual framework, Lloyd gathered data from samples of university students. The grid repertory test was used to collect the cognitive information, and multidimensional scaling was used to identify the underlying dimensions of the cognitive spaces. Similarly, Gould's rank-ordering technique was utilized to collect the preference data, with multidimensional scaling again determining the structure of the preference spaces. Finally, the behavior space was generated using a forty-eight-by-forty-eight origin-destination matrix and subjecting it to the revealed preference procedures used by Rushton (1981). A series of canonical correlation analyses suggested strong linkages between cognitions, preferences, and actual behavior. Lloyd ended by noting, however, that despite these encouraging results, considerably more work was needed to formally explicate the relationships between the cognitive constructs and actual behavior and also to identify how the cognitive information is translated into overall preferences for particular destinations, which are then translated into overt behavior.

Using twenty-five Kentucky cities, White (1974) also focused on the relationship between preferences and overt behavior. He provided evidence to support the hypothesis that the in-migration to a particular city is related to the preference value attributed to that city by a sample of potential migrants. Indeed, the correlation between residential preference and in-migration indicated that almost half the variation in migration behavior can be accounted for by preferences. In a later paper, however, using the same data set, White (1978) cautioned that models linking aggregated preference maps with aggregatede behavior are limited by the fact that preference patterns vary across different socioeconomic groups. This problem is compounded by the fact that socioeconomic groups vary in their propensity to migrate. White concluded by suggesting that the preferences of potential migrants might be usefully disaggregated on the basis of accessibility to alternative destinations, socioeconomic status, and awareness levels for alternative locations.

In a later study, using a data set involving metropolitan areas throughout the United States, White (1980a) showed that out-migration from Topeka, Kansas, to a selection of other cities was more closely related to awareness and preference indices than to such traditional

variables as size, distance, and economic and demographic characteristics. In further analyses of the same data set, White (1981) explored
the communality and content of residential preferences. First, there
seemed to be substantial common agreement among the more than
one thousand people in six different cities who indicated their preferences for twenty-six metropolitan areas. Second, residential preferences were more strongly related to the perceived characteristics of
cities than to either their objective or informational characteristics.

In a similar vein, Jones and Zannaras (1976) investigated the variation in young adult in-migration rates for thirty Venezuelan cities. A
multivariate regression model, involving traditional economic opportunity and quality of life variables, accounted for 65 percent of the
variation in migration behavior, but a second model, incorporating
measures of perceived economic opportunity and perceived quality of
life, improved the level of explanation to 83 percent. The authors noted
that the images held by youths do not necessarily reflect those of the
whole population but pointed out that youths tend to form the most
highly mobile segment of the population and are therefore the most
important source of potential migrants.

Jones (1978) extended this work in his discussion of so-called Venezuelan myth maps. In particular, he was able to show that these myth
maps, constructed on the basis of perceived economic opportunities
and quality of life characteristics, could be attributed to images projected by the national newspapers, which tend to popularize the regional development efforts of the public sector. Also within Venezuela,
the same author (Jones 1980) has attempted to articulate the role of
cognitive variables in migration through the construction of a path
model, thus isolating the direct and indirect effects of different variables.

Finally, Todd (1982) also used path analysis to explore the role of
subjective attributes in explaining small-town population change in
Manitoba. Given the divergence between objective and subjective correlates of place, he suggested that both kinds of variables could be
profitably included in regression models. This suggestion was supported by the fact that, in examining small-town stability as evidenced
by population change, Todd was able to show that the objective and
subjective variables can have independent associations with in- or out-
migration once the problem of multicollinearity has been identified.

Although the explication of the links between preferences and overt
behavior has been of the utmost importance, it has been equally important to explain the preferences themselves. In other words, can we
explain why certain individuals prefer certain locations? The answer to
this question involves trying to establish how individuals integrate var-

ious pieces of information into some kind of overall utility value that they can then use to rank alternatives (Timmermans and Golledge 1990). The migration literature offers three major approaches to this problem. The revealed preference approach involves the examination of observed behavior in order to uncover the underlying preference structure and so establish rules of behavior. For example, Schwind (1971) inductively derived the spatial preferences of migrants for regions by analyzing actual migration flows between State Economic Areas in Maine. Similarly, Tobler (1979) computed the relative attractiveness of states from data on interstate migration. It is important to remember, however, that only purely discretionary behavior should be analyzed through revealed preferences. In those instances where the choice is constrained in some way, a confounding of preferences and constraints will occur.

Since the revealed preference approach only allows one to deduce a preferential ordering for the range of spatial alternatives that are available in a particular study area, some researchers have attempted to develop experimental designs whereby attribute values can be manipulated to produce a variety of abstract combinations, thus creating a set of hypothetical alternatives that is independent of any particular spatial structure. One of the potentially most useful of these approaches is the conjoint measurement model. The conjoint measurement technique provides a method for defining a utility value for each alternative as a joint effect of its constituent attributes. The coefficients associated with those attributes indicate their individual contributions to the overall utility value.

Lieber (1979) has successfully used the conjoint measurement procedure within a migration context by asking subjects to evaluate both hypothetical and real destinations according to three predetermined attributes. The three attributes were travel time to a major city, travel time to a fresh-air recreational opportunity, and travel time to close relatives. The first two attributes were split into four levels, while the third attribute was split into two levels. As a result, the experimental design consisted of thirty-two treatment combinations, and Lieber concluded that a multiplying, or nonlinear, model may be more appropriate for describing preference judgments than a linear one.

The main advantage of the conjoint measurement model over the revealed preference approach is that subjects are directly evaluating the attributes assumed to underlie destination preferences, rather than simply the alternatives themselves. It is in this respect that the derived rules of spatial choice are considered to be independent of the particular opportunity set being considered. One of the major disadvantages of the technique, however, is that the experimental levels associated with each of the attributes have to be predetermined by the experimenter, and these levels will not necessarily coincide with the internalized thresholds for those attributes held by the subjects themselves.

A third type of methodology used to probe the individual decision-making process involves multidimensional scaling techniques. Such techniques can help to identify the cognitive attributes, or dimensions, that individuals use to differentiate between alternative choices. In more general terms, multidimensional scaling allows one to generate abstract variables that represent underlying dimensions, or patterns, in the original data. Unlike the variables used in factor analysis, however, these abstract variables are based upon information concerning interobject similarities rather than upon measurements across a set of empirical attributes. The output of a multidimensional scaling analysis consists of a set of coordinates for each object, representing its scaled value on each of the derived dimensions. Individual objects can thus be represented as points within an n-dimensional space. The distance between the points, or objects, in this n-dimensional space reflects their similarity. Spaces of minimum dimensionality are sought in order to assist the interpretation of the dimensions, and in practice the data are often presented as a two-dimensional perceptual map (Golledge, Rivizzigno, and Spector 1976).

Obviously, moving from a higher- to a lower-order dimensional representation of a given set of interobject distances results in sacrificing information concerning the true distances. A statistical measure of this loss of information is termed *stress*, and stress necessarily increases as we decrease dimensionality. Thus, when choosing the appropriate number of dimensions to adequately represent a given set of data, the researcher is faced with a trade-off between stress, or goodness-of-fit, and dimensionality. It is often best to plot the relation between stress and dimensionality and then hope that a significant "elbow" in the curve will indicate the appropriate number of dimensions (Golledge and Rushton 1972:14). The difficulties associated with selecting the correct number of dimensions are similar to those encountered in factor analysis, where one is guided by the eigenvalues. Also, similar numerical values for stress can be obtained for different dimensional configurations derived from the same set of data (Tobler 1982).

The collection of input data, often generated by a paired comparison experiment, is not unproblematic, as ideally the subjects are given all possible pairs of objects and are then asked to provide some kind of comparative judgment concerning those pairs. Obviously, the number of possible pairs increases quite dramatically as the number of objects increases. For example, if we assume that comparisons of the object with itself and complementary comparisons are ignored, then just 20 objects will generate 190 paired comparisons. Thus, with even moderately large numbers of stimuli, the pairwise judgment task becomes onerous for most subjects, and experimenters usually resort to some kind of incomplete experimental design involving a manageable subset of the total possible number of pairs (Spence 1982).

At least two issues must be considered, however, when choosing such a subset of pairs (Isaac 1982). First, not all distances are equally important for determining a configuration via nonmetric multidimensional scaling. Indeed, it seems that the long and short distances are particularly important, as the long distances help to outline the configuration, while the short distances provide local detail. The medium distances are therefore the most dispensable. The second issue concerns the reliability of judgments associated with particular distances, and here it appears intuitively logical that error will increase as the true distance increases. Cross-sectional reliability can be assessed by requiring repeated judgments within a single experiment, but any assessment of longitudinal reliability involves separating cross-sectional errors from those changes induced by a shift in attitudes (Deutscher 1982).

Finally, any interpretation of the dimensions obtained from a multidimensional scaling analysis is open to debate. In particular, it is unclear whether such dimensions are ultimately useful as causal or explanatory constructs within models of overt spatial behavior. The use of multidimensional scaling techniques often implies a structural rather than a process orientation that is more conducive to detailed description than process-related explanation (Pipkin 1982). This view is reinforced by the fact that most paired comparison tasks are undertaken in laboratory settings, and proximity judgments are usually elicited without reference to goals or intentions.

Within the context of migration, Demko (1974) sought to uncover subjects' images of a selected group of cities in southern Ontario which were treated as potential destinations. The generated similarities data were subjected to multidimensional scaling analysis, in order to obtain a set of derived cognitive spaces. Similarly, Lueck (1976) used multidimensional scaling analysis to investigate the cognition of nine cities in the United States. He concluded that a three-dimensional solution could adequately account for the variation in the original dissimilarities data. He described these three dimensions as representing an excitement scale, a cleanliness and safety scale, and a social milieu scale.

Like revealed preferences and conjoint measurement, however, multidimensional scaling has not been immune from criticism. Scholars have especially questioned whether it provides a useful model of the psychological processes involved in decision-making. A significant weakness is the fact that the cognitive dimensions have to be interpreted in an a posteriori fashion by the researcher, whereas in conjoint measurement the significant attributes are specified in advance. Also, the axes provided by multidimensional scaling are continuous in nature, although it is quite likely that individuals make decisions on the basis of certain threshold values, rather than on the basis of continuous referents (Harman and Betak 1976).

Information and Preference Surfaces

From the preceding discussion it can be argued that information and preferences play an important role in determining attitudes toward migration. The amount of information that individuals possess about particular places, and their preferences for those places, can be expressed as surfaces. Knowledge of such surfaces can enhance our understanding of migration patterns. For example, it has already been shown that a relationship exists between information levels and migrational search behavior (McCracken 1975). It should be noted, however, that the considerable body of work on mean information fields, associated mainly with investigations of spatial diffusion (L. A. Brown 1981), is not directly relevant to the present discussion for two major reasons. First, such investigations have not calibrated information levels directly but have relied on surrogate measures derived from patterns of spatial interaction (Morrill and Pitts 1967). Second, the reliance on distance-decay functions in these studies has necessitated the representation of surfaces as one-dimensional distributions. Such a representation has the unfortunate effect of filtering out any directional biases in these surfaces (Hanson, Marble, and Pitts 1972).

The purpose of the present discussion is to describe a detailed examination of the information and preference surfaces associated with a group of residents living in West Los Angeles (Cadwallader 1978). The aim is to account for any regularities in those surfaces and later to examine their underlying structures and structural interrelationships, in the hope that such structures will help to identify the variables used in the evaluation process. Using Gould's (1975b:20) terminology, then, an effort is being made to look backward from these surfaces to some of the causal influences that form them. To this end, trend surface analysis is used to generate the explanatory hypotheses, which are then tested by means of correlation and regression analysis. In the following section the underlying structures and their interrelationships are investigated using principal components analysis and canonical correlation procedures.

The data for the research were collected from fifty residents of West Los Angeles. The subjects were not chosen randomly, as the aim was to use individuals who all lived within three blocks of each other. In this way individual differences in the information and preference patterns could be compared, while holding location in physical space constant.

Obviously, it is no easy task to establish acceptable measures of information and preferences. Consequently, researchers have used a variety of approaches in the past. In most cases information levels have been measured using category rating scales. For example, Horton and Reynolds (1971) presented their subjects with a map showing the Cedar Rapids metropolitan area divided into twenty-seven subareas. The subjects were then asked to evaluate, using a five-point scale, their level of familiarity with each of the subareas. Similarly, Donaldson and Johnston (Donaldson 1973; Donaldson and Johnston 1973) asked subjects to rate their familiarity with forty-eight Christchurch suburbs, using a five-point scale ranging from very familiar to unknown. Respondents were requested to equate the term *familiar* with "how well they knew their way around both minor and major streets of the suburbs" (Donaldson and Johnston 1973:47). Although such five-point rating scales are comparatively easy for subjects to respond to, they do not provide detailed interval-level data. By contrast, Gould (1973), when studying the information surfaces held by Swedish schoolchildren, asked the children to write down, in the space of five minutes, the names of all the villages, towns, and cities in Sweden that they could remember. The raw counts were used to represent the levels of information, as the settlements were not weighted according to their positions in the individual lists. Again, this measurement procedure is fairly crude, as it fails to measure the actual amount of information associated with each settlement in the individual lists.

In the case of residential preference surfaces, the most popular methodology has been that developed by Gould (Gould and White 1986). The subjects are asked to rank, according to residential desirability, the forty-eight contiguous states of the United States. This methodology has been criticized on the grounds that subjects appear to experience difficulty discriminating between the states in this fashion, as they probably view some states as very desirable, others as very undesirable, and the rest simply somewhere in the middle (Clark and Cadwallader 1973b). Also, this ranking procedure provides only ordinal-level data. Other researchers have chosen to use a five-point rating scale, similar to that used for information surfaces. Johnston (1970), for example, used a five-point scale of desirability when measuring the residential attractiveness associated with thirty towns in New Zealand. Similarly, Horton and Reynolds (1971) also used a five-point scale, ranging from very poor to very good, to calibrate residential quality.

The present author (Cadwallader 1978) measured both the information and preference patterns by the method of direct magnitude estimation (Gescheider 1988; Lodge 1981). Each subject was asked to estimate his or her familiarity with and preference for thirty cities in the Los Angeles basin, although two of these cities were subsequently omitted from the statistical analysis because their associated variances were so small (fig. 4.3). The method of direct magnitude estimation is a technique that has been used by psychologists to establish scales of subjective magnitude (Stevens 1975). In general, the measurement procedure involves asking subjects to estimate the relative magnitudes of a set of stimuli by comparing them with a standard stimulus. It is advisable to select the standard so that it is in the middle range of the variable stimuli and to randomize the order in which the stimuli are presented to the subjects. The scale that results from such a measurement procedure possesses ratio-level properties, thus allowing all arithmetic operations to be performed with the numbers assigned to the subjective magnitudes. This attribute is highly desirable, as it removes the necessity of having to derive interval or ratio information from a ranked set of data.

Hypotheses concerning the variables used to account for the spatial configuration of the information and preference surfaces were generated by means of trend surface analysis. Trend surface analysis is essentially a multiple regression technique whereby the general trend in an areally distributed variable can be identified (Unwin 1981). In general, a surface can be expressed symbolically as follows:

$$Z = f(X, Y) \tag{4.2}$$

where Z is the mapped or areally distributed variable, X is latitude, and Y is longitude. The trend surface analysis assumes that the mapped variable can be decomposed into two components: a trend component, representing the large-scale systematic changes that extend across the map; and a local component, representing local fluctuations around the general trend. So for any particular location on a map, the observed height of the surface is made up of the trend component at that point plus the local component, or residual. This statement can be expressed as follows:

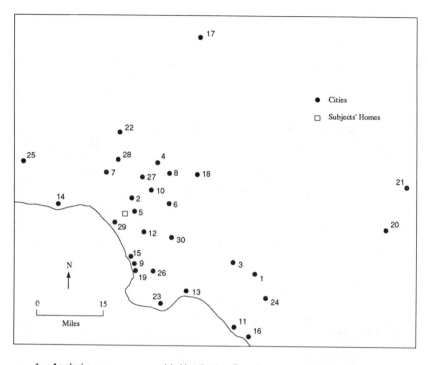

1. Anaheim	11. Huntington Beach	21. San Bernardino
2. Beverly Hills	12. Inglewood	22. San Fernando
3. Buena Park	13. Long Beach	23. San Pedro
4. Burbank	14. Malibu	24. Santa Ana
5. Culver City	15. Manhattan Beach	25. Thousand Oaks
6. Downtown L.A.	16. Newport Beach	26. Torrance
7. Encino	17. Palmdale	27. Universal City
8. Glendale	18. Pasadena	28. Van Nuys
9. Hermosa Beach	19. Redondo Beach	29. Venice
10. Hollywood	20. Riverside	30. Watts

Figure 4.3. Location of the cities involved in the information and preference study of Los Angeles.
Source: Cadwallader 1978:fig. 1.

$$Z_i = f(X_i, Y_i) \pm e_i \tag{4.3}$$

where Z_i is the height of the surface at location i, X_i and Y_i are the latitude and longitude associated with location i, and e_i is the local component, or residual, associated with location i.

The procedure involves fitting successively higher-order polynomials of the following form:

$$Z = a + b_1X + b_2Y \tag{4.4}$$

$$Z = a + b_1X + b_2Y + b_3X^2 + b_4XY + b_5Y^2 \tag{4.5}$$

$$Z = a + b_1X + b_2Y + b_3X^2 + b_4XY + b_5Y^2 + b_6X^3 + \\ b_7X^2Y + b_8XY^2 + b_9Y^3 \tag{4.6}$$

where the notation is the same as in equation 4.2 and a and the b terms are the regression coefficients. Equations 4.4, 4.5, and 4.6 represent linear, quadratic, and cubic surfaces, respectively. A quadratic surface contains one inflection point, while a cubic surface contains two inflection points, and so on. The extent to which the computed trend surface accounts for the variation in the mapped data can be measured by the coefficient of multiple determination.

Although trend surface analysis has been used in a variety of geographical contexts (Clark and Hosking 1986), there has been some disagreement about its appropriateness as a hypothesis-generating device. Norcliffe (1969), in particular, regards it as being basically a hypothesis-testing technique. Others, however, have taken a less-restricted view of the technique and have commented upon its usefulness as a search procedure (Cliff et al. 1975:56). It is in this latter capacity that the technique is being used here, as both the major regional trends and their more local deviations are used to identify variables associated with the spatial configurations of the information and preference surfaces.

It should be noted that the distribution of data points is not ideal for trend surface analysis, as relatively few observations occur in the eastern part of the area (fig. 4.3). In general, a clustering of data points will tend to inflate the R-squared value, and the area containing the cluster of data points will have an undue influence on the shape of the surface. Although a more even distribution of data points is certainly desirable, experimental evidence does suggest that trend surface analysis is fairly robust to departures from the ideal distribution (Unwin 1970). Also, as the technique is being used in a largely exploratory capacity, this problem is not considered critical.

The results from fitting linear, quadratic, and cubic surfaces are provided in table 4.1, although the significance levels associated with each surface are not reported, as these are notoriously difficult to interpret in trend surface analysis (Tinkler 1969). More complex surfaces were not computed for two reasons. First, it is often extremely difficult to determine the empirical meaning of anything beyond a third-order surface. Second, higher-order surfaces result in a significant loss of degrees of freedom. A fourth-order surface, for example, would entail the

Table 4.1. Trend surface analysis of the information and
preference surfaces for Los Angeles

	Information surface (R^2)	Preference surface (R^2)
Linear	.13	.15
Quadratic	.24	.34
Cubic	.53	.60

Source: Cadwallader 1978: table 1.

loss of fifteen degrees of freedom. Obviously, a perfect fit will be obtained whenever the number of terms in the trend function equals the number of data points. As one would expect, the best fit for both the information and preference surfaces is provided by the cubic surface, although even the cubic surfaces only account for just over half the total variation in the data. The comparatively small coefficients of determination indicate that the surfaces are extremely convoluted. Of greater interest, however, is the fact that the trend surface analysis successfully identified a number of potentially important explanatory variables.

Inspection of the preference surfaces and their residuals suggested the importance of distance from the Pacific Ocean as a determinant of residential desirability. Also, some measure of affluence appeared to be important, as cities such as Beverly Hills and Malibu were consistently given high ratings. In the information surface, distance again appeared to be a major factor, although in this case distance from the subject's home was important, rather than distance from the ocean. City size emerged as a second variable influencing information levels, with the larger cities tending to be more familiar than the smaller ones. The extent to which these four variables account for the variation in the information and preference surfaces was investigated by means of multiple correlation and regression analysis.

For the preference surface, the multiple regression model is as follows:

$$Y_i = a - b_1X_{i1} + b_2X_{i2} \tag{4.7}$$

where Y_i is the attractiveness of city i; X_{i1} is the distance of city i from the Pacific Ocean; X_{i2} is the average income of city i; and a, b_1, and b_2 are constants. The multiple correlation coefficient for this equation is .85, and the partial correlation coefficients suggest that average income is more important than distance from the ocean (table 4.2). Note that the coefficient for average income is positive, indicating that the affluent cities are more highly preferred, whereas the coefficient for distance

Table 4.2. Partial correlation coefficients
associated with the information
and preference surfaces for Los
Angeles

Information surface	
Distance from subjects' homes	–.54
City size	.15

Preference surface	
Distance from the ocean	–.44
Average income for city	.80

Source: Cadwallader 1978: table 2.

from the ocean is negative, indicating that residential desirability decreases with increasing distance from the ocean. It should be remembered, however, that extreme caution is required when interpreting the coefficients in models of this type, as empirical estimates of the distance coefficient can be influenced by the particular configuration of points, or cities (Sheppard 1984).

The variation in information levels was analyzed using the following multiple regression model:

$$Y_i = a - b_1 X_{i1} + b_2 X_{i2} \tag{4.8}$$

where Y_i is the information level for city i; X_{i1} is the distance of city i from the subjects' homes; X_{i2} is the population of city i; and a, b_1, and b_2 are constants. The multiple correlation coefficient for this equation is .58, with distance from the subjects' homes being more important than population size (table 4.2). Again, note that information levels decrease with increasing distance but increase with increasing population size. These results are similar to those obtained by Gould's (1973, 1975a,b) investigation of the information surfaces of Swedish schoolchildren, as he found that the configuration of those surfaces could be satisfactorily accounted for by population and distance variables. Similar results have also been reported when measurements were made concerning the accuracy of information rather than just the quantity (Webber, Symanski, and Root 1975).

Cognitive Structures

A more thorough investigation of the information and preference surfaces can be undertaken by identifying the underlying evaluative dimen-

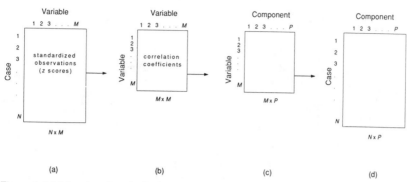

Figure 4.4. Major steps in principal components analysis.
Source: Cadwallader 1985a:fig. 5.9. (Martin Cadwallader, *Analytical Urban Geography,* © 1985, p. 129. Reprinted by permission of Prentice Hall, Inc., Englewood Cliffs, New Jersey.)

sions. Principal components analysis provides a suitable methodology for this purpose, as it was originally developed by psychologists to reduce a large number of variables to a smaller number of underlying components, or dimensions (Comrey 1973). These underlying components summarize the original variables, although as one moves from, say, twenty variables to only three components, some of the original variation is lost. Just how much of the original variation is lost, however, can be readily computed.

It is convenient to think of principal components analysis as four matrices. The first matrix (fig. 4.4a) is simply a data matrix, where the cases are the rows and the variables are the columns. As we have N cases and M variables, the overall size of the matrix is $N \times M$. The data in this matrix are standardized, so that each variable is expressed in terms of standard deviations from its mean. The data matrix is then transformed into a correlation matrix (fig. 4.4b). Each variable is correlated with every other variable, thus creating an $M \times M$ matrix of correlation coefficients. The diagonal cells are given the value of one, as they represent the correlation of each variable with itself.

The correlation matrix is then transformed into the components matrix (fig. 4.4c). Each column in the matrix is a component that represents a group of interrelated variables. The variables are the rows, so if we have P components, then the size of this matrix is $M \times P$. Each cell in the matrix contains a component loading, and these loadings indicate the strength of the relationships between the variables and the underlying components. Thus the component loadings are used to interpret which group of variables is summarized by each particular component. Finally, by multiplying the original data matrix by the components matrix, we obtain the matrix of component scores (fig. 4.4d). In

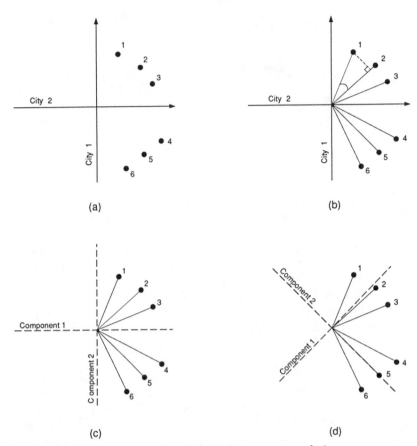

Figure 4.5. Geometric interpretation of principal components analysis.
Source: Cadwallader 1985a:fig. 5.11. (Martin Cadwallader, *Analytical Urban Geography,*
© 1985, p. 132. Reprinted by permission of Prentice Hall, Inc., Englewood Cliffs, New Jersey.)

this matrix the cases are once again the rows, while the components are
the columns. Each cell contains a component score, and these scores
indicate the value for each case on each component. In other words,
after starting with values for a large number of variables for each case,
we finish with values for a smaller number of components for each
case.

It is also helpful to visualize this statistical procedure in geometric
terms (Rummel 1970). First, imagine that we have two cities and six
variables (fig. 4.5a), although in reality we would need many more
cities for this type of analysis. Both cities have above-average values for
the first three variables, while city 1 is below average and city 2 is above
average for the remaining three variables. If we draw lines from the

origin to each of the six points in this two-dimensional space, we obtain six vectors, one for each variable (fig. 4.5b). The cosine of the angle between each pair of vectors, or variables, denotes the correlation coefficient between those variables. An angle between 0 and 90 degrees indicates a positive correlation, with 0 representing a perfect linear relationship and 90 degrees representing the complete absence of a linear relationship. Negative correlations are indicated by angles between 90 and 180 degrees. If the vectors are of unit length, then the same information is represented by the projection of one vector onto another. The longer the projection, the greater the correlation coefficient. In other words, the closer together the vectors are in this two-dimensional space, the more strongly the variables are related.

Having discussed correlation coefficients in geometric terms, we can now consider a geometric representation of the component loadings (fig. 4.5c). The first component is placed through the six vectors, or variables, in such a fashion that it maximizes the sum of the squared component loadings. The component loadings are analogous to the correlation coefficients in figure 4.4b, but in this case each vector is projected onto the components. In other words, variable 3 is quite closely related to the first component and thus has a relatively high component loading, while variable 1 has a relatively low component loading. If the loadings for all six variables are squared and summed, then the location of the first component maximizes that sum. This sum of the squared component loadings is called an eigenvalue, and it is used to determine the proportion of the total variation that is summarized by each component. The second component is introduced at right angles to the first, meaning that the two components are statistically independent of each other. The projections of each variable on this second axis provide the loadings for component 2. Further axes, or components, can be introduced at right angles to each other, although these axes cannot be represented in a two-dimensional diagram. In fact, as many axes can be fitted as there are variables.

In order to interpret and label the different components, it is obviously advantageous to have some very high loadings while the rest are very low. The situation represented in figure 4.5c is not ideal in this sense, as the loadings associated with the first component are neither exceptionally high nor exceptionally low. In other words, the component is not easily interpreted, or labeled, as a simple structure has not been achieved. This simple structure can often be obtained, however, by rotating the axes (fig. 4.5d). Now component 1 goes through the middle of the first three variables, while component 2 goes through the middle of the other three variables. As a result, both components have three high loadings and three low loadings, and thus each component summarizes three variables. If the axes, or components, are rotated while a right angle is maintained between them, the rotation is termed an orthogonal rotation. If, on the other hand, a right angle is not maintained, we have an oblique rotation, in which the components are no longer statistically independent of each other.

Using the data for Los Angeles described in the previous section, with the subjects as cases and the cities as variables, an orthogonal rotation was performed. In particular, a varimax rotation was chosen, in order to maximize the variance associated with each column of component loadings. Those cities with highly correlated familiarity, or preference ratings, were associated with the same components, and it was hoped that the interpretation of these components would suggest the underlying dimensions which the subjects had used to evaluate the cities.

The underlying structure of the preference surface is represented in table 4.3, and the highest loading for each city, on any of the four components, was used to interpret those components. The four components describing the preference pattern accounted for approximately 87 percent of the total variance, while the first two components alone accounted for over 65 percent. The first component is associated with interior cities such as San Bernardino, Thousand Oaks, and Riverside (fig. 4.3), whereas the second component is associated with cities on, or close to, the coastline. The latter cities include Hermosa Beach, Redondo Beach, Newport Beach, and Long Beach. The only exception to this general rule is Malibu, which loads more heavily on the first component. The overwhelming importance of the first two components in variance accounted for is significant. It suggests that the subjects, when asked to evaluate the cities according to their relative attractiveness, simply thought of two dimensions: coastal cities and interior cities. As a result, the coastal cities all received similar ratings, as did the interior cities. The relative attractiveness of coastal cities in general, as opposed to interior cities in general, however, varied across individuals.

The results of the principal components analysis of the information surface are less easily interpreted. To account for 76 percent of the total variance requires six components, and no single component accounts for more than approximately 17 percent (table 4.4). It is noteworthy, however, that cities grouped together in information space also tend to be grouped together in physical space (fig. 4.3). For example, San Bernardino and Riverside are associated with the same component, as are Long Beach and San Pedro and Hermosa Beach, Manhattan Beach, and Redondo Beach. This finding is not unexpected, as it means that if a

Table 4.3. The preference structure of cities in the Los Angeles Basin

City	Components			
	I	II	III	IV
Anaheim	.808	.383	.289	-.066
Beverly Hills	.656	.715	-.090	-.093
Buena Park	.778	.562	.153	-.120
Burbank	.890	.369	.140	-.034
Downtown L.A.	-.031	-.005	.816	.260
Encino	.724	.603	.070	-.153
Glendale	.855	.317	.215	.223
Hermosa Beach	.481	.817	.094	.174
Huntington Beach	.415	.766	-.001	.269
Inglewood	.660	.681	.062	.018
Long Beach	.442	.780	.323	-.227
Malibu	.786	.549	-.100	.023
Manhattan Beach	.442	.834	.061	.193
Newport Beach	.370	.770	-.053	.006
Palmdale	.253	-.120	.768	.115
Pasadena	.844	.293	.213	.217
Redondo Beach	.491	.786	.096	.203
Riverside	.830	.380	.326	.008
San Bernardino	.723	.570	.290	-.041
San Fernando	.502	.075	.736	-.072
San Pedro	.014	.624	.632	.071
Santa Ana	.857	.350	.328	-.023
Thousand Oaks	.864	.449	-.029	-.060
Torrance	.345	.780	.357	-.208
Universal City	.519	.249	.623	-.149
Van Nuys	.328	.185	.719	-.347
Venice	.064	.153	.334	.817
Watts	-.122	.096	.810	.278
Percent of total variance:	36.4	29.0	16.7	5.0

Source: Cadwallader 1978: table 3.
Note: Underscores indicate highest component loading for each variable.

person possesses a great deal of information about a city in one particular part of the Los Angeles basin, he or she is also likely to be very familiar with other cities in the same area. The relative amount of information associated with each group of cities, however, again varies from person to person.

The final step in the analysis involves an investigation of the interrelationships between the two underlying structures. Canonical correlation analysis was deemed appropriate for this task, as it allows one to measure the relationships between two sets of variables or, as in this case, two sets of components (Kachigan 1986). Canonical analysis,

Table 4.4. The information structure of cities in the Los Angeles Basin

City	Components					
	I	II	III	IV	V	VI
Anaheim	.333	.611	.261	.141	.504	.234
Beverly Hills	.624	.268	.153	.425	−.145	.000
Buena Park	.792	.103	.253	.030	.363	.214
Burbank	.232	.566	−.024	.031	.493	−.008
Downtown L.A.	.324	−.017	.105	.749	.206	.188
Encino	.644	.041	.566	.115	−.141	.154
Glendale	.071	.131	.183	.193	.789	.119
Hermosa Beach	.358	−.069	.116	.015	.285	.779
Huntington Beach	.750	.036	.006	.390	.246	.272
Inglewood	.605	.113	.037	−.017	.139	.040
Long Beach	.281	.124	.571	.215	.507	.297
Malibu	.672	.423	.046	.376	−.114	.236
Manhattan Beach	.132	.234	.123	.038	.026	.905
Newport Beach	.112	.205	.068	.365	.067	.657
Palmdale	.143	.259	.568	.073	.427	.152
Pasadena	.196	.044	.425	.642	.132	.237
Redondo Beach	.132	−.001	.303	.502	.150	.581
Riverside	.438	.588	.263	.022	.436	.288
San Bernardino	.064	.936	.094	.177	.077	.058
San Fernando	.155	.879	.183	−.082	.009	.055
San Pedro	.296	.140	.512	.258	.506	.175
Santa Ana	.616	.155	.280	.176	.522	.206
Thousand Oaks	.801	.063	.356	.053	.205	.163
Torrance	−.048	−.036	−.285	.862	.040	.007
Universal City	.029	.897	.168	−.027	.127	.118
Van Nuys	.088	.399	.777	−.025	.001	.125
Venice	.203	.204	.324	.473	.326	.125
Watts	.254	.073	.638	−.036	.322	.034
Percent of total variance:	17.3	15.1	11.7	11.0	10.7	10.4

Source: Cadwallader 1978: table 4.
Note: Underscores indicate highest component loading for each variable.

which was referred to earlier as a means of operationalizing migration fields, was developed by Hotelling (1936) and involves identifying linear composites of each set of variables such that the relationships between the composites are maximized. By tradition, the two groups of variables are labeled the "criterion," or dependent set, and the "predictor," or independent set. Canonical analysis is most often used in those instances where a single observed variable is inadequate to represent the criterion dimension of interest. In all cases, however, the overriding concern when employing canonical analysis is to identify the structural relationships between two groups of variables as a whole, rather than the relationships between individual variables.

The procedure involves deriving successive linear composites of both sets of variables in such a way that the correlation between each successive pair of composites is maximized. The first pair of composites identifies the most important pattern that is common to both groups of variables, and succeeding pairs of composites are uncorrelated with each other. In other words, the two sets of variables are transformed into orthogonal canonical vectors, where the canonical vectors are linear functions of the original variables, such that the correlations between certain variables of the two sets are maximized. The canonical correlations express the degree of association between the two sets of variables for each canonical vector. The square of the largest canonical correlation is the proportion of the variance in the first composite of the criterion set that is accounted for by the first composite of the predictor set. In this sense it is important to note that the canonical correlation provides a measure of the association between a pair of linear composites derived from the criterion and predictor variables, rather than a measure of the association between the two sets of variables themselves. Finally, the canonical weights express the degree of association between the original variables and the canonical vectors. These weights are like the loadings in a factor matrix and thus represent standardized measures which enable one to determine the relative contribution of each of the variables to each of the canonical vectors.

In the present instance, the component scores, rather than measurements on the original variables, were used as input to the canonical analysis. This approach has been used before (Bourne and Murdie 1972). The major problem with using measurements on the individual variables as input data is that the importance of the canonical vectors is not determined by how well they account for the variation within the two sets of variables; they simply optimize the relationships between the two sets. It seems logical, therefore, to first determine the underlying structures and then to relate those structures.

The first four components in the canonical analysis represent the preference structure, while the remaining six represent the information structure (table 4.5). The canonical correlations associated with three of the four canonical vectors are very low, suggesting that the two structures are only loosely related. Consequently, no attempt is made to interpret the canonical vectors. The results of the canonical analysis are thus somewhat disappointing, as some evidence of an interrelationship between the two structures was expected. In order to explore

Table 4.5. Results of the canonical analysis of cities in the Los Angeles Basin

Components	Canonical vectors			
	I	II	III	IV
I	.048	.350	.116	.929
II	.248	.494	−.830	−.080
III	−.218	.803	.455	−.319
IV	.930	.056	.354	−.097
V	.005	−.066	−.046	−.081
VI	−.104	−.095	.373	−.788
VII	−.541	−.143	.400	−.145
VIII	.876	−.117	.283	−.213
IX	−.059	.006	.759	.574
X	−.063	−.973	−.136	.159
Canonical correlations:	.714	.450	.270	.100

Source: Cadwallader 1978: table 5.

Table 4.6. The individual correlations between information and preferences for cities in the Los Angeles Basin

Correlation coefficient	Frequency (no. of individuals)
0 to .25	23
.26 to .50	18
.51 to .75	9
.76 to 1.00	0

Source: Cadwallader 1978: table 6.

this line of reasoning more fully, the correlations between the information and preference patterns for each individual were computed (table 4.6). The preponderance of correlation coefficients below .51, however, provides further evidence that no simple relationship exists between information and preferences.

A Synthesis of Macro and Micro Approaches

Having discussed some of the concepts and procedures involved in the behavioral approach to interregional migration, we can now explore how the macro- and micro-level approaches might be most usefully combined. The macro approach, with its roots in neoclassical economics, accounts for migration by examining characteristics of the socio-economic and physical environments, such as wage rates, unemployment, and climate. The micro approach, on the other hand, is more concerned with the decision-making process involved in how people choose between alternatives and thus borrows from the theories of choice behavior developed by psychologists. Although both these approaches have provided valuable insights, a synthesis seems appropriate; these two lines of inquiry should be regarded as complementary rather than competitive (Golledge 1980).

Such a synthesis can best be achieved by combining objectively calibrated characteristics of regions or places with their subjectively measured counterparts (Cadwallader 1989b). For example, although migration flows are undoubtedly sensitive to interregional wage differentials (Greenwood 1985), the cognition, or perception, of those differentials must also be taken into account. A fundamental axiom of the micro-level, or behavioral, approach is that a person's behavior is based on his or her perception of the environment, not on the environment as it actually exists. In other words, preferences and attitudes toward the characteristics of places are likely to play a significant role in explaining migration.

Within this general context, the purpose of the present section is to explore the relative contributions of objective and subjective variables in explaining migration patterns in the United States. The variables and measurement procedures are briefly described, and the relationships between the objective variables and their subjective counterparts are analyzed. Both sets of variables are then used to explain residential preferences and migration behavior. Finally, a series of path models is constructed to indicate how the subjective variables intervene between their objective counterparts and migration.

Net migration rates for each state in the United States were obtained from the *Current Population Reports* published by the U.S. Bureau of the Census. In each case the net migration from 1970 to 1979 was divided by the population of the state in 1970. Six so-called objective variables, describing individual characteristics of each state, were then chosen on the basis of their effectiveness in previous research on migration. Moreover, an attempt was made to use variables describing both the socio-economic and physical environments.

In particular, income, cost of living, and employment opportunities were chosen to represent the socioeconomic environment. Labor tends to migrate from low- to high-income areas, so income should be positively associated with net migration. Many authors argue, however, that the cost of living tends to negate income benefits (Cebula 1983:175), and empirical evidence suggests that living-cost differentials have a significant impact on migration patterns (Renas and Kumar 1981). Finally, migration rates are also sensitive to employment opportunities (Congdon 1988).

Characteristics of the physical environment were represented by recreational opportunities, climatic attractiveness, and population density. Quality of life variables have become increasingly popular in migration models (Isserman 1985). For example, Liu (1975) used recreational acres per capita when explaining differential net migration rates. A number of studies have used climatic variables, often involving some kind of temperature measurement, as indicators of quality of life (Ballard and Clark 1981). Renas and Kumar (1983), when investigating net migration into large metropolitan areas, concluded that people generally prefer regions which have moderate climates, rather than extremely hot or cold climates. Population density has also been used to measure physical quality of life (Porell 1982).

Data for the objective variables describing each state were culled from a variety of sources. The employment, income, and population density variables were taken from the *Statistical Abstract of the United States, 1982–83*, published by the U.S. Bureau of the Census. Measures of cost of living, outdoor recreational opportunities per capita, and climatic attractiveness were taken from Liu (1973). In particular, the index of climatic attractiveness incorporates data concerning relative humidity and amount of sunshine.

The data for the subjectively measured counterparts of these six variables were collected, via questionnaires, from a sample of Madison, Wisconsin, households. The sample was obtained using a three-stage method. First, a census tract was identified that represented the Madison population, especially its socioeconomic characteristics. Second, nine blocks were selected from this census tract in an attempt to generate a spatially distributed sample that was representative in house and lot size, housing age, and housing type. Third, within the nine selected blocks, every household was included in the survey. During the door-to-door collection procedure, the interviewer contacted 160 households, yielding 120 completed and usable questionnaires, for a response rate of 75 percent.

The subjective variables were calibrated using the previously described method of direct magnitude estimation. The method of direct magnitude estimation has two major advantages compared with the more widely used category rating scales (Lodge 1981). First, category rating scales force subjects to use a fixed range of categories that might not correspond to the true range of the stimuli, whereas direct magnitude estimation allows the subjects to express their judgments as precisely as possible. Second, category rating scales generate only ordinal, or at best quasi–interval-level data, thus prohibiting the use of some of the more powerful statistical techniques, whereas magnitude scaling procedures generate ratio-preserving measures of attitude strength. Indeed, the relatively crude measurement provided by category scaling might be partly responsible for the often disappointingly low correspondence between social attitudes and behavior.

A limited number of authors have employed both objective and subjective variables to measure levels of social well-being or quality of life (Pacione 1982). A major attempt to investigate the link between these subjective and objective indicators was made by Knox and Mac-Laran (1978), using data from the city of Dundee, Scotland. Individuals from different neighborhoods were asked to assess their level of satisfaction with each of ten major life-domains, using an eleven-point scale. The phrases "completely dissatisfied" and "completely satisfied" were associated with the extreme values of zero and ten. Correlations between these subjective scores and their objective counterparts proved to be generally positive, although some fairly weak, and even negative, associations were also found.

Similar, although rather less direct, studies have been carried out by other researchers. Todd (1982) investigated the association between objective and subjective characteristics of small towns in Manitoba. Six community satisfaction measures, involving such factors as shopping and medical facilities, were obtained from a sample of residents living in seventy-one settlements. These were then correlated with a functional index based upon the distribution of thirty-eight central functions. The correlation coefficients between the functional index of service provision and the six subjective measures of community satisfaction were all positive, although only one of these six bivariate correlations exceeded .5, leading Todd to conclude that subjective variables are not merely duplicates of their objective counterparts. Likewise, using principal components analysis on twenty-one objective and thirteen subjective attributes of places, Kuz (1978) found little overlap between the two subsets. Moreover, he reported a correlation coefficient of only .07 between objective and subjective indices constructed from the key variables in the two subsets.

Overall, previous research suggests that the correspondence between objective and subjective measures of the same phenomenon can vary from a very strong to a comparatively weak relationship. Such variation is not surprising, however, as environmental cognition is a complex process and the relationship between a so-called objective reality and an individual's cognition of that reality will be mediated by such factors as age, socioeconomic status, and aspiration level. Methodological factors may also be partly responsible for the different results. First, the values generated for the subjective indicators are unlikely to be completely independent of the techniques used to obtain those values. Second, while objective indicators can be collected for well-defined administrative units, individuals will not all be thinking of exactly the same territorial boundaries when providing their subjective evaluations.

The relationship between magnitude judgments and unidimensional stimuli is usually described by a power function (Stevens 1975). This curvilinear relationship reflects the fact that two stimuli close together on the low end of the scale appear to be more easily discriminated than those on the high end of the scale. In other words, it becomes increasingly difficult to distinguish between two stimuli as their magnitudes increase. Most of the classical work in psychophysics, however, has focused upon the measurement of such sensory magnitudes as loudness, where the experiments can be carried out under laboratory conditions. Less is known about the cognition of environmental variables (Evans 1980). Given our present rather limited knowledge, therefore, the objective and subjective variables involved in the study under discussion were expressed as both linear and power functions.

In all cases the correlation coefficient between an objective variable and its subjective counterpart is in the expected positive direction (table 4.7). The coefficients associated with the linear and power functions were generally indistinguishable, except for population density, where the correlation for the linear function was .548, while that for the power function was .847. Of greater interest, however, is the fact that the correlation coefficients for the previously defined environmental characteristics appear to be consistently lower than those for the socioeconomic characteristics, although employment opportunities also had a rather weak relationship between its objective and subjective measures. This finding suggests that the conflicting results reported in the recent literature might be explained by examining the types of variables being studied. In other words, certain categories of variables might exhibit uniformly stronger associations in a particular context than would other categories.

Few authors have explicitly attempted to explain the variation in residential preferences. White (1981), however, has analyzed the factors influencing the preference scores associated with a set of U.S. cities. A seven-point scale was used to measure the subjects' prefer-

Table 4.7. The relationships between the objective and
subjective variables for migration in the United States

	Linear function	Power function
Employment opportunities	.238	.265
Cost of living	.680	.670
Recreational opportunities	.112	.290
Income	.654	.669
Population density	.548	.847
Climatic attractiveness	.284	.261

Source: Cadwallader 1989b: table 1.

ences for twenty-six different cities, and a similar scale was used to obtain judgments about three attributes of those cities: climatic desirability, cost of living, and access to recreational opportunities. In addition, values for a set of objective attributes were also collected, including size, economic conditions, environmental and demographic factors, crime, and educational and recreational opportunities. The 1970 population was used as the measure of size for each city, while the other four variables were calibrated by using composite indices constructed from a much larger set of initial variables.

For all six cities surveyed, the subjective variables accounted for more of the variation in residential preferences than did the objective variables. The coefficients of determination associated with the equations containing the subjective variables ranged from .735 to .847, while those for the objective variables ranged from .281 to .589. Standardized regression coefficients were used to determine the relative importance of the individual variables in accounting for the variance in preferences. In their relation to the subjective attributes, residential preferences turned out to be much more dependent upon perceived access to recreational opportunities than upon either perceived cost of living or climatic desirability. For five of the six cities, cost of living proved to be more important than climate, and in every case climatic desirability and access to recreation were both positively related to preferences, while cost of living had a negative relationship. Regarding the objective attributes, the standardized regression coefficients suggested that the economic index was the most closely associated with preferences, followed by the crime and educational and recreational indices.

The results obtained in the Madison study were remarkably similar to those reported by White, even though in this case exactly the same number of variables were used in both sets of equations (table 4.8). First, the equation containing the subjective variables produced an

Table 4.8. The partial correlations with overall preferences for
migration in the United States

	Subjective variables	Objective variables
Employment opportunities	.128	.089
Cost of living	−.020	.269*
Recreational opportunities	.620**	.039
Income	.022	.113
Population density	−.158	−.287*
Climatic attractiveness	.236	.009
Coefficient of determination	.6930**	.1599
Multiple correlation coefficient	.8324	.3999

Source: Cadwallader 1989b: table 2.
Note: * is significant at .10; ** is significant at .05.

overall coefficient of determination of .6930, while that containing the objective variables had a coefficient of only .1599. Second, the partial correlation coefficients of the subjective variables indicate that recreational opportunities had by far the most important association with preferences and that climatic attractiveness also appeared to be more important than the economic measures such as cost of living, employment opportunities, and income. Third, among the objective variables, cost of living and population density turned out to be more important than either recreational opportunities or climatic attractiveness. In sum, then, as with White's results, the subjective variables were better predictors of preferences than their objective counterparts; the environmental characteristics were more important in the subjective context, while the socioeconomic characteristics were more important in the objective context.

Having examined how well the objective and subjective variables account for preferences, we now turn our attention to the relationship between preferences and migration. In a study based upon twenty-five Kentucky cities, White (1974) calculated a correlation coefficient of .67 between residential preferences and in-migration. In a later study, based upon twenty-six American cities, the same author (White 1981) found a correlation of .70 between a set of composite preference scores and net migration. Using the Madison data described above, a correlation coefficient of only .27 was found between overall preferences and net migration. It should be remembered, however, that the preferences have been aggregated across the sample, and the relationship might well be much stronger at the individual level.

Using the Kentucky data, White (1974) regressed in-migration on

Table 4.9. The partial correlations with migration for the United States

	Subjective variables	Objective variables
Employment opportunities	−.047	−.076
Cost of living	−.293*	−.427**
Recreational opportunities	.340**	.258*
Income	.248	.616**
Population density	−.336**	−.321**
Climatic attractiveness	.194	.489**
Coefficient of determination	.3768**	.5813**
Multiple correlation coefficient	.6138	.7624

Source: Cadwallader 1989b: table 3.
Note: * is significant at .10; ** is significant at .05.

seven independent variables and found that residential preferences were the best single predictor. Similarly, when focusing on Topeka, Kansas, White (1980a) suggested that the perceived attributes of urban places add more to the explanation of migration from Topeka than do objective characteristics. The analysis of young adult in-migration rates for thirty Venezuelan cities reenforced these results (Jones 1978), as the incorporation of variables which measured perceived economic opportunity and perceived quality of life improved the level of explanation relative to models containing only objective variables. In particular, objective economic opportunities and objective quality of life explained 55 and 61 percent, respectively, of the variation in migration rates. The introduction of perceived economic opportunities and perceived quality of life, however, increased the levels of explanation to 61 and 76 percent, respectively, leading Jones to conclude that perception appears to play a significant supplemental role in explaining migration.

Rather than using the subjective variables as supplemental to their objective counterparts, however, in the present study the relative importance of these two sets of variables was directly analyzed (table 4.9). When regressed on net migration, the multiple coefficient of determination for the six subjective variables was .3768, compared with .5813 for the six objective variables. This result suggests that the objective variables perform better in a purely predictive context, although the subjective variables would presumably increase the explained variation if they were combined with their objective counterparts. Such an integration of the two sets of variables, however, would probably lead to problems of multicollinearity. Interestingly enough, among the individual objective variables, income, climatic attractiveness, and cost of living have the three highest partial correlation coefficients, and recre-

Table 4.10. The partial correlations for the hybrid
model of migration for the United States

Recreational opportunities (subjective)	.507**
Population density (subjective)	−.265*
Cost of living (objective)	−.499**
Income (objective)	.573**
Climatic attractiveness (objective)	.491**
Coefficient of determination	.6305**
Multiple correlation coefficient	.7940

Source: Cadwallader 1989b: table 4.
Note: * is significant at .10; ** is significant at .05.

ational opportunities and population density turn out to be the most important subjective variables.

A composite model combining these five variables was therefore calibrated. This combined model had a higher coefficient of determination that those obtained when using either the subjective or objective variables on their own, even though one fewer explanatory variable was included (table 4.10). As expected, recreational opportunities, income, and climatic attractiveness are all positively related to migration, while population density and cost of living have negative relationships. All five coefficients are significantly different from zero at the .10 level, while four of them are also significant at .05.

Path models provide a useful way of exploring the interrelationships among a set of variables. In the context of the study examined here, the subjective variables seem to act as intervening variables between their objective counterparts and migration. More specifically, we can expect the objective characteristics of the states to affect migration not only directly but also indirectly through their impact on the cognition of those states. The aim of the analysis is to assess explicitly the relative magnitudes of these direct and indirect effects.

A somewhat similar analytical framework was used by Desbarats (1983a), who investigated the migration flows of a sample of applicants to British universities. A series of path models were employed to decompose the direct and indirect effects of destination characteristics on migration and to analyze the influence of various constraints. Although she found a high association between the subjective variables and migration, the objective variables were equally effective in accounting for migration. In addition, the objective variables not only acted as a constraint upon overt behavior but also appeared to constrain the preferences. In a similar vein, Jones (1980) constructed a path model to assess the influence of objective and subjective variables on urban in-migra-

where X_5 is either preferences or migration; O_1 and O_2 are the objective variables; S_1 and S_2 are their subjective counterparts; and e_3, e_4, and e_5 are the disturbance terms, or residual path coefficients. The standardized regression coefficients associated with these structural equations represent the path coefficients, while the path coefficient associated with each disturbance term is the square root of the unexplained variation in the dependent variable under consideration. As in all recursive models where there are no simultaneous relationships, the path coefficients can be estimated from ordinary least-squares regression analysis.

In the context of preferences (fig. 4.7), it is clear that the physical characteristics of the states, specifically climatic attractiveness and recreational opportunities, play a more decisive role than their socioeconomic counterparts. Of greater interest, however, is the fact that, for both climatic attractiveness and recreational opportunities, the indirect effects via the corresponding subjective variables are as great as the direct effects. For example, in the case of climatic attractiveness, the indirect effect is represented by the product of the path coefficients between X_2 and X_4, and X_5 and X_4. This product gives an indirect effect of .20, as opposed to the direct effect of –.22. In this case, then, the direct and indirect effects counteract each other.

A somewhat different picture emerges when migration behavior itself is used as the dependent variable (fig. 4.8). In this situation the socioeconomic characteristics are as important as the physical characteristics, and the direct effects are uniformly more important than the indirect effects. For example, income and climatic attractiveness have significant direct effects on migration but only minor indirect effects via their subjective counterparts. For all four models the path coefficients associated with the disturbance terms are relatively high, suggesting that other variables might profitably be included.

The data analyses suggest a number of tentative conclusions. First, the relationship between the objective variables and their subjective counterparts appears to be stronger for the socioeconomic characteristics than for the environmental characteristics. Second, the subjective variables accounted for more of the variation in residential preferences than did the objective variables. Third, the objective variables performed better in predicting actual migration patterns, although a composite model containing both objective and subjective variables proved to be the most effective. Fourth, a series of path models explored the degree to which the objective characteristics of states affect migration not only directly but also indirectly through their impact on the cognition of those states. The results suggest that such indirect effects play a more important role in the context of preferences than in the context of migration.

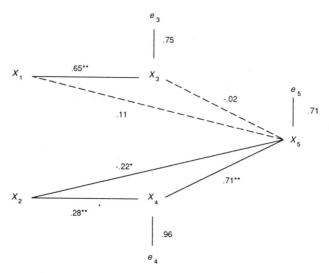

X_1 is income (objective), X_2 is climatic attractiveness (objective), X_3 is income (subjective), X_4 is climatic attractiveness (subjective), and X_5 is overall attractiveness.

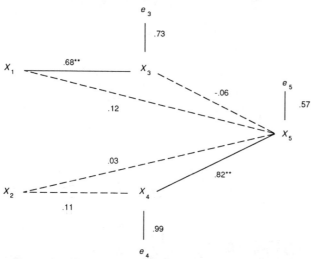

X_1 is cost of living (objective), X_2 is recreational opportunities (objective), X_3 is cost of living (subjective), X_4 is recreational opportunities (subjective), and X_5 is overall attractiveness.

Figure 4.7. The preference path models for migration in the United States.
Source: Cadwallader 1989b:fig. 2.
Note: ** indicates path coefficients that are significant at .05; * indicates path coefficients that are significant at .10; hashed lines indicate path coefficients that are not significant at .10.

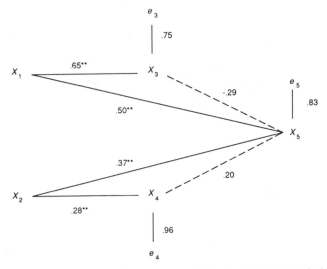

X_1 is income (objective), X_2 is climatic attractiveness (objective), X_3 is income (subjective), X_4 is climatic attractiveness (subjective), and X_5 is migration.

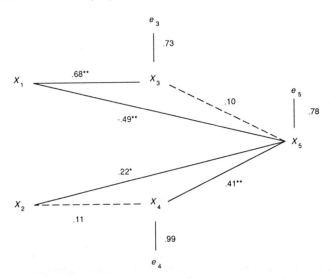

X_1 is cost of living (objective), X_2 is recreational opportunities (objective), X_3 is cost of living (subjective), X_4 is recreational opportunities (subjective), and X_5 is migration.

Figure 4.8. The migration path models for the United States.
Source: Cadwallader 1989b:fig. 3.
Note: ** indicates path coefficients that are significant at .05; * indicates path coefficients that are significant at .10; hashed lines indicate path coefficients that are not significant at .10.

5

Patterns of
Residential Mobility

In the present chapter we turn our attention to migration within cities, more commonly known as residential mobility. With approximately 20 percent of the U.S. population changing residence every year, residential mobility characterizes, to varying degrees, all urban neighborhoods. Indeed, this mobility is largely responsible for the changing socioeconomic structure of neighborhoods and is generally associated with the deterioration and decline of particular regions within cities. Almost half of the U.S. population made at least one residential move during the five-year period from 1970 to 1975, and 45 percent of those moves represented changes of residence within the same metropolitan area (Quigley and Weinberg 1977). Similarly high rates of mobility have been reported for Australian cities, where between 40 and 50 percent of the population in most large cities changed residence between 1971 and 1976 (Maher 1982).

More recently, however, the annual mobility rate for the United States has exhibited a general downward trend, to a low of about 17 percent in 1982 (Rogerson 1987). There are a number of potential reasons for declining mobility during the 1970s and early 1980s. First, the slow economic growth during parts of the 1970s may have reduced the employment opportunities for prospective migrants. Second, unfavorable housing market conditions, including rapid inflation and high interest rates, made moving more difficult. Third, and perhaps most important, the increased labor force participation among females tended to foster declining mobility rates, as it has been empirically demonstrated that two-worker households are less likely to move than their single-worker counterparts (Krumm 1983; Linneman and Graves 1983).

Finally, Rogerson (1987) suggests that an inverse relationship exists between national mobility levels and generation size. In particular, he argues that large generations are characterized by lower mobility rates because of the increased competition in the labor and housing markets. For the twenty-eight years for which data were available to him, he showed a negative correlation between the fraction of the total population in the twenty-to-twenty-four age group and the overall mobility rate. Note that generation size was assumed to be a surrogate for housing and labor market conditions, so such economic variables were not controlled for. A more explicit model of the underlying causal relations would postulate that the demographic variable of generation size has an indirect effect on mobility rates through the operation of labor and housing market variables. In any event, demographic impacts have often been neglected in investigations of residential mobility.

The remainder of this chapter is divided into four parts. First, the spatial distribution of mobility rates is discussed, both across different metropolitan areas and within individual cities. Second, the variation in turnover rates within cities is related to housing and social structure using path models and simultaneous equations. Third, the notion of structural equation models with unobserved variables is introduced, and fourth, a LISREL model of residential mobility is briefly described.

The Spatial Pattern of Mobility Rates

When local mobility rates are computed for different cities, substantial variation is observed. In general, data are consistent with arguments that higher turnover rates are associated with high immigration, employment, and housing growth rates (Moore and Clark 1986). For example, the proportion of households moving within a given time period has been much smaller in the northern metropolitan areas of high stability or out-migration, such as Scranton or Johnstown, than in the faster-growing cities of the Southwest, such as Reno or Colorado Springs (Adams and Gilder 1976). More specifically, a strong positive correlation has been shown between in-migration rates for Standard Metropolitan Statistical Areas and the local mobility rates for those same areas (Goodman 1982).

There are two main explanations for this relationship. First, the repeat migration theory suggests that a number of moves by the same individuals are responsible for the aggregate-level correlations. In particular, long-distance migrants are often uncertain concerning the nature of the local housing market when they first arrive in a new city. As a result, their initial choice of housing is often temporary while they explore different neighborhoods and housing opportunities. Second, it has also been argued that in-migration to an area often induces the original residents to leave (Stone 1971). That is, according to the so-called place-effect theory, in-migration can increase the mobility of current residents by altering the demographic or social composition of the neighborhood and by changing housing market conditions. Goodman (1982) has provided empirical support for both the repeat mover and the place-effect theory.

Besides this variation between cities there is also substantial variation in turnover rates within cities (Morrill 1988). For example, the present author (Cadwallader 1982) analyzed the spatial pattern of mobility rates for Portland, Oregon, for three different time periods. Data for the study were derived from census tract material for Portland, using Multnomah County to identify the spatial extent of the city. The amount of residential mobility, or rather the lack of it, was defined as the number of people residing in the same house in 1970 as in 1965, as a percentage of persons five years old and over in 1970, for each census tract. This measure of an area's mobility status is similar to that used by Speare, Goldstein, and Frey (1974), and values for 1950 and 1960 were derived in exactly the same fashion as for 1970, except that the data for 1950 involved the number of people residing in the same house in 1950 as in 1949. Although this modification obviously changes the absolute values, the spatial patterns associated with 1950, 1960, and 1970 can still be meaningfully compared in a relative, or distributional, sense.

The initial analysis involved investigating the relationship between residential mobility and distance from the central business district, by calibrating the following three equations:

$$RM = a + bD \tag{5.1}$$

$$RM = ae^{bD} \tag{5.2}$$

$$RM = aD^b \tag{5.3}$$

where RM is residential mobility as previously defined, and D is straight-line distance from the central business district. These three equations represent linear, exponential, and power functions, respec-

Table 5.1. The coefficients of determination
for residential mobility and distance
from the central business district

	1950	1960	1970
Linear	.09	.17	.16
Power	.26	.33	.34
Exponential	.10	.19	.18

Source: Cadwallader 1982: table 1.

tively, and the latter two can be fitted using least-squares analysis by making the following logarithmic transformations:

$$\ln RM = \ln a - bD \tag{5.4}$$

$$\log RM = \log a - b(\log D) \tag{5.5}$$

where the notation is the same as in equations 5.1, 5.2, and 5.3 and *ln* refers to natural, or naperian, logarithms, and *log* refers to common logarithms to the base ten.

The results of this curve-fitting exercise demonstrated that, for all three time periods, the amount of residential stability increases with increasing distance (table 5.1). These results are similar to those reported by Moore's (1971) study of residential mobility in Brisbane, Australia, although he used four different measures of distance from the central business district. He measured accessibility in mileage distance, car travel time in minutes, and public transport travel time in minutes, both including an excluding waiting time. Of these four measures, public transport travel time, excluding waiting time, provided the best fit to the data. He ascribed this result to the comparative rarity of two-car families.

Returning to the case of Portland, the coefficients of determination indicate that the power function is the most appropriate form for specifying this relationship, although clearly there is still a relatively large proportion of unexplained variation, suggesting that more complex functional relationships might be profitably explored. Trend surface analysis was used to facilitate this exploration, as it allows the pattern of residential mobility to be conceptualized as a surface, rather than simply averaging the mobility rates across different directions from the city center. As previously noted, the distribution of data points in trend surface analysis is often important, as a clustering of data points will tend to inflate the goodness-of-fit, as measured by the coefficient of determination. The distribution of data points is not a problem in the

Table 5.2. The coefficients of determination
for the trend surface analyses of
the residential mobility surfaces

	1950	1960	1970
Linear	.24	.08	.02
Quadratic	.45	.40	.10
Cubic	.57	.52	.21

Source: Cadwallader 1982: table 2.

present instance, however, as the points represent the centroids of census tracts and are thus fairly evenly distributed throughout the city. What little clustering there is is associated with the smaller tracts toward the center of the city and is not considered critical.

The results of fitting linear, quadratic, and cubic surfaces are reported in table 5.2. For all three years the best fit is provided by the cubic surface, with between 21 and 57 percent of the variation in mobility rates being accounted for, although the comparatively small coefficients of determination indicate that the actual surfaces are extremely convoluted. Of greater interest, however, is the change over time. For all three surfaces, the amount of explained variation is greatest for 1950 and least for 1970. This situation, which remains the same even after the corrected coefficients of determination are calculated, in order to take into account the different numbers of census tracts for each time period, indicates that the mobility surface has become increasingly complex over time. Significantly, previous researchers have obtained similar kinds of results when investigating the configuration of population density surfaces over time (Hill 1973).

Of course, the overall pattern of residential mobility in any given city is composed of individual decisions to move and their associated spatial flows. The most frequently reported correlate of movement propensity is stage in the life cycle (Doorn and Van Rietbergen 1990; Gober, McHugh, and Reid 1991). This relationship between stage in the life cycle and residential mobility is primarily a response to the changing dwelling-space needs of the family (Clark and Onaka 1983). The highest probability of moving occurs between the ages of twenty and thirty, with the beginning of married life and the arrival of children. There tends to be greater stability while the children are at school and the head of household is consolidating his or her career, and then mobility often increases again when the children leave home and less living space is required.

Most descriptions of individual mobility have focused on the biases associated with distance and direction. There is strong evidence to suggest that the distribution of distances can be adequately represented by a family of negative exponential functions (Morrill and Pitts 1967), reflecting the greater frequency of short- as opposed to long-distance moves. Indeed, for the city of Seattle, it has been estimated that the average distance of an intracity move is less than three miles, with 16 percent being less than half a mile (Boyce 1969). Researchers have reported similar results for a number of other U.S. cities (Knox 1987:175–76).

Regarding directional biases associated with mobility patterns, Clark (1971) has suggested that although central-area moves appear to be random in direction, the moves within the suburban areas of the city tend to be biased in a sectoral fashion. This sectoral bias has been related to the idea that urban residents might possess mental images of the city that are predominantly sectoral rather than zonal (Johnston 1972; Smith and Ford 1985) and also to the fact that the underlying socioeconomic structure of the city often has a strong sectoral component (Clark 1972). Efforts to generalize the nature of directional biases across different cities have failed, however, largely due to the fact that the direction of moves will be as sensitive to the idiosyncratic location of new housing opportunities in a particular city as it is to the overall spatial pattern of cities in general.

Perhaps the most significant regularity in mobility patterns, however, is that households tend to move between areas of similar socioeconomic status. Most moves, often up to as many as 70 percent, take place within or between census tracts of similar socioeconomic characteristics (Clark 1976). This phenomenon emphasizes the considerable economic constraints provided by income and housing costs and suggests that, at the aggregate level at least, intraurban migration flows are remarkably predictable. Similar conclusions are implied by Alperovich (1983), who constructed a multiple regression model to assess the influence of several variables on migration within the Israeli city of Tel Aviv–Yafo. The estimated coefficients suggested the importance of such origin and destination characteristics as housing quality and resident age and educational level.

Besides regression analyses, entropy-maximizing models also appear to have some potential for predicting migration flows. Using data for Amsterdam, Clark and Avery (1978) concluded that an entropy-maximizing model provides an adequate representation of the basic structure of population flows, especially given the difficulties of finding an appropriate cost function for movements between small areas of a city. Graph analytical methods associated with network analysis have also proven useful for exploring intraurban migration flows (Kipnis 1985).

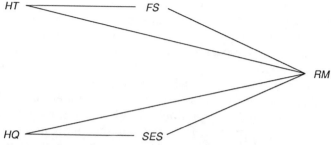

Figure 5.1. A causal model representing the interrelationships among housing patterns, social patterns, and residential mobility.
Source: Cadwallader 1985a:fig. 9.1. (Martin Cadwallader, *Analytical Urban Geography,* © 1985, p. 236. Reprinted by permission of Prentice Hall, Inc. Englewood Cliffs, New Jersey.)

Mobility Rates and Social Structure

In addition to identifying the spatial pattern of mobility rates, establishing the interrelationships between mobility rates and other features of the urban environment, such as socioeconomic, demographic, and housing characteristics, is also of interest. In this section we will explore explicitly the interaction between the demand for housing, as expressed by different social groups, and the supply of housing, as represented by different types and quality of housing, and try to establish the interrelationships between housing patterns and social patterns, on the one hand, and rates of residential mobility, on the other. These interrelationships are expressed in the form of a causal model (fig. 5.1), which is analyzed by means of path analysis (Cadwallader 1981b).

The general framework of the causal model is based upon the essential interplay between households and housing stock. As the housing stock of an area changes, we might expect a simultaneous adjustment of the population characteristics of that area. For example, the aging and extensive subdivision of a particular neighborhood will lead to a higher proportion of multifamily dwelling units and thus a higher proportion of small and often low-income families. In many ways, this association between housing stock and housing characteristics is dynamically articulated by the filtering process, whereby housing that is occupied by one income group deteriorates over time and thus becomes available to the next-lower income group (Cadwallader 1985a:122–24). Intermediaries, such as financial institutions and real estate agents, also play an important role in this matching of demand and supply in the housing market, although these social institutions are not explicitly considered in the present analysis.

As it can be argued that the housing stock is generally less mobile, at least in the short run, than the consumers, or occupants, it seems plausible to suggest that housing characteristics should be placed causally prior to population characteristics. In other words, the housing is considered to be a constraint on the pattern of housing opportunities and thus represents a major mechanism responsible for the evolution of residential differentiation in general and social areas in particular. Changes in the supply, or evolution, of the housing stock arise largely because of the aging process. Differences in the timing of housing development, due to building cycles and prevailing economic conditions, thus produce different residential patterns within cities (Adams 1970).

Bourne (1976) suggests that housing stock can be divided according to type, ownership, and costs. For the purpose of the present model, type and ownership, or tenure status, are collapsed into one dimension, and costs are reinterpreted more broadly as housing quality. As such, the two housing dimensions used here, representing type and quality, closely parallel the type and value and quality dimensions suggested by Rees (1970). Population characteristics are also divided into two major dimensions, socioeconomic status and family status, based on the classical social area analysis studies (Bell 1955; Van Arsdol, Camilleri, and Schmid 1958). Thus it is postulated that when choosing a home the prospective buyer must select the type and quality of housing and that this decision will be primarily influenced by the buyer's stage in the life cycle and socioeconomic status. For example, those areas of the city containing spacious homes and yards will tend to be particularly attractive to large families with young children. Hence, a neighborhood occupying a particular location in social space, defined by socioeconomic and family status, is liable to occupy an analogous location in housing space, where the major axes represent the type and quality of housing (Rees 1970). Also, we might expect socioeconomic status to be especially associated with type of housing. In other words, it is assumed that socioeconomic status primarily determines the quality of housing purchased, while stage in the life cycle primarily determines the type of housing purchased.

Finally, residential mobility is interpreted as a phenomenon of the housing market, with families changing their housing stock as they experience changes in both family status and socioeconomic status. More specifically, the pattern of residential mobility, as measured by turnover rates, is expected to be primarily related to housing type and family status, rather than to housing quality and socioeconomic status, as previous research has shown stage in the life cycle to be one of the dominant forces behind the decision to move (Webber 1983). As Rossi

(1980:61) stresses, residential mobility is the process by which families adjust their housing to meet the demands for space generated by changing family composition. In an aggregate sense, low family status areas are disproportionately inhabited by young people, renters, and apartment dwellers, all of whom normally exhibit high mobility rates. On the other hand, families with children, homeowners, and single-family dwelling units characterize high family status areas; these are usually associated with high rates of stability (Speare, Goldstein, and Frey 1974:100).

By contrast, the effects of socioeconomic status on residential mobility are extremely difficult to disentangle. While Abu-Lughod and Foley (1960) were able to show that movers have lower incomes than nonmovers, Fredland (1974) suggests that mobility increases slightly with increasing income. Higher educational levels appear to be associated with higher mobility rates (Abu-Lughod and Foley 1960), but in some instances there is no evidence of a relationship (Speare, Goldstein, and Frey 1974). Finally, the occupation of the head of the household has generally been a poor predictor of mobility (Long 1972).

This overall conceptual schema can be formally expressed as follows:

$$H_i = f(HT_i, HQ_i) \tag{5.6}$$

$$S_i = f(SES_i, FS_i) \tag{5.7}$$

where H_i is the location of area i in housing space, HT_i is the type of housing associated with area i, HQ_i is the quality of housing associated with area i, S_i is the location of area i in social space, SES_i is the socioeconomic status associated with area i, and FS_i is the family status associated with area i. In addition,

$$S_i = f(H_i) \tag{5.8}$$

More specifically,

$$FS_i = f(HT_i) \tag{5.9}$$

$$SES_i = f(HQ_i) \tag{5.10}$$

where the notation is the same as in equations 5.6 and 5.7. Finally,

$$RM_i = f(FS_i, HT_i) \tag{5.11}$$

where RM_i is the amount of residential mobility associated with area i. The corresponding hypothesized causal model (fig. 5.1) also shows links between housing quality and residential mobility, but these were not expected to be statistically significant.

It is appropriate to emphasize at this point that the proposed model is calibrated using aggregated data and therefore represents a macro- rather than a micro-level approach. Such macro-level analyses can help to identify the ecological factors associated with spatial variations in mobility rates. The macro analyst is concerned with the collective outcome of individual decisons to migrate, rather than with monitoring and modeling the individual decision-making process itself. Within this context, the use of aggregated data allows one to focus on the general pattern of mobility, without being distracted by the complexity of individual differences. As yet, only limited research has been conducted on the relationship between urban structure and intraurban mobility, but it seems plausible to suggest that the macro-analytic approach will prove to be valuable in linking spatial behavior and spatial structure.

In accordance with the proposed theoretical framework, the empirical analyses are divided into four parts: the postulated major dimensions, or axes, of social space are verified via principal components analysis; the major dimensions of housing space are examined in a similar fashion; the hypothesized interrelationships between the social and housing patterns are tested using correlation analysis; and their relationships with residential mobility, as expressed in the causal model, are explored by means of path analysis. Census tract–level information was used in the empirical analysis, with appropriate data being collected from the 1970 U.S. Census of Population and Housing for four U.S. cities: Canton, Ohio; Des Moines, Iowa; Knoxville, Tennessee; and Portland, Oregon. Four cities were chosen in order to test the robustness of the conceptual schema in different contexts, and these particular cities were chosen to provide variation in size, with one large and three smaller, and spatial location. The data for each city included split tracts but excluded those tracts containing zero for any of the selected variables.

Studies of residential differentiation based on social variables, such as income, family size, and race, have invariably produced three major dimensions which summarize social variation in urban populations (Davies 1984). These dimensions are generally labeled socioeconomic status, family status, and ethnic status. In order to determine whether this broad generalization applies to the cities selected for this study, six variables were chosen to represent socioeconomic status and family status. The socioeconomic status variables consisted of median income, median school years completed by persons aged twenty-five years or over, and the number of professional, technical, and kindred workers as a percentage of the total employed. The family status variables were persons per household, percentage of females sixteen years old and over in the labor force, and persons under eighteen as a percentage of the total population. The choice of both sets of variables was circumscribed by the desire to maintain comparability with the classic studies in the field, although it was decided not to include the ethnic status variables, as their role in determining patterns of social variation is less important in smaller cities.

The underlying dimensions produced by these six variables were identified, as in most factorial ecological studies, by the use of principal components analysis with a varimax rotation. It has sometimes been argued that the orthogonality constraint associated with the varimax rotation is unnecessarily restrictive, as we might well expect the underlying dimensions to be related (Johnston 1976). Evidence suggests, however, that in the present substantive context the orthogonal and oblique solutions are very similar (Hughes and Carey 1972). In such situations, the simplicity and mathematical elegance of the orthogonal solution are preferred.

The dimensions generated by the principal components analyses correspond closely to the socioeconomic status and family status dimensions found in previous studies (table 5.3). The only variable that is inadequately represented in this structure is the percentage of females sixteen years old and over in the labor force, which has communalities ranging from .59 in the case of Canton to only .09 in the case of Knoxville. Despite these low communalities, however, the variable behaves as expected, in that it is always negatively associated with the family status component. Its declining importance as an indicator of social differentiation since the pioneering studies of the 1950s is undoubtedly due to the increased labor force participation of females from all levels of the socioeconomic hierarchy.

In order to formally verify the apparent similarity between the dimensions obtained for the four cities, coefficients of congruence were calculated for each pair of cities (Harman 1967:270). The coefficient of congruence is a measure of similarity between component loadings, which ranges in value from +1 for perfect agreement, through 0 for no agreement, to −1 for perfect inverse agreement. In the present instance the coefficients for both socioeconomic status and family status are all extremely high, indicating that the dimensions of social space are almost identical for all four cities (table 5.4). For example, the coefficients

Table 5.3. The principal components analyses of the population characteristics

	Canton			Des Moines		
	SES	FS	Comm.	SES	FS	Comm.
Education	.95	-.08	.91	.96	-.03	.92
Income	.94	.07	.89	.91	.34	.94
Occupation	.94	-.07	.89	.88	-.27	.85
Persons per household	.21	.95	.95	.05	.95	.91
Percentage under eighteen	-.04	.93	.87	-.01	.95	.90
Women in labor force	.20	-.74	.59	.03	-.61	.37
Percentage total variance	46.0	38.9		42.2	39.5	

	Knoxville			Portland		
	SES	FS	Comm.	SES	FS	Comm.
Education	.94	-.14	.91	.95	.04	.90
Income	.91	.21	.86	.90	.33	.92
Occupation	.87	-.09	.76	.91	-.06	.83
Persons per household	.02	.97	.93	.12	.95	.92
Percentage under eighteen	-.17	.95	.93	-.05	.95	.91
Women in labor force	-.03	-.29	.09	-.10	-.58	.35
Percentage total variance	41.7	33.3		42.8	37.6	

Source: Cadwallader 1981b: table 1.

of congruence for Canton and Des Moines are .99 for the socioeconomic status dimension and .97 for the family status dimension. These results are especially reassuring in light of some previous work suggesting much lower degrees of factorial similarity across cities, although this finding had been primarily due to the pattern of minor, rather than major, factor loadings (Palm and Caruso 1972).

Analyses similar to those undertaken for social space were used to identify and describe the major dimensions of housing space. In this case, however, the previous literature was far less helpful as a guide to the selection of variables, because there has been no consistent approach

Table 5.4. The coefficients of congruence for social space

	(1)	(2)	(3)	(4)
Canton (1)	—	.97	.95	.98
Des Moines (2)	.99	—	.96	.99
Knoxville (3)	.98	.99	—	.97
Portland (4)	.98	.99	.99	—

Source: Cadwallader 1981b: table 2.
Note: Coefficients for family status are above the diagonal; coefficients for socioeconomic status are below the diagonal.

to the definition of housing submarkets, especially in a spatial context (Bourne 1981). As a result, two major criteria were used when choosing the housing variables. First, they should represent the mix of attributes that together make up the housing package, or bundle, as identified in previous studies (Kain and Quigley 1970). Second, they should have theoretical implications for patterns of residential mobility.

With these criteria in mind, the following six variables were chosen to represent housing space: percentage of year-round owner-occupied housing units, number of single-family dwelling units as a percentage of year-round housing units, median number of rooms, median housing value for owner-occupied dwelling units, percentage of year-round housing units with more than one bathroom, and percentage of year-round housing units built in 1939 or earlier. The tenure status and single-family dwelling unit variables were chosen because they have been found to be among the most powerful predictors of residential mobility (Michelson 1977; Speare, Goldstein, and Frey 1974). Part of the reason for the stability of owner-occupiers lies in higher moving costs, combined with a greater flexibility in being able to adjust in situ by remodeling and their greater social commitment to the local neighborhood. Dwelling unit size, especially when related to household size, is also an important determinant of mobility (Rossi 1980). The remaining three variables—housing value, number of bathrooms, and housing age—generally indicate housing quality. Housing value in particular is obviously a very direct indicator of housing quality, while a number of studies have shown how housing values are associated with a variety of other housing attributes, such as age and number of bathrooms (Blumner and Johnson 1975; Mark 1977). Previous researchers have also used the age of the dwelling unit as a surrogate for housing quality (Quigley 1976).

The principal components analyses of the housing variables, again using a varimax rotation, revealed two distinct dimensions labeled housing type and housing quality (table 5.5). Housing type consists of owner-occupancy rates, number of single-family dwelling units, and number of rooms, while housing quality is composed of housing value, number of bathrooms, and housing age. It is interesting to note that the number of rooms loads consistently high on housing type rather than on housing quality, while housing age is predominantly associated with housing quality, although in the case of Des Moines it loads more highly on housing type. Overall, the variation in housing age is the least satisfactorily accounted for of the housing measures, with communalities ranging from .77 to .30.

The congruency coefficients between the housing dimensions re-

Table 5.5. The principal components analyses of the housing characteristics

	Canton			Des Moines		
	HT	HQ	Comm.	HT	HQ	Comm.
Housing value	.28	.94	.96	.14	.97	.96
Number of bathrooms	.24	.94	.94	.23	.96	.97
Age of housing	-.46	-.75	.77	-.65	-.40	.58
Percentage owner-occupied	.90	.39	.96	.97	.20	.98
Percentage single-family dwelling units	.96	.19	.96	.99	.03	.98
Number of rooms	.75	.35	.69	.70	.55	.79
Percentage total variance	44.0	44.0		48.5	39.5	

	Knoxville			Portland		
	HT	HQ	Comm.	HT	HQ	Comm.
Housing value	.03	.97	.94	-.02	.95	.90
Number of bathrooms	.42	.87	.93	.31	.86	.84
Age of housing	-.53	-.63	.67	-.30	-.46	.30
Percentage owner-occupied	.94	.29	.96	.96	.23	.97
Percentage single-family dwelling units	.99	.06	.97	.98	.05	.96
Number of rooms	.82	.52	.94	.84	.43	.89
Percentage total variance	49.8	40.8		46.2	34.8	

Source: Cadwallader 1981b: table 3.

veal that the cities are remarkably similar in housing structure, with the coefficients for both housing type and housing quality being as high as those previously reported for the social space dimensions (table 5.6). For example, in the cases of Knoxville and Canton, the coefficient of congruence is .99 for housing quality and .98 for housing type. The interpretability of the components and their obvious similarity across the four cities suggest that an orthogonal rotation is quite capable of identifying simple structure, thus obviating the necessity for employing more complex and sophisticated oblique rotations.

After identifying two distinctive and recurring sets of dimensions

Table 5.6. The coefficients of congruence for housing space

	(1)	(2)	(3)	(4)
Canton (1)	—	.96	.99	.98
Des Moines (2)	.99	—	.99	.99
Knoxville (3)	.98	.99	—	.99
Portland (4)	.98	.97	.99	—

Source: Cadwallader 1981b: table 4.
Note: Coefficients for housing quality are above the diagonal; coefficients for housing type are below the diagonal.

Table 5.7. The correlation coefficients between the population and housing dimensions

	Canton	Des Moines	Knoxville	Portland
Socioeconomic status and housing quality	.855	.928	.910	.885
Socioeconomic status and housing type	.296	.023	.114	.044
Family status and housing quality	.015	.115	.057	.018
Family status and housing type	.685	.857	.723	.827

Source: Cadwallader 1981b: table 5.

associated with social space and housing space, the next step in the analysis was to investigate the interrelationships between these dimensions. These interrelationships were analyzed by calculating the zero-order correlation coefficients between the social and housing dimensions. The results of the zero-order correlation analysis indicate quite clearly that socioeconomic status is closely related to housing quality and family status is equally closely related to housing type (table 5.7). In the case of Portland, for example, socioeconomic status and housing quality have a correlation of .885, while family status and housing type have a correlation of .827. By contrast, family status and housing quality, and socioeconomic status and housing type have correlations of only .018 and .044, respectively. The unambiguous nature of these results is especially encouraging; they provide extremely strong evidence for the relationships postulated in equations 5.9 and 5.10.

Further evidence for the validity of these interrelationships was obtained by carrying out a single principal components analysis of the original twelve variables for each city. This analysis was undertaken for two reasons: to demonstrate that the previously identified housing and social space factors were not simply methodological artifacts produced by the prior separation of the housing and socioeconomic variables, and to show that the socioeconomic status and housing quality dimensions, on the one hand, and the family status and housing type dimensions, on the other, are indeed as closely integrated as the zero-order correlations suggest.

As expected, the residential variation in each of the four cities was well summarized by two major components, with approximately 80 percent of the total variance being accounted for. In each case there was one component composed of the socioeconomic status and housing quality variables and a second component composed of the family status and housing type variables. Thus, the interrelationships between the variables identified by the initial principal components analyses were remarkably stable, even when both sets of variables were combined. Also, the pairings of dimensions postulated in the original equations and substantiated by the zero-order correlations emerged equally strongly from this combined analysis. The only exception to these findings was the age of housing variable, which, for both Knoxville and Des Moines, was most closely associated with family status and housing type, rather than with socioeconomic status and housing quality. In addition, age of housing and women in the labor force also had the lowest communalities associated with them.

The interrelationships among the social space and housing space dimensions and residential mobility were analyzed by means of path analysis, with the amount of residential mobility, or rather the lack of it, being defined as in the section "The Spatial Pattern of Mobility Rates." Path analysis allows one to estimate the magnitude of the linkages between variables, which then provide information about the underlying causal processes. In the present instance, the causal model being postulated is recursive, as the dependent variables have an unambiguous causal ordering. In this situation, ordinary least-squares regression techniques can be used to obtain the path coefficients, provided, or course, that the normal regression assumptions are met. The path coefficient associated with the disturbance terms, incorporating the combined effect of all unspecified variables, is simply the square root of the unexplained variation in the dependent variable under consideration (Asher 1976:31).

The causal model to be calibrated is represented by the following set of structural equations (see also fig. 5.1):

$$FS = b_1 HT \tag{5.12}$$

$$SES = b_1 HQ \tag{5.13}$$

$$RM = b_1 HT + b_2 HQ + b_3 SES + b_4 FS \tag{5.14}$$

where the notation is the same as in equations 5.6–5.11. There are no values for the intercepts, as the variables are all in standardized form, and the standardized regression coefficients for these equations provide the path coefficients (Turner and Stevens 1971). Note that there are no links between housing type and housing quality or family status and socioeconomic status, as these variables represent independent components derived from the principal components analyses. Also, there are no paths between housing type and socioeconomic status or housing quality and family status, as these interrelationships were found to be insignificant in the correlation analysis (table 5.7).

The results of the path analysis (figs. 5.2–5.5) are strikingly similar for all four cities. In every case, the path coefficients for housing type

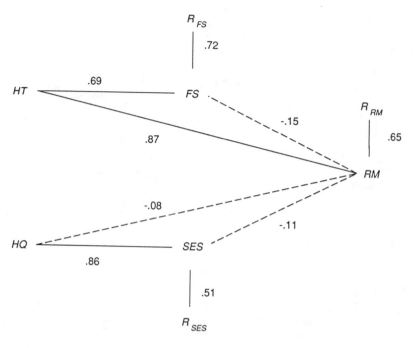

Figure 5.2. The path coefficients for Canton.
Source: Cadwallader 1981b:fig. 1.
Note: The broken lines represent paths that are not statistically significant at .05.

and family status, and housing quality and socioeconomic status are very large and in the expected positive direction. Similarly, in all cases, the path coefficient between housing type and residential mobility is significant and positive, indicating that those census tracts with high proportions of owner-occupied and single-family dwelling units experience the least amount of residential mobility. For three of the four cities, there are no other significant links between any of the causally prior variables and residential mobility; but in the case of Portland, housing type also has an indirect effect via family status. These results indicate that the same comparatively simple causal structure can be postulated for all four cities. Moreover, the path coefficients associated with the causal structure are strikingly similar for each city. Nevertheless, as the path coefficients connected with the distrubance term testify, there remain other as yet unidentified variables that should be included in the analysis.

Given the encouraging nature of the results, the author decided to

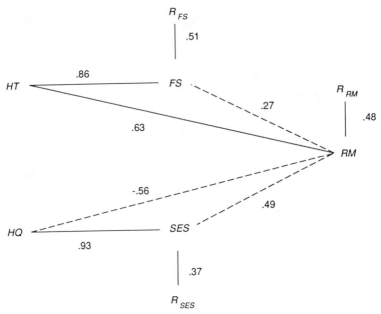

Figure 5.3. The path coefficients for Des Moines.
Source: Cadwallader 1981b:fig. 2.

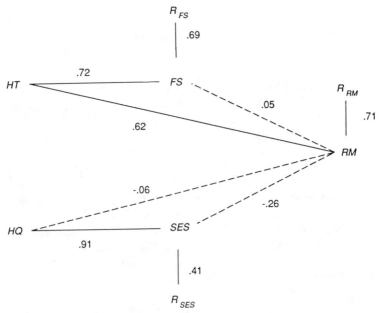

Figure 5.4. The path coefficients for Knoxville.
Source: Cadwallader 1981b:fig. 3.

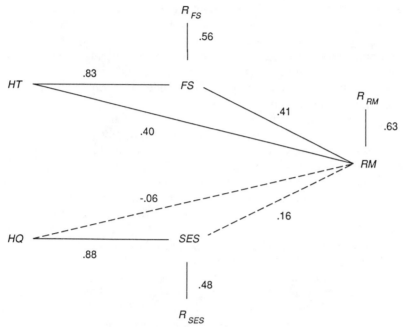

Figure 5.5. The path coefficients for Portland.
Source: Cadwallader 1981b:fig. 4.

investigate whether the causal structure had remained stable over time. To accomplish this, the 1950 and 1960 data for Portland were analyzed in a similar fashion to that used for the 1970 data. With respect to the hypothesized causal model, the path coefficients indicate that in statistically significant relationships the causal structures for 1950 and 1960 were identical to that for 1970. The only difference between the situation for 1970 and those for the preceding time periods was the emerging association between family status and residential mobility. In sum, evidence strongly suggests that the causal structure not only is very similar across cities but also appears to have remained fairly stable over time.

Thus far, then, this analysis has yielded four major results. First, it has been confirmed that the social attributes of urban subareas can be decomposed into socioeconomic status and family status dimensions. Second, it has been demonstrated that the housing attributes of urban subareas can be decomposed into housing quality and housing type dimensions. Third, evidence has been presented to support the hypothesis that the social space and housing space dimensions are significantly interrelated and, more specifically, that socioeconomic status is a direct function of variation in housing quality and family status is a direct function of variation in housing type. Fourth, a causal model, constructed to elucidate the interrelationships between the social space and housing space dimensions and residential mobility, generated remarkably consistent results across both space and time, with the housing type dimension proving to be the single most important determinant of residential mobility.

The path models of residential mobility that have been described thus far are recursive in nature, however, and do not consider the possibility of two-way, or reciprocal causation. The exclusion of two-way causuality presents a potential theoretical problem, as it can be reasonably argued that although the socioeconomic characteristics of urban subareas undoubtedly influence the magnitude of residential mobility rates, the reverse is also equally true. With this problem in mind, the present author (Cadwallader 1982), using the data for Portland, Oregon, described previously, estimated a simultaneous equation model of mobility rates for 1950, 1960, and 1970.

The two housing dimensions of quality and type emerge quite clearly from the principal components analyses for 1960 and 1970 (table 5.8), although somewhat less clearly for 1950. In this latter context, it should be noted that the number of rooms variable is not present in the 1950 component structure, as the 1950 census did not report that information. Despite this missing variable, however, it is still significant that for 1950 all the variables except housing value load most heavily on the housing type dimension. In contrast, the component loadings for 1960 and 1970 are as expected, except that in 1960 the age of housing variable loads slightly more heavily on housing type than on housing quality. In all three years more than 80 percent of the total variation is accounted for by the two major components, and all the communalities, except those for age of housing, indicate that more than 80 percent of the variation associated with each variable is accounted for by these two components.

The population characteristics decompose into the usual socioeconomic status and family status dimensions for all three time periods (table 5.9), with education, income, and occupation in every case loading most heavily on socioeconomic status, while persons per household, percentage under eighteen, and women in the labor force are most closely related to family status. Again, for all three years, these two components account for over 80 percent of the total variation. Also, all the communalities indicate that over 80 percent of the variation in individual variables is accounted for, except for the women in the labor force variable in 1970. In this latter instance, the women in the labor

Table 5.8. The principal components analyses of the housing
characteristics for Portland

	1950		
	HT	HQ	Communality
Housing value	.15	.96	.94
Number of bathrooms	.85	.36	.85
Age of housing	-.68	-.51	.72
Percentage owner-occupied	.95	.15	.92
Percentage single-family dwelling units	.97	.10	.96
Percentage total variance	60.6	26.8	

	1960		
	HT	HQ	Communality
Housing value	.00	.97	.95
Number of bathrooms	.38	.86	.88
Age of housing	-.54	-.40	.44
Percentage owner-occupied	.97	.15	.97
Percentage single-family dwelling units	.99	.00	.98
Number of rooms	.85	.33	.82
Percentage total variance	51.5	32.6	

	1970		
	HT	HQ	Communality
Housing value	-.02	.95	.90
Number of bathrooms	.31	.86	.84
Age of housing	-.30	-.46	.30
Percentage owner-occupied	.96	.23	.97
Percentage single-family dwelling units	.98	.05	.96
Number of rooms	.84	.43	.89
Percentage total variance	46.2	34.8	

Source: Cadwallader 1982: table 3.

force variable is still negatively related to family status but has obviously lost much of its power as an important element of residential differentiation.

In order to statistically document the apparent similarity between these four major dimensions over time, the corresponding coefficients of congruence were calculated. To retain comparability with the 1950 data, the housing components for 1960 and 1970 were recomputed without the number of rooms variable. The congruency coefficients for 1960 and 1970, however, were based on all six variables. The results of this analysis are as expected (table 5.10). In every case the coefficients are greater than .9, indicating a striking degree of stability over time. The coefficients for the population dimensions are particularly high, while, as previously implied, the housing quality dimension for 1950 is somewhat different from its counterparts for 1960 and 1970.

Table 5.9. The principal components analyses of the population characteristics for Portland

| | 1950 | | |
	FS	SES	Communality
Education	−.01	.96	.92
Income	.58	.75	.89
Occupation	−.20	.89	.83
Persons per household	.96	.04	.93
Percentage under eighteen	.95	−.17	.93
Women in labor force	−.93	−.06	.86
Percentage total variance	51.0	38.4	

| | 1960 | | |
	FS	SES	Communality
Education	.03	.93	.87
Income	.33	.90	.92
Occupation	−.09	.92	.85
Persons per household	.96	.17	.95
Percentage under eighteen	.97	.03	.94
Women in labor force	−.91	.00	.84
Percentage total variance	47.0	42.5	

| | 1970 | | |
	FS	SES	Communality
Education	.04	.95	.90
Income	.33	.90	.92
Occupation	−.06	.91	.83
Persons per household	.95	.12	.92
Percentage under eighteen	.95	−.05	.91
Women in labor force	−.58	−.10	.35
Percentage total variance	42.8	37.6	

Source: Cadwallader 1982: table 4.

These housing and population dimensions were used as input for the simultaneous equations model (fig. 5.6). This model is described by the following three equations:

$$RM = a + b_1 SES + b_2 FS \tag{5.15}$$

$$SES = a + b_1 RM + b_2 HQ \tag{5.16}$$

$$FS = a + b_1 RM + b_2 HT \tag{5.17}$$

where *RM* is residential mobility, *SES* is socioeconomic status, *FS* is family status, *HQ* is housing quality, and *HT* is housing type. Note that,

Table 5.10. The matrices of congruency
coefficients for Portland

	Housing components		
	1950	1960	1970
1950	—	.9269	.9097
1960	.9528	—	.9943
1970	.9227	.9906	—

Note: The coefficients for housing
quality are above the diagonal, while
those for housing type are below the
diagonal.

	Population components		
	1950	1960	1970
1950	—	.9879	.9724
1960	.9838	—	.9841
1970	.9921	.9963	—

Source: Cadwallader 1982: table 5.
Note: The coefficients for family status
are above the diagonal, while those for
socioeconomic status are below the
diagonal.

unlike the path models described previously, here residential mobility
is expected to exhibit reciprocal relationships with both socioeconomic
status and family status. Given the definition of residential mobility, all
the relationships are expected to be positive.

Reduced-form equations were calibrated to derive estimates for the
three endogenous variables: residential mobility, socioeconomic status, and family status (table 5.11). Housing quality and housing type,
the two exogenous, or predetermined variables, were used to obtain
these estimates. In all cases the coefficients of determination are greater
than .5, and most of them are above .7. Housing type is a consistently
more important predictor of residential mobility than is housing qual-

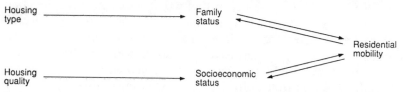

Figure 5.6. The causal structure represented by the simultaneous equation model.
Source: Cadwallader 1982:fig. 1.

Table 5.11. The estimated reduced-form
equations using components

1950

$RM = 76.05 + 4.87HT^* + 1.02HQ \qquad R^2 = .74$
$\qquad\quad (.41) \qquad (.42) \qquad\quad (.42)$
$SES = -.01 + .34HT^* + .82HQ^* \qquad R^2 = .79$
$\qquad\quad (.06) \qquad (.06) \qquad\quad (.06)$
$FS \;\; = -.01 + .79HT^* - .06HQ \qquad R^2 = .62$
$\qquad\quad (.09) \qquad (.09) \qquad\quad (.09)$

1960

$RM = 50.25 + 6.07HT^* - 1.19HQ \qquad R^2 = .52$
$\qquad\quad (.64) \qquad (.64) \qquad\quad (.64)$
$SES = .02 + .22HT^* + .88HQ^* \qquad R^2 = .80$
$\qquad\quad (.05) \qquad (.05) \qquad\quad (.05)$
$FS \;\; = .00 + .91HT^* - .09HQ \qquad R^2 = .84$
$\qquad\quad (.04) \qquad (.04) \qquad\quad (.04)$

1970

$RM = 50.67 + 6.99HT^* + .86HQ \qquad R^2 = .55$
$\qquad\quad (.67) \qquad (.60) \qquad\quad (.68)$
$SES = -.01 + .03HT + .89HQ^* \qquad R^2 = .78$
$\qquad\quad (.04) \qquad (.04) \qquad\quad (.04)$
$FS \;\; = .05 + .74HT^* + .01HQ \qquad R^2 = .68$
$\qquad\quad (.05) \qquad (.05) \qquad\quad (.05)$

Source: Cadwallader 1982: table 6.
Note: The values in the parentheses are standard
errors. Asterisks indicate those coefficients that
are significantly different from zero at .01.

ity, and as anticipated, the direction of the relationship is positive. Also as expected, housing type is by far the major determinant of family status, and housing quality is the major determinant of socioeconomic status, although in this latter case housing type also plays a minor role.

The structural equations, using the estimated values for the endogenous variables, exhibit reassuringly high coefficients of determination (table 5.12). For all three time periods, family status is significantly related to residential mobility in the hypothesized positive direction. The coefficient for socioeconomic status, however, is not significantly different from zero at the .01 significance level. The equations for socioeconomic status are generally as hypothesized, with both housing quality and residential mobility exhibiting positive coefficients that are significantly different from zero. The only exception to this pattern is the coefficient associated with the residential mobility variable for 1970, which is positive, but not significantly different from zero.

Table 5.12. The estimated structural equations
using components

	1950

$RM = 76.11 + 1.65\hat{S}ES + 5.47\hat{F}S^*$ $R^2 = .40$
      (.63)   (.75)   (.85)
$SES = -5.24 + .07\hat{R}M^* + .75HQ^*$ $R^2 = .81$
      (.98)   (.01)   (.06)
$FS = 4.56 - .06\hat{R}M + 1.08HT^*$ $R^2 = .65$
     (6.33)   (.08)   (.42)

	1960

$RM = 50.27 - .69\hat{S}ES + 6.81\hat{F}S^*$ $R^2 = .29$
      (.77)   (.86)   (.85)
$SES = -1.79 + .04\hat{R}M^* + .92HQ^*$ $R^2 = .78$
      (.43)   (.01)   (.05)
$FS = -3.61 + .07\hat{R}M + .48HT$ $R^2 = .58$
     (2.94)   (.06)   (.36)

	1970

$RM = 50.23 + .86\hat{S}ES + 9.47\hat{F}S^*$ $R^2 = .52$
      (.69)   (.79)   (.84)
$SES = -.24 + .01\hat{R}M + .89HQ^*$ $R^2 = .78$
      (.28)   (.01)   (.04)
$FS = -.57 + .01\hat{R}M + .65HT$ $R^2 = .71$
     (3.01)   (.06)   (.42)

Source: Cadwallader 1982: table 7.
Note: $\hat{S}ES$, $\hat{F}S$, and $\hat{R}M$, refer to the estimated
values derived from the reduced-form equations.
Asterisks indicate those coefficients that are
significantly different from zero at .01.

In contrast, family status is somewhat less satisfactorily accounted
for in all three years. Housing type has the expected positive relationship with family status in all cases but is only significantly different
from zero in 1950. Residential mobility, on the other hand, has an unexpected negative relationship for 1950 and is not significantly different
from zero for any of the three time periods. In other words, the amount
of residential mobility appears to influence primarily the socioeconomic status of an area rather than the family status. Regarding change
over time in the structural coefficients, the overall impression is one of
remarkable stability. The coefficients have generally similar signs for all
three years, and the pattern of statistically significant relationships is
also noticeably similar. This temporal stability parallels that found for
the housing and population dimensions themselves.

In order to further verify these results, the same structural equations were estimated using a subgroup of the original housing and population variables, rather than the derived components. This second test was performed as a response to the argument that component scores might be misleading as overall indicators, in that their values depend, to a certain extent at least, on variables that are only slightly associated with the particular component under investigation (Joshi, 1972). This problem is especially apparent when a large number of variables is involved in the study; then the minor variables, in concert, can have a major influence on the component scores. The diagnostic variables used to represent each component were chosen on the basis of the component loadings (tables 5.8 and 5.9). Housing value was used to measure housing quality, percentage of single-family dwelling units to measure housing type, income to measure socioeconomic status, and persons per household to measure family status. In general, the variable with the highest loadings was chosen to represent each particular component, although in the case of socioeconomic status income seemed a more appropriate indicator than either education or occupation.

Using these individual variables, both the reduced-form and structural equations are similar to those when the components are used (tables 5.13 and 5.14). In the reduced-form equations, percentage living in single-family dwelling units is more highly associated with residential mobility than is housing value, and this same variable is also the major determinant of population per household. As expected, however, income is associated with both percentage living in single-family dwelling units and housing value. Overall, then, the pattern of statistically significant relationships is almost identical when we compare the coefficients for the individual variables with the coefficients for the components. With respect to the structural equations, based upon this same set of diagnostic variables, residential mobility is mainly associated with persons per household, although income plays a role in 1950. Persons per household is not particularly well predicted by either percentage of single-family dwelling units or residential mobility, except for the significant coefficient associated with percentage of single-family dwelling units in 1960. Finally, income levels are associated with both housing value and residential mobility, with all relationships being in the expected positive direction.

Of course, the results presented here need to be interpreted with some caution, as they are based upon the analysis of aggregate-level data. These macro-level, or ecological relationships are essentially descriptive, as they do not necessarily directly reflect the underlying behavioral proccesses. As has been suggested elsewhere (Clark and Avery

Table 5.13. The estimated reduced-form equations
using variables

1950			
RM =	60.81 +	.19$SFDU$* + .01HV	R^2 = .79
	(1.39)	(.02) (.01)	
INC =	1181.92 +	18.17$SFDU$* + .10HV*	R^2 = .78
	(167.09)	(1.86) (.02)	
PPH =	2.32 +	.01$SFDU$* - .01HV	R^2 = .48
	(.14)	(.00) (.01)	

1960			
RM =	35.23 +	.23$SFDU$* - .01HV	R^2 = .51
	(2.71)	(.02) (.01)	
INC =	770.30 +	26.89$SFDU$* + .31HV*	R^2 = .85
	(264.55)	(2.32) (.02)	
PPH =	1.55 +	.02$SFDU$* + .01HV	R^2 = .85
	(.09)	(.00) (.01)	

1970			
RM =	24.81 +	.32$SFDU$* + .01HV	R^2 = .63
	(2.26)	(.02) (.01)	
INC =	158.04 +	38.64$SFDU$* + .35HV*	R^2 = .78
	(488.53)	(5.06) (.02)	
PPH =	1.41 +	.02$SFDU$* + .01HV	R^2 = .80
	(.07)	(.00) (.01)	

Source: Cadwallader 1982: table 8.
Note: SFDU is single-family dwelling units, HV is
housing value, INC is median income, and PPH is
persons per household. Asterisks indicate those
coefficients that are significantly different from zero
at .01.

1978), however, it is important that residential mobility be studied at both the macro and microlevels of analysis, with a major objective of the former approach being the specification of the relationship between urban structure and residential mobility. Within this context, the simultaneous equation model that has been described here goes some way toward clarifying this relationship. Two avenues for further research are readily apparent, however. First, more work needs to be done with respect to the formal specification of the structural equations. For example, the present equations do not allow for multiplicative relationships. Also, and perhaps more important, a series of lagged variables might be usefully included. Besides providing a clearer indication of the causal processes, such variables would also help mitigate against identification problems in the estimation process.

Table 5.14. The estimated structural equations using
variables

	1950			
$RM =$	$32.74 +$	$.05\hat{I}NC^* +$	$9.68\hat{P}PH^*$	$R^2 = .45$
	(7.59)	$(.02)$	(3.83)	
$INC =$	$-4666.69 +$	$96.18\hat{R}M^* +$	$.07HV^*$	$R^2 = .75$
	(756.75)	(10.62)	$(.02)$	
$PPH =$	$6.43 -$	$.07\hat{R}M +$	$.02SFDU$	$R^2 = .40$
	(3.38)	$(.05)$	$(.01)$	

	1960			
$RM =$	$12.64 -$	$.07\hat{I}NC +$	$14.91\hat{P}PH^*$	$R^2 = .21$
	(5.35)	$(.07)$	(2.16)	
$INC =$	$-3385.60 +$	$117.96\hat{R}M^* +$	$.34HV^*$	$R^2 = .62$
	(897.59)	(16.05)	$(.03)$	
$PPH =$	$1.62 -$	$.01\hat{R}M +$	$.02SFDU^*$	$R^2 = .86$
	$(.80)$	$(.24)$	$(.01)$	

	1970			
$RM =$	$-2.82 +$	$.02\hat{I}NC +$	$19.41\hat{P}PH^*$	$R^2 = .42$
	(4.89)	$(.03)$	(2.07)	
$INC =$	$-1415.31 +$	$120.71\hat{R}M^* +$	$.33HV^*$	$R^2 = .71$
	(938.18)	(18.14)	$(.02)$	
$PPH =$	$.63 +$	$.03\hat{R}M +$	$.01SFDU$	$R^2 = .57$
	$(.80)$	$(.03)$	$(.01)$	

Source: Cadwallader 1982: table 9.
Note: $\hat{I}NC$, $\hat{P}PH$, and $\hat{R}M$ refer to the estimated values
derived from the reduced-form equations. Asterisks
indicate those coefficients that are significantly different
from zero at .01.

Models with Unobserved Variables

Models with unobserved, or latent, variables are usually specified in
either of two contexts (Cadwallader 1986b): where measured variables,
like income and occupation, are subject to measurement error due to
factors such as faulty recall or inaccurate coding and where accurately
measured observed variables are considered to be merely indicators, or
reflections, of underlying theoretical constructs that are inherently unobservable. In practice, it is difficult to distinguish between these two
interpretations, as from a statistical point of view they are both treated
in the same way (Bielby and Hauser 1977).

Different disciplines tend to use different terminology in referring
to observed and unobserved variables. In economics, the existence of

either measurement error or hypothetical constructs is often recognized by referring to observed variables as proxy variables, while in sociology the term *indicator* has become popular for such proxy variables. In psychology, the distinction tends to be made between measured, or manifest variables and latent variables, where latent variables represent hypothetical constructs, or factors, that cannot be directly measured.

Like models with observed variables, models containing unobserved variables can be either recursive or nonrecursive. It has been argued, however, that models using only measured variables are more appropriate for description and prediction than explanation and causal understanding, as measured variables will seldom correspond in a one-to-one fashion with the fundamental concepts of interest to the researcher (Bentler 1980). Consequently, the parameters associated with such models might be expected to vary across populations, as they are only an inaccurate reflection of the true underlying causal mechanism. For this reason, causal models that are used to represent the basic theory of interest are often augmented by an auxiliary, or measurement model that identifies the linkages between true scores and measured variables.

These auxiliary models might try to deal with measurement error by using either single or multiple indicators. The traditional regression approach assumes perfect measurement of all but the dependent variable, but in recent years this restriction has been remedied by the development of confirmatory factor analysis and the more general model for the analysis of covariance structures (Jöreskog 1973). In particular, the development of structural equation models has integrated a number of originally disparate research traditions in econometrics, psychometrics, and sociometrics. While econometricians have traditionally favored simultaneous equation models, involving nonrecursive relationships among a set of variables that contain negligible measurement error, psychometricians have tended to emphasize the problems of measurement error and have thus pursued the areas of inquiry known as factor analysis and reliability theory. At the same time the work on path analysis in sociology has encouraged the realization that identification can be attained in the presence of both measurement error and simultaneous relationships.

The introduction of unmeasured variables into the causal system, however, tends to generate a large number of unknowns, and this in turn leads to problems of identification. In general, the more complex the causal model, the greater must be the ratio of measured to unmeasured variables. Thus, we are often faced with a disturbing trade-off if we want to construct highly overidentified models that are easily rejec-

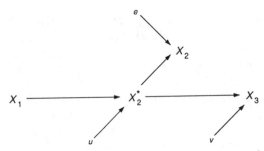

Figure 5.7. A model with measurement error in one of the variables.
Source: Cadwallader 1986b:fig. 7.

table (Namboodiri, Carter, and Blalock 1975: 537). If our general theories are very complex, containing many unknown coefficients, then the measurement model must be simple. But if the measurement model is very complex, then the basic theory must be comparatively simple.

It is perhaps easiest to start by considering a model that contains measurement error in just one of the variables (fig. 5.7). The causal chain of interest is represented by the variables X_1, X_2^*, and X_3, but X_2^* is not observed directly. Rather, its observed counterpart X_2 is contaminated with an error, denoted as e. The term e refers to measurement errors, or errors-in-variables, as distinct from u and v, which refer to the unobserved disturbance terms, or error-in-equations. To simplify the example, it can be assumed that e is uncorrelated with X_2^* or with X_1 and X_3. In other words, the error is regarded as being random rather than systematic (Duncan 1975:115). This simple model can be represented by the following three equations:

$$X_2 = X_2^* + e \tag{5.18}$$

$$X_2^* = b_{21}X_1 + u \tag{5.19}$$

$$X_3 = b_{32}X_2^* + v \tag{5.20}$$

where equation 5.18 describes the measurement model and equations 5.19 and 5.20 constitute the causal model.

More often, however, multiple rather than single indicators are utilized in the context of measurement error. Typically, no observed variable is an indicator of more than one latent variable, and the structural disturbances of the measurement equations are mutually independent (Bielby and Hauser 1977). In some circumstances these specifications can be relaxed, thus allowing an observed variable to be an indicator of

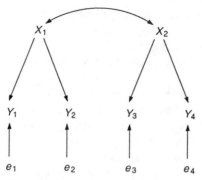

Figure 5.8. A confirmatory factor model.
Source: Cadwallader 1986b:fig. 8.

more than one latent variable and also allowing certain correlations to exist among the disturbances in the measurement equations.

The confirmatory factor model represents a measurement model containing multiple indicators that is not attached to a causal or structural equation model, as the factors, or latent variables, are merely correlated, rather than linked by explicit causal connections. Figure 5.8 shows a confirmatory factor model that contains two factors, X_1 and X_2, that each have two indicators, with the arrows pointing from the latent variables to the measured variables. This diagram can be represented by the following four equations:

$$Y_1 = b_1X_1 + e_1 \tag{5.21}$$

$$Y_2 = b_2X_1 + e_2 \tag{5.22}$$

$$Y_3 = b_3X_2 + e_3 \tag{5.23}$$

$$Y_4 = b_4X_2 + e_4 \tag{5.24}$$

in which the predictors X and e are independent in each of the four equations and the e's are mutually independent, thus generating the classical factor analysis model. Note that the diagram contains more explicit information about the behavior of the disturbance terms than do the equations.

Traditionally, three different types of factors are distinguished (Kenny 1979:110). A common factor appears in the equation of two or more variables, a specific factor appears in a single equation, and an error factor is simply the measurement error associated with a particular variable. In practical terms it is difficult to distinguish between specific and error factors, so they are usually combined to form the unique factor, represented by the e's in figure 5.8. In our example, the two common factors, X_1 and X_2, are expected to be correlated, implying an oblique, rather than an orthogonal, factor model.

In exploratory factor analysis the researcher is forced to make a number of restrictive assumptions (Carmines 1986). First, all common factors, or latent variables, must be either correlated or uncorrelated. Second, all observed variables must be directly affected by all common factors. Third, the unique factors, or errors-in-variables, must be uncorrelated with one another. In contrast, the confirmatory factor model represents a more flexible approach, allowing the researcher to impose a series of substantively motivated, rather than statistically dictated, series of constraints. These constraints determine which pairs of common factors are correlated, which observed variables are affected by which common factors, and which pairs of unique factors are correlated. The model is confirmatory in the sense that statistical tests can be performed to confirm that sample data are consistent with the imposed constraints. That is, the investigator is required to hypothesize the relationships between the latent variables and observed indicators, and the model can always be rejected by the data.

Most often, parameters are given a fixed value, usually either zero or one, or two parameter estimates are forced to be equal. For example, a factor loading or the correlation between two factors can be set equal to zero, or a factor loading, or factor variance, can be set equal to one. In the context of figure 5.8, one common factor regression weight must be fixed to identify each factor, or else the factor variance must be fixed. In other words, b_1 and b_3 can be set equal to one, thus allowing the two factor variances to be free parameters, or the two factor variances can be set equal to one thus allowing the four regression weights, b_1, b_2, b_3, and b_4, to be free parameters. The present model contains nine parameters (Bentler 1980). If the common factor variances are fixed, then we have the four variances associated with the unique factors, one correlation, and four regression weights. Alternatively, if two of the regression weights are fixed, then we have the two common factor variances, the four unique factor variances, one correlation, and two regression weights.

By contrast, figure 5.9 represents a simple two-factor, two-indicator model that indicates an explicit causal connection, rather than a mere correlation, between the two latent variables, X_1 and X_2. In factor analysis there is no structural model describing the relationships among the latent variables. In other words, they are simply correlated (oblique) or

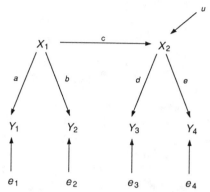

Figure 5.9. A causal model with latent variables.
Source: Cadwallader 1986b:fig. 9.

independent (orthogonal) factors. Figure 5.9, however, indicates a recursive structural model in which X_1 affects X_2. A disturbance term u has been added to X_2, in order to denote the errors-in-equation term associated with the hypothesized structural relationship between X_1 and X_2.

Following Costner (1985), we can label the path coefficients a, b, c, d, and e, and note that six correlations can be obtained from the data in order to estimate these five coefficients. Obviously, since X_1 and X_2 are both unmeasured and all the path coefficients connect some variable to either X_1 or X_2, none of the path coefficients can be directly computed from the data (Namboodiri, Carter, and Blalock 1975:556). The excess equation can provide a test of this overidentified system, as there is one degree of freedom. If additional indicators of each variable are introduced, then the system becomes highly overidentified, thus allowing multiple tests to be made. Also, additional indicators enable one to permit certain relatively simple kinds of nonrandom measurement errors.

Returning to figure 5.9, we have two correlations for pairs of indicators of the same variable (Y_1, Y_2) and (Y_3, Y_4), plus four correlations using the pairs (Y_1, Y_3), (Y_1, Y_4), (Y_2, Y_3) and (Y_2, Y_4). The following equations can then be obtained for these six correlations:

$$r_{Y_1 Y_2} = ab \tag{5.25}$$

$$r_{Y_3 Y_4} = de \tag{5.26}$$

$$r_{Y_1 Y_3} = acd \tag{5.27}$$

$$r_{Y_1Y_4} = ace \tag{5.28}$$

$$r_{Y_2Y_3} = bcd \tag{5.29}$$

$$r_{Y_2Y_4} = bce \tag{5.30}$$

If we have three indicators of both X_1 and X_2, and strictly random errors can be assumed for all indicators, then we have increased the number of empirical correlations to fifteen, while only increasing the number of unknown path coefficients to seven. In those instances where there is not a unique estimate of each of the path coefficients, Hauser and Goldberger (1971) suggest that a weighted average favoring indicators having the smallest error variances is maximally efficient.

For such overidentified systems containing latent variables, Jöreskog (1973) has developed a procedure that provides maximum-likelihood estimators. An example of this so-called LISREL model will be provided in the next section. In its most general form, the model allows one to estimate identified structural equation models that include both errors-in-variables and error-in-equations. Because parameters within the model can be chosen to be fixed, free, or constrained, the general model contains a wide range of specific models, including the classical econometric models, where there are errors-in-equations but no errors-in-variables, and the factor analysis models in psychometrics, where there are errors-in-variables but no errors-in-equations.

Finally, a rather different kind of latent variable model is represented in figure 5.10a. In this case we have multiple causes and multiple indicators of a single unobserved variable, Y^*. In other words, the unmeasured variable is an intervening variable. A linear equation expresses the unobserved variable Y^* as being a function of its observed causes, X_1, X_2, and X_3, plus an unobserved disturbance e. The observed indicators, Y_1, Y_2, and Y_3, are each expressed in terms of Y^* and an unobserved disturbance, u_1, u_2, or u_3. In figure 5.10b these indicator disturbances are assumed to be freely correlated, so the model can be rewritten to make Y^* an exact function of its causes, thus absorbing the term e into the u's and relabeling the latter as v's. When the disturbances associated with the indicator variables are allowed to be freely correlated, nothing is gained by retaining a disturbance term in the causal equation, as it would be impossible to distinguish empirically between effects due to the disturbance e or to inherent correlation among the u disturbances (Hauser and Goldberger 1971).

In the model in figure 5.10b, the unobserved variable Y^* is simply a

a full information, maximum-likelihood method. The estimation technique generates parameter estimates such that the implied variances and covariances resemble, as closely as possible, their observed counterparts. That is, the aim is to generate estimates of the parameters that most closely reproduce the sample variance-covariance matrix of the observed variables.

Obviously, estimation is quite a complex task, as the measurement model represents a factor analytic approach, while the structural model involves multiple regression. It turns out, however, that the full-information methods of unweighted least squares, generalized least squares, and maximum likelihood can all be used to estimate covariance structure models, although maximum likelihood is generally preferred. Maximum likelihood is approximately normally distributed and has a comparatively small sampling variance (Long 1983). Because of maximum likelihood's asymptotic properties, the sample size should be as large as possible, and Boomsma (1982) suggests that it is dangerous to use sample sizes of less than one hundred. As estimation is an iterative procedure, the necessary computer time can be quite costly. The rate of convergence toward the final estimates, however, can be greatly facilitated by the selection of appropriate starting values.

The software to estimate such models is well documented in the widely available series of LISREL programs (Jöreskog and Sorbom 1981), which includes a number of informative empirical examples. Input involves specifying eight parameter matrices, in which each element represents a fixed, constrained, or free parameter. The eight parameter matrices include four coefficient matrices and four covariance matrices. The coefficient matrices contain the following information: the loadings for the indicators of the latent exogenous variables, the loadings for the indicators of the latent endogenous variables, the paths from the latent exogenous variables to the latent endogenous variables, and the paths from the latent endogenous variables to other latent endogenous variables. Similarly, the four covariance matrices specify the covariances between the latent exogenous variables, the errors in equations, the errors in exogenous indicators, and the errors in endogenous indicators.

For determining goodness-of-fit, the difference between the implied and observed variance-covariance matrices can be statistically assessed using a chi-square statistic (Bentler and Weeks 1980). The degrees of freedom for this likelihood ratio test statistic are equal to the number of overidentifying restrictions in the model, and a comparison is made between the constraints imposed by the model, or the null hypothesis, and the unrestricted moments matrix (Bielby and Hauser 1977). Jöreskog's approach to the measurement model allows the researcher to generalize the traditional factor model by enabling the relaxation of the assumption of no correlations between the errors, as well as between factors (Zeller and Carmines 1980:174). If one retains the assumption that the error terms are uncorrelated, then the common factors are considered to account for all the covariance in the observed variables, while the residuals only contribute to the variance of each variable (Long 1981).

If the value of the likelihood ratio is large compared with the degrees of freedom, then it is concluded that the overall model does not represent the causal mechanisms that generated the data. It should be noted, however, that in very large samples even a minor discrepancy between model and data can lead one to reject the model, as the chi-square statistic is a function of sample size as well as the closeness of the estimated and observed covariance matrices. Consequently, the probability of rejecting a model increases with increasing sample size, even if the residual matrix contains only trivial discrepancies between observed and predicted values. In situations involving extremely large samples, virtually all models would be rejected on purely statistical grounds. This underlines the need for researchers to develop a goodness-of-fit test that is less sensitive to sample size.

The standard error associated with each parameter estimate provides an indication of the importance of that parameter to the model. Parameters whose estimates are small compared with their standard errors, as determined using the standard normal curve, can be eliminated from the model (Bentler 1980). In this way certain paths can be removed from the causal structure, while an examination of the residuals might suggest the addition of other links, including those representing the correlations between errors. After such modifications the resulting model must be reestimated.

In those situations where an alternative model is a subset of the initial model, the difference in chi-square values between the two models is itself a chi-square statistic, which can thus be used to indicate the importance of the parameters that differentiate between the two models. In other words, in a series of hierarchical models, where restrictions are successively added or deleted in a systematic fashion, the likelihood-ratio statistics can be compared in order to test the significance of the restrictions imposed at each level of the hierarchy (Bielby and Hauser 1977). The most powerful test of competing theories can be made when one theory is embedded within another, such that their path diagrams are identical except that certain paths are set equal to zero.

Higher-order measurement models can also be conceived. Here there are several levels, or orders, of latent variables, unlike the traditional factors model, which simply contains a first-order factor analytic measurement structure, where the measured variables are directly expressed via latent variables. In higher-order models, the influence of the higher-order latent variables on the measured variables is only indirect, thus blurring the distinction between the measurement model and the causal model, as the various levels of latent variables affect each other through regression structures (Bentler 1982). Irrespective of whether one is using a first order or a higher-order measurement structure, however, it is difficult to settle on the appropriate number of indicators for each latent variable. In theory, the more the better, but in practice a large number of indicators can make it difficult to fit a model to the data. One possible strategy is to estimate the measurement model in association with a just-identified structural model. Any significant lack of fit can then be attributed to the structural model (Kenny 1979:182).

If a hypothesized model does not provide a good fit to the data, it can be modified in a number of ways. For example, parameters can be either eliminated or added to the model. A modification index is used to assess the likely result of relaxing a particular constraint (Jöreskog and Sorbom 1981). The greatest improvement in goodness-of-fit is achieved by freeing the parameter with the largest modification index, although care should be taken to ensure that such inductively generated changes make theoretical sense. Latent exogenous variables can be left free to correlate, as in an oblique factor analysis. Similarly, an observed variable can become an indicator for more than one latent variable, although Browne (1982) criticizes the tendency to specify correlated error terms simply to obtain an improved fit; there should always be sound theoretical reasons why particular errors are related. Finally, nonrecursive relationships can be specified, and selected parameters can be constrained to be equal.

Because of the presence of unobserved variables, identification can be a complicated matter in LISREL models, and unlike simultanous equation and exploratory factor models, the LISREL model offers few general guidelines. Identification involves ensuring that the parameters of the model are uniquely determined; it addresses the question of whether or not there is a unique set of parameter values consistent with the data (Everitt 1984:7). Attempts to estimate underidentified models can result in arbitrary estimates of the parameters. In all situations, therefore, it is important to remember that a LISREL model cannot be identified until the metric, or scale, of the latent variables has been established. In other words, one cannot estimate both the loadings and the variances associated with the latent variables. Thus, a latent variable should be scaled either by using standard deviation

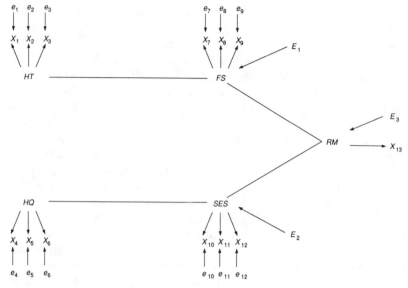

Figure 5.11. Residential mobility: Model 1.
Source: Cadwallader 1987:fig. 2.
Note: HT, HQ, FS, SES, and RM are latent variables representing housing type, housing quality, family status, socioeconomic status, and residential mobility, respectively; X_1–X_{13} are measured indicators of the latent variables; e_1–e_{12} represent errors in variables; and E_1–E_3 represent errors in equations.

units or by fixing one loading to a nonzero value. When a loading is fixed to one, the latent variable is given the same scale as the observed variable.

In general, identification is achieved by the imposition of constraints on the parameters. For example, in figure 5.9 only two observed variables have nonzero loadings on each of the factors, thus restricting certain parameters to zero. Similarly, the error terms are unrelated, thus fixing another set of parameters. Equality constraints can also be imposed, whereby the values of the parameters are constrained to be equal. The only way to guarantee that parameters are uniquely identified, however, is to obtain algebraic solutions for them that incorporate the variances and covariances of the observed variables (Long 1981). In some instances an overidentified structural model can help secure the identification of an underidentified measurement model (Kenny 1979:182).

The general framework of the residential mobility model shown in figure 5.11 is based on the previous discussion concerning the essential interplay between households and housing stock (Cadwallader 1987).

To briefly summarize, as the housing stock of an area changes, we might expect a simultaneous adjustment of the population characteristics of that area. Housing stock is divided according to housing type and housing quality, while population characteristics are classified into family status and socioeconomic status. It is postulated, therefore, that a prospective buyer choosing a home must select based on the type and quality of housing and that this decision will be primarily influenced by the buyer's stage in the life cycle and socioeconomic status. In particular, we might expect socioeconomic status to be associated with housing quality and family status to be associated with housing type. Finally, residential mobility is interpreted as a phenomenon of the housing market, with families changing their housing stock as they experience changes in both family status and socioeconomic status.

Each of the four major latent variables—housing type, housing quality, family status, and socioeconomic status is measured by three indicator variables: percentage owner-occupied (X_1), percentage single-family dwelling units (X_2), number of rooms (X_3); housing value (X_4), number of bathrooms (X_5), age of housing (X_6); persons per household (X_7), percentage under eighteen (X_8), women in labor force (X_9); and education (X_{10}), income (X_{11}), and occupation (X_{12}). The remaining latent variable, residential mobility, is simply measured by the proportion of people residing in the same house as they did five years previously (X_{13}). Thus the measurement model, specifying the relationships between the observed and latent variables, can be formally expressed by the following set of equations:

$$X_1 = b_1 HT + e_1 \tag{5.31}$$

$$X_2 = b_2 HT + e_2 \tag{5.32}$$

$$X_3 = b_3 HT + e_3 \tag{5.33}$$

$$X_4 = b_4 HQ + e_4 \tag{5.34}$$

$$X_5 = b_5 HQ + e_5 \tag{5.35}$$

$$X_6 = b_6 HQ + e_6 \tag{5.36}$$

$$X_7 = b_7 FS + e_7 \tag{5.37}$$

$$X_8 = b_8 FS + e_8 \tag{5.38}$$

$$X_9 = b_9 FS + e_9 \tag{5.39}$$

$$X_{10} = b_{10} SES + e_{10} \tag{5.40}$$

$$X_{11} = b_{11} SES + e_{11} \tag{5.41}$$

$$X_{12} = b_{12} SES + e_{12} \tag{5.42}$$

$$X_{13} = b_{13} RM \tag{5.43}$$

where the notation is the same as in figure 5.11.

Housing type and housing quality are treated as latent exogenous variables, while family status, socioeconomic status, and residential mobility are all latent endogenous variables. There are consequently three structural equations, one for each latent endogenous variable:

$$FS = b_{14} HT + E_1 \tag{5.44}$$

$$SES = b_{15} HQ + E_2 \tag{5.45}$$

$$RM = b_{16} FS + b_{17} SES + E_3 \tag{5.46}$$

The hypothesized structural model is recursive, as there are no reciprocal relationships between the endogenous variables.

Using Version 5 of the LISREL computer program (Jöreskog and Sorbom 1981), this model was tested with 1970 census tract data for the city of Portland, Oregon. Examination of the residuals and modification indices suggested that certain respecifications might improve the fit of the model. In general, the residuals indicate discrepancies between the covariances implied by the estimated model and the corresponding covariances that are observed in the data. These residuals can be examined one by one, and large residual covariances imply a specification error in that part of the model involving those two variables. The modification index, on the other hand, focuses on the fixed parameters of the model and indicates by how much the overall chi-square would decrease if any of these fixed parameters were made free. A relatively large modification index, therefore, suggests that the fit of the model can be substantially improved by freeing that particular parameter.

In this instance, the modification indices indicated that the model should be changed in order to include direct effects between the two exogenous latent variables, housing type and housing quality, and residential mobility (fig. 5.12). The original structural model had thus been

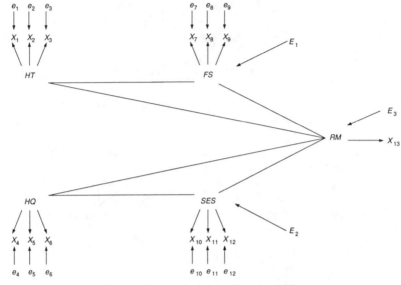

Figure 5.12. Residential mobility: Model 2.
Source: Cadwallader 1987:fig. 3.

misspecified; housing type and housing quality not only influence residential mobility via family status and socioeconomic status, respectively, but also have a direct influence on residential mobility. Freeing a
previously fixed parameter means losing one degree of freedom for
chi-square, so in this case the degrees of freedom were reduced by two
(table 5.15).

Fortunately, the difference between the chi-square values of two
nested models is also distributed as a chi-square distribution, with
degrees of freedom equal to the difference in degrees of freedom between the two alternative models. This property is thus extremely useful when the researcher is involved in the process of model building
(Herting 1985). Adding parameters creates a less-restrictive model,

Table 5.15. Successive improvements in the residential mobility
model

	Reduction in chi-square	Reduction in degrees of freedom
Model 1 to model 2	136	2
Model 2 to model 3	10	1
Model 3 to model 4	222	2

Source: Cadwallader 1987: table 1.

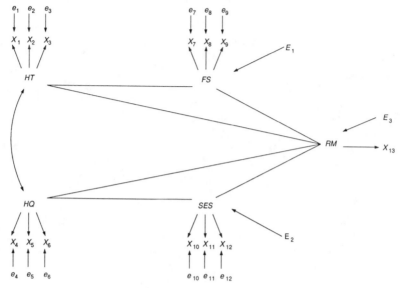

Figure 5.13. Residential mobility: Model 3.
Source: Cadwallader 1987:fig. 4.

while removing paths would create a more-restrictive model. The chi-square test thus addresses the issue of whether the improvement of fit in the less-restrictive model is statistically significant. In this particular instance, the reestimated model showed a reduction in chi-square of 136, which is a statistically significant improvement (table 5.15).

Examination of the modification indices for Model 2 suggested that further improvement might be achieved by allowing the two exogenous latent variables, housing type and housing quality, to be correlated, as in Model 3 (fig. 5.13). This change provides a further reduction in chi-square of ten for the loss of one degree of freedom. Finally, the modification indices and residuals associated with Model 3 suggest that correlated errors might be profitably introduced into the measurement model (fig. 5.14). In particular, variables X_1 and X_4, and X_2 and X_3 appear to have correlated errors, thus illustrating the fact that some of the indicators have spurious sources of covariation with other indicators. That is, pairs of indicators may have common sources of variation that have been omitted from the estimated models. Such appears to be the case in the present example, as the introduction of correlated errors reduces the chi-square value by 222 for the loss of only two more degrees of freedom.

In general, many different types of specification error can occur in

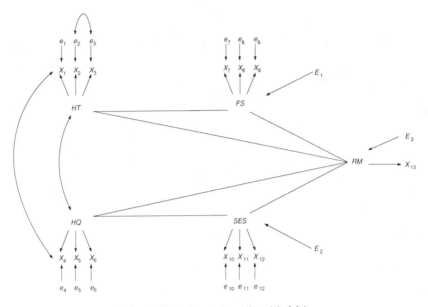

Figure 5.14. Residential mobility: Model 4.
Source: Cadwallader 1987:fig. 5.

causal models involving unmeasured variables (Herting and Costner 1985). First, additivity specification error occurs if one mistakenly assumes that the effects of two or more variables are additive. Similarly, linearity specification error is present if one mistakenly assumes that all the relationships are linear. Second, direction-of-effect specification error is encountered if a stated dependency between two variables is in the opposite direction to the true dependence. Third, omitted path specification error entails omitting a causal link between two variables. Fourth, recursive specification error involves assuming a unidirectional effect when the true effect is reciprocal. Finally, spurious association specification error involves omitting a common source of variation between two variables.

It can be seen, therefore, that the LISREL model represents an extremely general approach that allows one to estimate structural equation models that contain both errors-in-variables and errors-in-equations. By judiciously fixing or freeing selected parameters, the general model contains a wide range of more specific models, such as simultaneous equation systems and confirmatory factor analysis. Higher-order factor models, in which the various levels of latent variables affect each other through regression structures, can also be constructed (Bentler 1982). In addition, certain nonlinearities can be introduced, as long as they can be transformed to achieve linearity. For example, psychophysicists often express the relationships between estimates of magnitudes and true magnitudes as power functions (Stevens 1975). Such power functions can be incorporated into measurement models by logarithmically transforming the observed scores prior to calculating the covariance matrix (Dwyer 1983:273).

6

The Decision-Making Process in Residential Mobility

In contrast to the aggregated models described in the previous chapter, behavioral models of residential mobility focus on the individual decision-maker. Traditionally, the decision-making process has been conceptually partitioned into three stages: the decision to move, the search for available alternatives, and the evaluation of those alternatives (Brown and Moore 1971). Although this compartmentalization of the decision-making process obviously represents an oversimplification (Popp 1976), it has had the advantage of allowing researchers to focus their attention on different parts of the whole. The present chapter parallels this framework by discussing, in sequence, the decision to move, residential search, neighborhood evaluation, and neighborhood choice.

The Decision to Move

Investigations of the initial decision to seek a new residence have emphasized the importance of prior mobility history as a determinant of subsequent behavior. In particular, the duration-of-residence effect, whereby the longer a household remains in a particular location the less likely it is to move, has been termed the principle of cumulative inertia (McGinnis 1968). As always, there are exceptions to the rule, and for certain subpopulations the probability of a move appears to actually increase with increasing duration of stay (Clark and Huff 1977). In general, however, several variables can be used to distinguish between movers and stayers (Poot 1987). For example, besides the duration-of-residence effect, renters are more likely to move than owners, and there is some evidence that females are less mobile than males (Stapleton-Concord 1982).

In the context of voluntary mobility, classifications of the reasons for moving often make a distinction between so-called adjustment and induced moves (Clark and Onaka 1983). Adjustment moves are related to dissatisfaction with various attributes of the housing unit, such as its size, quality, neighborhood location, or accessibility. Space considerations are a particularly central stimuli in the mobility process, with the amount of space per person being a consistent predictor of the propensity to move (Clark, Deurloo, and Dieleman 1984). This relationship between residential mobility and housing space is primarily a response to changing household needs associated with different stages in the family life cycle. For example, the highest probability of moving occurs between the ages of twenty and thirty; this is associated with the beginning of married life and the arrival of children. There tends to be greater stability while the children are at school and the head of household is consolidating his or her career, and then mobility often increases again when the children leave home and less living space is required.

Induced moves, on the other hand, are related to specific household events, such as a change in marital status or retirement. Indeed, Sell (1983) has estimated that as much as 25 percent of residential mobility occurs under conditions of substantial constraint associated with family dynamics. In this context, the traditional concept of a linear progression through a conventional life cycle has become increasingly dated. Patterns of family structure and behavior have become progressively diversified, with an increase in the number of single-headed and single-person households. An expanded conceptualization of the family life cycle is required in order to encompass the wide variety of potential living arrangements and the transitions between them (Stapleton 1980). In addition, the complexity and the relationship to mobility patterns of such transitions can only be fully appreciated through the analysis of various interaction effects. For example, Clark, Deurloo, and Dieleman (1986) effectively utilized logit analysis to demonstrate that the evaluation of interaction effects between such variables as age, income, and tenure status can significantly enhance our understanding of the reasons to move or stay. The importance of interaction effects has been similarly documented in the context of residential mobility of the aged (Stapleton-Concord 1984).

Attempts to formally model the propensity to move of individual households has often revolved around the concept of locational or residential stress (Clark and Cadwallader 1973a; Brummell 1981; Phipps 1989). The decision to move can be viewed as a function both of the household's present level of satisfaction and of the level of satisfaction it believes may be attained elsewhere. The difference between these levels can then be viewed as a measure of stress created by the present residential location. The decision of the household to actually go ahead and seek a new residence represents an adjustment to that stress. The term *stress*, of course, has many different meanings, and our techniques for measuring stress and its effects are as yet rather crude compared with our ability to measure intelligence, attitude, or perceptual skills (McGrath 1970:3). Selye (1956), however, has proposed a set of terms that have been accepted by many psychologists and physiologists. He uses *stress* to refer to the state of the organism, *stressors* to refer to stress-producing agents, and *stress reactions* to refer to those responses which characterize a stressed organism.

Using this terminology, we can turn our attention to identifying the stressors. The overall amount of stress experienced by an individual household can be measured across a fairly simple set of stressors. In one study (Clark and Cadwallader 1973a), the level of stress was measured with regard to the size and facilities of the dwelling unit, the kind of people living in the neighborhood, the accessibility to friends and relatives, proximity to the workplace, and the amount of air pollution in the neighborhood. These stressors represent both the physical aspects of the dwelling and the social conditions of the neighborhood, but additional and alternative stressors are not precluded in extensions of the model. An additional proximity variable, accessibility to goods and services, was considered but not included in the analysis, principally because of the difficulty of aggregating all goods and services into one stressor. Other stressors used in the study involve essentially a single element. It seemed that respondents might be confused and seek to understand which particular good or service they were to consider. To give them a variety of potential goods and services would have considerably enlarged the questionnaire.

The size and facilities of the dwelling unit were included because these, in conjunction with the household's position in the life cycle, have been found to be of great importance for residential satisfaction. For example, Rossi (1980:61) has indicated that the major function of mobility is to enable families to adjust their housing to the housing needs that are generated by the shifts in family composition that accompany changes in the life cycle. The kind of people living in the neighborhood provides a measure of the relative importance of the social environment. How the household sees itself in relation to that environment is significant, as it has been suggested that residential mobility is sometimes the spatial expression of vertical mobility (Simmons 1968). The influx of a different socioeconomic class into a neighborhood may be particularly influential in inducing residents to move. The distance variables involved are proximity to friends and relatives and distance to work. Some studies have rejected job location as an important variable (Simmons 1968), but some evidence indicates that the length of the journey to work is a significant factor in the relocation of households (Clark and Burt 1980). Finally, numerous studies have found that smog contributes to residential dissatisfaction (Schusky 1966). As the study under discussion was carried out in Los Angeles, such a variable seems especially appropriate.

The effects of these stressors can be combined in order to calculate an overall measure of residential stress. The stress value for an individual household i is expressed as follows:

$$S_i = \text{Md of } [(EOS_j - LS_j) + 7] \qquad (6.1)$$

where S denotes the household's median level of stress, EOS is the household's ease of obtaining satisfaction at another location, and LS is its present level of satisfaction. The function is calculated over the j stressors already outlined.

To measure ease of obtaining greater satisfaction elsewhere (EOS), each household was requested to consider how easy or difficult it would be to find a more desirable location elsewhere in Los Angeles. The respondent was asked to use a seven-point attitude scale, going from very difficult (1) to very easy (7), for each of the five characteristics. Similarly, the household was asked to evaluate its present level of satisfaction (LS) on a seven-point attitude scale, going from very dissatisfied (1) to very satisfied (7), for each of the five characteristics. The greatest amount of stress is experienced when the household thinks that it is very easy to find better housing elsewhere while being very dissatisfied with the present location. In this situation the household is most likely to exhibit a strong desire to move. The problem of obtaining negative stress values, as a result of the subtraction involved in equation 6.1, is circumvented by adding seven to each median stress level. The stress scale then varies from 1 (lowest possible stress) to 13 (highest possible stress).

A modified stress value, with a weighting factor, was also calculated. The magnitude of this weighting factor is based on the importance of a particular characteristic j to an individual household, as revealed in its ranking of the relationship of those factors to having a satisfactory home. The weighted stress function can be expressed as follows:

$$S_i = \text{Md of } [(EOS_j - LS_j) + 7 + w_j] \tag{6.2}$$

where the notation is the same as in equation 6.1, except for the addition of the weighting factor, w_j.

The data used to calibrate equations 6.1 and 6.2 were obtained from a random sample of 169 households in the city of Santa Monica, within the Los Angeles metropolitan area. The sample was derived by first choosing a simple random sample of 40 equal-sized blocks and then systematically sampling households within those blocks. Of the 169 households, 39 refused to be interviewed, and 21 could not be contacted after three call-backs. The results of the sampling yielded 106 usable interviews. Thirty-seven percent of the respondents lived in houses, and the remainder lived in apartments.

First, the relationship between a household's median stress level and the household's desire to move was investigated, and then the individual stressors were analyzed. The household's desire to move was measured on a seven-point attitude scale going from 1 to 7, with 1 denoting no desire to move and 7 denoting a very strong desire to move. According to the model, higher levels of stress should be associated with a strong desire to move. As the attitude scales provide ordinal-level data, Kendall's Tau was utilized to examine the relationship between the desire to move and residential stress. Kendall's Tau is an appropriate measure of association when both variables are measured at the ordinal level, and its values range from –1.0 for a perfect negative relationship to +1.0 for a perfect positive relationship.

Even though Kendall coefficients are generally thought to be especially appropriate when the data contain a large number of tied ranks or when a large number of cases are classified into a relatively smaller number of categories, it should be recognized that the numerical value of tau can be relatively small even in the presence of a moderately strong relationship. The numerical value of tau depends on the marginal totals of the categories, and we can seldom expect to get a value of tau approaching unity. In the present instance, the correlation between the desire to move and residential stress is .384 (table 6.1). As expected, then, the greater the household's level of stress, the greater the potential mobility exhibited by the household. Note, however, that the weighted stress formulation does not improve the strength of the relationship.

Table 6.1. The relationship between the desire to move and residential stress

Correlation between the household's median stress level and desire to move	
Kendall's Tau	.384
Correlation between the household's weighted median stress level and desire to move	
Kendall's Tau	.343

Source: Clark and Cadwallader 1973a: table 3. (Clark, W.A.V., and Cadwallader, M. T., "Locational stress and residential mobility." *Environment and Behavior* 5: 29–41, copyright © 1973 by Sage Publications, Inc. Reprinted by permission of Sage Publications, Inc.)
Note: Both values are significant at the .001 level.

Table 6.2. The stressors

	Median value on the	
Stressor	Stress scale: 1 to 13	Weighted stress scale: 2 to 18
Proximity to friends and relatives	6.091	7.921
Proximity to work	5.417	8.056
Kind of people living in the neighborhood	5.231	8.038
Size and facilities of the dwelling unit	5.094	8.821
Amount of smog in the area	3.000	5.974

Source: Clark and Cadwallader 1973a: table 4. (Clark, W.A.V., and Cadwallader, M. T., "Locational stress and residential mobility." *Environment and Behavior* 5: 29–41, copyright © 1973 by Sage Publications, Inc. Reprinted by permission of Sage Publications, Inc.)

The different amounts of stress produced by each of the five stressors can be most conveniently compared on the basis of the median stress value generated by each stressor (table 6.2). The differences between the median stress levels are very small, suggesting that apart from the smog stressor, each of the other four stressors is equally important in generating the overall level of stress. The small difference among the stressors partially explains the lack of improvement in the weighted stress model. Correlations between the stressors and the desire to move give a clearer indication of the relative importance of each stressor. In this case, stress due to the size and facilities of the dwelling unit appears to be the most important factor, and proximity to work seems to be somewhat less important than the other factors (table 6.3).

A further test of this model of residential stress and mobility has been undertaken in Auckland, New Zealand (Clark 1975). One hundred thirty-nine recent movers were interviewed, and the basic structure of the model was the same, except that one of the stressors was changed. The availability of parks and playgrounds was substituted for smog, as air pollution is not a significant problem in New Zealand cities. On the other hand, outdoor activities are important for many New Zealand families. The Spearman correlation between median residential stress and desire to move was .32, which is significant at the

Table 6.3. The relationships between the individual stressors and the desire to move

1. Correlation between the household's stress due to the size and facilities of the dwelling unit and desire to move

	Coefficient	Significance
Tau	.352	.001

2. Correlation between the household's stress due to the kind of people living in the neighborhood and desire to move

	Coefficient	Significance
Tau	.343	.001

3. Correlation between the household's stress due to the distance from friends and relatives and desire to move

	Coefficient	Significance
Tau	.253	.001

4. Correlation between the household's stress due to the amount of smog in the area and desire to move

	Coefficient	Significance
Tau	.181	.005

5. Correlation between the household's stress due to the distance from work and desire to move

	Coefficient	Significance
Tau	.082	.137

Source: Clark and Cadwallader 1973a: table 5. (Clark, W.A.V., and Cadwallader, M. T., "Locational stress and residential mobility." *Environment and Behavior* 5: 29–41, copyright © 1973 by Sage Publications, Inc. Reprinted by permission of Sage Publications, Inc.)

.001 level. As expected, the greater the household's level of stress, the greater the desire to move. Of the individual stressors, size and facilities of the dwelling unit was most highly correlated with desire to move. The correlation between stress due to the kind of people living in the neighborhood and desire to more was much lower than in the Los Angeles study.

More recent formulations of residential stress have incorporated the duration-of-residence effect by postulating a trade-off between dissatisfaction and inertia (Huff and Clark 1978a). The level of stress, or dissatisfaction, is assumed to increase over time, as the household falls out of adjustment with its present situation. Similarly, however, the resistance to moving, or inertia, is also expected to increase with increasing duration of stay. Thus the probability of moving represents a trade-off between stress and inertia, where both components can be expressed as exponential functions of change over time. Despite the analytical appeal of such a conceptualization, however, the black-box nature of the stress and inertia functions indicates that the model is best suited to a predictive rather than an explanatory role (Clark, Huff, and Burt 1979).

Attempts to further refine the stress-inertia, or stress-resistance, model have suggested that households might be as sensitive to the direction and rate of change of stress as they are to its absolute level at any specific time. Using data from the Canadian city of Saskatoon, Phipps and Carter (1984) were able to show that intention to move was greatest for those households experiencing relatively high levels of stress that had increased over the preceding two years. The effects of resistance on mobility were also strong, although somewhat more complex.

It is worth noting at this point that opinions differ about the strength of the relationship between desire to move and actual mobility behavior. Using data from the United States and Canada, Moore (1986) argued that the relationship between the expectation of moving and the actual fulfillment of those expectations is sometimes quite limited. Not only do many respondents fail to move in a manner consistent with expectations, but disadvantaged groups are less likely to translate expectation into action than is the population in general. Other studies suggest that short-term migration intentions are an excellent predictor of subsequent behavior and that ambiguities arrive partly because of the failure to distinguish between local and nonlocal moves (McHugh 1984). Suffice it to say, however, that supply-side constraints obviously play an important role in the relationship betwen mobility intention and subsequent behavior. In particular, the availability of suitable alternatives to current consumption is crucial.

In efforts to resolve the complex interactions between residential satisfaction, desire to move, and actual mobility behavior, researchers have often employed various kinds of structural equation models. For example, using path analysis, Pickvance (1974) demonstrated that life cycle and tenure status play an important role in determining both desired and expected mobility. Speare (1974) also constructed a path analytical model to explore the interrelationships between five background variables, representing individual or household characteristics, location characteristics, and social bonds; an index of residential satisfaction; and two mobility variables, involving desire to move and actual mobility. In particular, Speare's model proposed that residential satisfaction is the proximate determinant of the decision to consider moving and that satisfaction is determined by the five background variables. That is, the key hypothesis to be tested was that the background variables would operate on the desire to move through the intervening variable of residential satisfaction. Using data from a sample of seven hundred residents of Rhode Island, Speare provided empirical support for his model.

A comparable study by Landale and Guest (1985), however, suggested that Speare's formulation is only partially appropriate. Using a series of logit models, they supported Speare's contention that subjective satisfaction is a strong predictor of thoughts about moving and that thoughts about moving are good predictors of actual mobility. On the other hand, they found three major problems with Speare's model. First, residential stress, as measured by satisfaction, is not a particularly good predictor of actual mobility, although it does have an indirect effect via thoughts about moving. Second, the background variables affect mobility independently, not just indirectly through satisfaction. Third, the satisfaction variables have little impact in mediating the effects of the background variables on thoughts and behavior concerning mobility.

In a similar vein, Hourihan (1984) developed a path model to explore how personal characteristics cause the perception of neighborhood attributes. Finally, Preston (1984) estimated a series of path models designed to elucidate the relationships between duration of residence, personal characteristics, and residential stress. Data were obtained from a survey of 513 elderly residents of the Kansas City SMSA, with each person being interviewed about present living conditions, individual and household characteristics, and residential history. In order to maximize internal homogeneity, the sample was divided into three groups: white home owners, black home owners, and renters. The results of the analyses suggested that residential stress and inertia are influenced by both years of residence and personal characteristics but that personal characteristics have the larger impact. The strength of the observed relationships differed across the three subpopulations, thus confirming the notion that models of residential mobility should be disaggregated whenever possible.

Residential Search

If a household is experiencing high levels of stress, and thus a strong desire to move, it must then either modify its present home or begin an explicit search for alternative accommodation. Three interrelated questions are crucial to any understanding of the residential search process (Clark 1981a). First, what information sources are used to find vacant dwellings in the city? Second, how intense is the search activity? Third, what is the spatial pattern associated with that search activity? In the present section we address each of these questions in turn.

By far the most important sources of information to prospective movers are newspaper advertisements, personal contacts, personal observation of "For Sale" signs, and real estate agents. Rossi (1980:209) has concluded that personal contacts, the second most frequently used medium, after newspapers, are by far the most effective. The use of different sources of information varies, however, according to the type of dwelling unit that is desired. For example, Michelson (1977) suggests that prospective movers more often use newspaper advertisements when searching for an apartment than when seeking a house. Real estate agents are an effective source for house hunters, especially out-of-town buyers (Clark and Smith 1982). These results are generally substantiated by those of Rossi (1980:209), although he emphasizes the particular significance of personal contacts and direct search when a household plans to rent rather than purchase.

Analyses of the sequential structure of information collection suggest that the preliminary stages of search are characterized by a greater dependence on newspaper advertisements, while in the later stages home buyers rely increasingly on real estate agents (Clark and Smith 1979). In a particularly detailed study of the residential search process, Talarchek (1982) used a questionnaire survey of recent intraurban migrants in the Syracuse, New York, metropolitan area. He detected a two-stage process in the acquisition of information on specific variables. First, households obtain information on neighborhood and locational variables, such as quality of schools, property taxes, and distance to the nearest shopping center. Second, as the residential search progresses, households begin to collect information on the attributes of individual housing units, such as lot size, number of rooms, and floor plan. As might be expected, housing costs seem to be monitored throughout these two stages. While this two-stage process can be identified for the sequential acquisition of information on specific variables, no such pattern appears to exist for the sequential utilization of information sources. Indeed, Talarchek warns that a great diversity of search behavior characterizes the population, even within specific income and household composition groups.

The characteristics of the different information sources are also of some interest. Smith, Clark, and Onaka (1982) have conducted an exhaustive examination of newspaper housing advertisements, with the specific aim of comparing the behavior of private sellers and real estate agents. Housing advertisements were sampled over a twenty-year period for Santa Barbara, California, and over a nineteen-year period for Stockton, California. In general, the data provided support for three major hypotheses. First, real estate agents make substitutions between price and locational information in order to achieve a desired level of ambiguity, whereas owners do not appear to make such trade-offs. Second, owners provide relatively more locational information than do real estate agents, while real estate agents are more specific about price. Third, both owners and real estate agents tend to increase the level of price ambiguity when faced with increasing uncertainty concerning bid price distributions.

Real estate agents are perhaps the most complex channel of information transmission, as they act as both recipients and transmitters of information (Palm 1976). Prospective buyers pass messages about housing preferences, while real estate agents may either intentionally or unintentionally transform and filter vacancy messages. Various characteristics of real estate agents can affect the nature and extent of their influence on the search process. For example, the ethnicity of the real estate agent contributes a particular set of dimensions to real estate practice. Using a survey of Anglo, black, and Hispanic real estate agents in Denver, Palm (1985) was able to substantiate three research hypotheses. First, sellers tend to select real estate agents of the same ethnic background as themselves. Second, the ethnicity of the real estate agent affects the size and location of territories in which he or she seeks new listings. Third, the ethnicity of the agent substantially shapes his or her network of business contacts.

The intensity of search activity has been addressed in a major empirical investigation of search behavior in Toronto. Using a sample of 380 cases drawn from a population of 1,486 movers, Barrett (1976) computed the amount of time spent searching and the number of houses searched. Simply summarized, the absence of an extensive search phase was the major behavioral characteristic, as a large majority of households spent approximately one month looking at between two and four houses. As might be expected, the search behavior of low-income and minority populations is especially restricted, due to poor access to private transportation and relatively small amounts of previously uncommitted time (Cronin 1982).

The length of time spent searching depends on the degree of satisfaction associated with present alternatives combined with the time and money costs that would be incurred by further search. In this context, researchers have constructed a variety of probability models to devise optimal "stopping rules" for housing search activity (Flowerdew 1976; Phipps and Laverty 1983). Most search theories tend to incorporate the idea of a critical utility value which differentiates acceptable and unacceptable alternatives, but this threshold value will change during the course of searching, due to learning and preference adjustment (Smith et al. 1979). Personality factors are also likely to be involved, with conservative households being prepared to follow a satisfying rather than an optimising strategy.

Meyer (1980) has outlined a less-formal model of decision-making under uncertainty. Altohugh it represents a stopping rule model, in this case the cutoff level is an empirical parameter unique to the individual. Studying hypothetical apartment searches by undergraduate students, Meyer showed that the decision to stop searching is based on three factors: inferences about the distribution of utilities associated with the population of alternatives, the amount of time available for search, and the quality of the particular apartment currently being considered. Efforts to link these stopping rule models with the information acquisition approach have focused on the relationship between the costs of information derived from different sources and the length of search (Smith and Clark 1980).

Finally, Barrett (1976) suggests that the spatial pattern of search is remarkably constrained. For example, of his sample of 380 Toronto respondents, more than 92 percent restricted themselves to average search distances of less than three miles. In addition, Brown and Holmes (1971) have demonstrated that the search activity of low-income inner-city residents is more localized than that of their higher-income suburban counterparts. Huff (1984) has attempted to formalize this constraining influence of distance by a series of distance-decay models of residential search. In particular , the intensity of search is expected to decline with increasing distance from certain key reference points in the household's search space, such as current residential location, location of the workplace, and the locations of friends and relatives. Nearby possibilities are rejected before search occurs in areas at increasing distances from these various anchor points. The parameters which govern the actual shape of the distance-decay function depend upon a combination of the household attributes and the characteristics of the present residence. For example, if a household is dissatisfied with the size of its present residence but is satisfied with the general location, then search activity will tend to be concentrated in the local neighborhood.

Clark and Smith (1982) conducted a detailed empirical analysis of spatial search behavior within the San Fernando Valley region of the Los Angeles metropolitan area. A series of regression equations was constructed, with variables such as the number of different neighborhoods searched and the distance of search serving as the dependent variables of interest. These equations were then estimated using individual data on two distinctive samples: a longitudinal sample of households still actively involved in the search process and a retrospective sample of households who had already bought a house. Despite some noticeable differences between the two groups, the length of residence and number of real estate agents used appeared to perform consistently well as explanatory variables. For example, for the retrospective sample, length of residence had the highest standardized regression coefficient in the number of areas searched equation. The direction of the relationship was negative, indicating that length of residence acts as a surrogate for information levels. The greater the information is about potential areas, the fewer areas have to be actively searched. In constrast, as might be expected, the number of real estate agents used was positively related to the spatial extent of search.

More formal, theoretical models of spatial search are still comparatively rare, with the notable exception of those developed by Huff (1982, 1986). Each of Huff's models is designed to generate a search pattern which can be compared with an observed distribution. The generating rules are the assumptions concerning the nature of the search process, and the resulting set of searched vacancies is represented by some kind of spatial pattern. Huff describes residential search behavior as a two-step process, consisting of the initial selection of an area in which search is to be concentrated, followed by the actual selection of vacancies within the targeted area. The decision to search in any particular area is assumed to be a function of the household's expected utility from searching in that area, which depends upon the relative concentration of potentially acceptable vacancies. Those vacancies located in areas of the city with relatively low expected search costs have a higher probability of being visited than vacancies located elsewhere. Thus, under certain simplifying conditions, the search process can be described as a first-order Markov chain, in which the probabilty of searching in a given area is a function of three elements: the indirect cost of identifying a member of the opportunity set in that area, the direct cost of actually visiting a member of that opportunity set, and the location of the last vacancy visited.

In general, Huff (1986) successfully contends that geographic regularities exist in the spatial pattern of vacancies visited by potential movers and that these regularities primarily arise from two distinct but interrelated sources: the spatial distribution of potential opportunities and the spatial biases in the search strategies employed. Huff is thus able to formally integrate the behavioral approach, with its emphasis on individual choice and decision-making, with the constraints approach, which focuses on the structural issues associated with the supply of housing. He effectively demonstrates that these approaches are complementary, in that they highlight different sources of spatial regularity in observed behavior. In sum, his constrained choice set model, area-based search model, and anchor points models exemplarily illustrate a formal, theory-based empirical analysis that goes well beyond descriptive generalizations.

Neighborhood Evaluation

The third part of the residential decision-making process, the process of neighborhood evaluation and choice, involves two major questions (Hourihan 1979a,b). First, what are the evaluative dimensions across which people assess the relative desirability of alternative neighborhoods? Second, once those evaluative dimensions have been identified, what are the appropriate rules for combining them into an overall utility value for each neighborhood? The present section addresses the first of these two questions, and the second question is taken up in the following section.

An initial study by Johnston (1973) suggested that neighborhood preferences can be understood as resulting from three underlying cognitive categories, or evaluative dimensions: the impersonal environment, composed mainly of the physical attributes of the neighborhood; the interpersonal environment, composed mainly of the social attributes of the neighborhood; and the locational attributes of the neighborhood. Unfortunately, however, the data for Johnston's study were aggregated across different neighborhoods, thus masking the possibility that different sets of evaluative dimensions might be associated with different individual neighborhoods. With this aggregation problem in mind, the present author (Cadwallader 1979a) examined, first, whether the same evaluative dimensions are used for different types of neighborhoods and, second, whether the relative importance of these dimensions, in determining residential preferences, is the same for all neighborhoods. In other words, can the evaluative process be easily generalized, or is it largely context-specific?

The data used for this study were obtained, in questionnaire form, from 148 residents of Madison, Wisconsin. The original sample size of 255 households yielded 189 completed questionnaires. Of these completed questionnaires, however, 41 were considered unusable, mainly because of missing data. The sample design required the selection of all households within an area containing approximately ten city blocks, as it was felt that all the subjects should be located in the same neighborhood, thus ensuring some measure of comparability for their ratings of other neighborhoods. In this respect, the subjects represent a statistical population, rather than a sample drawn from such a population. The city blocks were composed of single-family dwelling units, and on average, the subjects had lived at their present addresses for approximately twelve years, although all portions of the duration-of-residence curve were well represented.

Each subject was asked to rate eight Madison neighborhoods on eleven seven-point rating scales. The neighborhoods were chosen by

Table 6.4. The neighborhood attributes

1	Crowded	— Spacious
2	Poorly kept yards	— Well-kept yards
3	Open	— Private
4	Poor reputation	— Good reputation
5	Poor-quality housing	— Good-quality housing
6	Noisy	— Quiet
7	People dissimilar to me	— People similar to me
8	Unsafe	— Safe
9	Inconvenient location	— Convenient location
10	Poor park facilities	— Good park facilities
11	Ordinary	— Distinctive

Source: Cadwallader 1979a: table 1.

the experimenter with a view toward maximizing ease of recognition on the part of the subjects. If a subject so desired, he or she was shown a map of Madison that outlined the eight neighborhoods. The comparatively long residence in Madison of most of the subjects ensured few problems associated with neighborhood identification.

The subjects were presented with the eleven rating scales, across which the neighborhoods were to be evaluated, in the form of a semantic differential test. The semantic differential technique was originally developed by psychologists to investigate the meaning of words (Osgood, Suci, and Tannenbaum 1957), but it has also been used in the analysis of environmental images (Downs 1970; Norcliffe 1974). The methodological procedure involves presenting the subjects with a set of stimuli, or concepts, which they are required to evaluate across a series of scales consisting of bipolar adjectives. In the present context, the neighborhoods represent the stimuli, while the eleven rating scales represent the bipolar adjectives (table 6.4). These particular rating scales were chosen partly to maintain comparability with Johnston's study and partly to reflect the selection of attributes used in other studies involving some aspect of residential preferences (Chapin 1974:63; Ermuth 1974:62; Root 1975). Care was taken to randomize the order of both neighborhoods and scales and also to ensure that no regular sequence occurred with respect to whether the right-hand or the left-hand member of the polar terms represented the positive one.

The data derived from the semantic differential procedure provided a 148 × 11 data matrix for each of the eight neighborhoods. These matrices were subjected to principal components analyses in order to identify any underlying evaluative dimensions. Components with eigenvalues greater than one were extracted and then rotated to simple structure according to the varimax criterion. For each neighborhood

Table 6.5. The evaluative dimensions

Dimension	I	II	III	I	II	III	I	II	III	I	II	III
	Middleton			Maple Bluff			Shorewood Hills			Monona		
Spaciousness	.72			.75			.65			.75		
Yard upkeep	.66				.59		.73			.55		
Privacy	.50				.72			.41				.75
Reputation	.61				.49			.78			.75	
Housing	.60			.78			.82			.52		
Quiet	.75			.68				.70		.78		
People			.61			.78			.85		.52	
Safety	.72				.60				.41	.58		
Location		.74				.78		.77				.56
Park facilities			.84		.70			.65			.78	
Distinctiveness		.68		.86			.77					.60
Variance (percentage of total)	28	16	13	25	19	13	26	25	10	21	18	14
	Indian Hills			Hilldale			Nakoma			Odana		
Spaciousness	.71			.79			.71			.69		
Yard upkeep	.49				.60			.59			.81	
Privacy			-.70	.52					.87	.69		
Reputation	.66				.83			.79			.65	
Housing	.79			.60			.81			.62		
Quiet	.53			.77					.64			.65
People		.51			.73			.53			.76	
Safety	.62				.82		.68					.77
Location			.71			.71		.68				-.51
Park facilities		.86				.75		.74		.46		
Distinctiveness	.71			.74			.69					.50
Variance (percentage of total)	30	15	10	23	22	25	26	23	12	18	18	16

Source: Cadwallader 1979a: table 2.

there were three components with eigenvalues greater than one, and the highest loading for each scale on these components is reported in table 6.5. In almost every case the percentage of the total variance accounted for by these three components is fairly low, with the first component accounting for approximately 20–30 percent of the total variance. Such low levels of explained variation suggest that the eleven scales are not easily collapsed into significant underlying dimensions.

The structures of these components were analyzed, however, in order to determine whether they matched those postulated by Johnston (1973). For this purpose a matrix was constructed to show how

Table 6.6. The associations between neighborhood attributes

		1	2	3	4	5	6	7	8	9	10	11
1	Spaciousness	—										
2	Yard upkeep	4	—									
3	Privacy	3	2	—								
4	Reputation	2	6	3	—							
5	Housing	8	4	3	2	—						
6	Quiet	5	3	4	3	5	—					
7	People	0	3	0	4	0	0	—				
8	Safety	4	5	2	4	4	4	2	—			
9	Location	0	1	3	2	0	2	2	1	—		
10	Park facilities	1	2	3	4	1	1	4	1	3	—	
11	Distinctiveness	5	2	2	1	5	4	0	3	3	0	—

Source: Cadwallader 1979a: table 3.

many times the highest loading for each scale was associated with the same component as the highest loading for every other scale (table 6.6). For example, for four neighborhoods, the highest loadings for quiet and privacy were on the same component, and for five of the eight neighborhoods the highest loadings for quiet and spaciousness were on the same component. The major variable groupings in this matrix were then uncovered by means of elementary linkage analysis (Yeates 1974:96).

Two major groupings emerged. The first contained the scales representing spaciousness, housing quality, distinctiveness, quiet, and privacy, and the second contained the scales representing neighborhood reputation, yard upkeep, safety, type of people, and park facilities. The location variable was not included in either of these typal structures, as its highest loading was not regularly associated with the same component as the highest loading of any other variable. In general, then, these variable groupings are of great interest, as they can be conveniently categorized as representing physical characteristics, social characteristics, and location. As such, they are encouragingly similar to the three evaluative dimensions postulated by Johnston (1973).

Despite this general similarity, however, it is obvious that the factor structures associated with each neighborhood are far from identical (table 6.5). For this reason, further analysis was pursued to see if any evidence existed for similar neighborhoods being cognized through similar evaluative dimensions. The perceived similarity between the neighborhoods was measured by a similarity rating, which was obtained by asking the subjects to take each neighborhood in turn as an anchor neighborhood and to identify the three other neighborhoods which they regarded as most similar to it. Political scientists investigating the

Table 6.7. The matrix of similarity ratings and congruency coefficients

	1	2	3	4	5	6	7	8
1 Middleton	—	.01	.18	.19	.02	.30	.02	.22
2 Maple Bluff	.77	—	.06	.02	.41	.05	.35	.02
3 Indian Hills	.91	.88	—	.16	.09	.20	.07	.23
4 Hilldale	.74	.87	.82	—	.06	.15	.09	.29
5 Shorewood Hills	.86	.91	.92	.85	—	.04	.38	.04
6 Monona	.88	.89	.86	.84	.84	—	.05	.20
7 Nakoma	.83	.94	.94	.78	.90	.92	—	.10
8 Odana	.68	.55	.67	.76	.59	.53	.58	—

Source: Cadwallader 1979a: table 4.

perception of cross-national similarities have used such a procedure (Hefner, Levy, and Warner 1967). The similarity rating for each pair of neighborhoods is shown by the values above the diagonal in table 6.7, with the highest values indicating the greatest similarity.

The degree of factorial similarity across the neighborhoods was measured by the coefficient of congruence. Usually each component from one factor structure is compared with the components from all other factor structures and then is paired with the one with which it has the highest coefficient of congruence (Harman 1967:271). In the present instance, however, only the first components from each factor structure were compared, as the eigenvalues associated with the remaining components were rather small. The congruency coefficients are show below the diagonal in table 6.7.

Inspection of the similarity ratings and congruency coefficients suggests that neighborhoods perceived to be similar are indeed cognized through similar evaluative dimensions. The three neighborhoods of Maple Bluff, Shorewood Hills, and Nakoma especially illustrate this phenomenon. The congruency coefficients between these three are all equal to or greater than .90, while these neighborhoods also have the three highest similarity ratings. In sum, although the evaluative dimensions are not the same for all neighborhoods, it does appear that subjects utilize similar dimensions when evaluating similar neighborhoods.

Before considering the relative importance of the neighborhood attributes in explaining neighborhood preferences, it is worth noting the important roles that some of the attributes have been assigned in various theories of urban residential differentiation. Alonso (1964), for example, has distinguished between the historic and structural theories of urban form. The historic theory, associated mainly with the name of Burgess (Cadwallader 1985a:118), is essentially the spatial manifestation of the filtering process, whereby new houses are built for upper-income houses and in time are filtered down to lower-income families. An important element of this theory, then, is the assumption that households locate in order to maximize their satisfaction with housing quality.

The structural theory, on the other hand, places the emphasis on the trade-off between the demand for accessibility and the demand for land. It is assumed that accessibility behaves as an "inferior good," so that as families increase their incomes they prefer to substitute land for accessibility. In other words, it is postulated that lower-income households will locate in order to maximize locational advantages, whereas upper-income households will attempt to maximize their desire for spacious lots.

A third major theory of residential differentiation can be conveniently labeled the segregation theory. This theory is implicit in factorial ecological studies, which purport to demonstrate that people attempt to live apart from those unlike themselves and thus minimize the possibility of conflict because of class, generational, racial, and religious or national differences (Davies 1984). The segregation theory therefore assumes that, when evaluating neighborhoods for residential desirability, households will focus particular attention on the kind of people living in the neighborhoods.

The relative importance of the neighborhood attributes was first examined by analyzing how the subjects rated the attributes on a seven-point scale, going from very unimportant (1) to very important (7). The mean rating is used as the aggregate measure of importance for each attribute, while the standard deviation provides a measure of the level of agreement between the subjects (table 6.8). As expected from the preceding theoretical discussion, the attributes of location and housing quality were both considered very important. The type of people living in the neighborhood was considered somewhat less important, although the influence of this variable might have been muted by the fact that Madison is not characterized by large ethnic or racial differences. Also considered of relatively minor importance was the spaciousness scale; thus some doubt was cast on one of the major ingredients of the structural theory of urban form, although this result could be somewhat misleading, given the strong association between housing and spaciousness (table 6.6). In general, the standard deviations indicate that the amount of agreement between the subjects is inversely related to the perceived importance of the attributes.

Further analysis was required, however, to determine whether these attribute rankings remained constant when subjects were asked to think of particular neighborhoods. That is, are the weights attached to the

Table 6.8. The relative importance of the neighborhood attributes

	Mean	Standard deviation		Mean	Standard deviation
1 Location	6.12	1.31	7 Spaciousness	5.53	1.44
2 Housing	6.06	1.21	8 Yard upkeep	5.49	1.45
3 Safety	6.02	1.45	9 Park facilities	4.87	1.54
4 Noise	5.94	1.41	10 Reputation	4.82	1.72
5 Privacy	5.67	1.54	11 Distinctiveness	4.41	1.66
6 People	5.55	1.45			

Source: Cadwallader 1979a: table 5.

different attributes invariant across neighborhoods? In order to address this question, a stepwise regression analysis was performed for each of the eight neighborhoods. The overall preference rating for the neighborhood, as evaluated by each subject, acted as the dependent variable, while the eleven attributes, or scales, acted as the independent variables.

The particular form of stepwise regression used for this analysis was the backward elimination procedure (Draper and Smith 1966:167). This procedure involves computing a regression equation containing all the variables and calculating the partial F value for each variable, treating it as though it were the last variable to enter the equation. The lowest partial F value is then compared with a preselected significance level, in this case .10, and if the F value is lower, then the corresponding variable is removed. The regression equation is then recomputed, and the process is continued until no more variables can be removed. The value of this particular procedure lies in the fact that all variables are first included in the equation and then the insignificant variables are removed in the interests of parsimony.

The results of the stepwise regression analysis (table 6.9) are a little confusing when compared with the original rankings (table 6.8). The standardized regression coefficients reflect the relative importance of the variables in determining the preference ratings, and it can be seen that the distinctiveness variable appears in more equations than any other, although it previously obtained the lowest ranking. Conversely, the previously important location variable appears in only one of the eight regression equations. Although one should remember that the multiple correlation coefficients are rather small and there is obviously some multicollinearity among the variables, these results clearly indicate the potential hazards involved in attempting to analyze preferences independently of any particular context. By contrast, Preston

Table 6.9. The stepwise regression models

Middleton	$Y = 1.32 + .31X_1 - .17X_6 + .32X_9 + .16X_{11}$	$R = .51$
Maple Bluff	$Y = 1.25 - .17X_1 + .18X_4 + .24X_7 + .20X_{11}$	$R = .40$
Indian Hills	$Y = .96 + .37X_4 + .40X_{10} + .19X_{11}$	$R = .52$
Hilldale	$Y = .45 + .29X_5 + .27X_6 - .14X_8 + .32X_{11}$	$R = .66$
Shorewood Hills	$Y = 1.56 + .15X_1 + .15X_2 + .28X_7$	$R = .40$
Monona	$Y = 2.76 - .18X_2 - .27X_3 + .24X_4 + .36X_{11}$	$R = .45$
Nakoma	$Y = 2.65 - .32X_2 + .39X_4 + .30X_7 + .17X_{11}$	$R = .52$
Odana	$Y = .14 + .28X_1 - .18X_2 + .28X_7 + .17X_8 + .17X_{10} + .15X_{11}$	$R = .51$

Source: Cadwallader 1979a: table 6.
Note: X_1–X_{11} are in the same order as the neighborhood attributes in table 6.4.

(1986) suggests that such context effects are comparatively weak and can be reduced by controlling for individual differences in the perceived levels of residential area attributes.

Like the present author (Cadwallader 1979a), Hourihan (1984) also used semantic differential scales and principal components analysis to uncover the evaluative dimensions used by a sample of residents in Cork, Ireland. For the purposes of constructing a path model of residential satisfaction, an initial group of seven components was later reduced to four. These four components summarized the appearance, life-style, quality of life, and stability associated with each neighborhood.

An alternative methodology for capturing these underlying dimensions is available in the form of multidimensional scaling analysis. Based on data derived from a survey of women in Hamilton, Ontario, Preston (1982) concluded that land use, lot size, social character, and housing quality are considered in the evaluation of residential areas. Hourihan (1979a) also used multidimensional scaling analysis when examining neighborhood perception among a sample of residents in Dublin, Ireland. The social status of the evaluated neighborhoods turned out to be the most important differentiating characteristic, followed by familiarity and housing style. Individual differences in the importance attached to those dimensions, however, were apparently unrelated to the socioeconomic status of the subjects. Like principal components analysis, multidimensional scaling is primarily an inductive approach in which the dimensions are subjectively interpreted by the researcher. Unlike the more restrictive orthogonal rotations that have characterized the semantic differential investigations, however, multidimensional scaling allows the evaluative dimensions to be related.

Neighborhood Choice

Having identified the major evaluative dimensions involved in the residential choice process, we will next explore how the subjective ratings associated with those three evaluative dimensions are integrated into an overall utility value for a particular neighborhood. As location, housing, and safety proved to be the three most important attributes, these were used to represent the locational, physical, and social characteristics dimensions, respectively. A series of multiattribute attitude models was used to determine whether the attributes should be combined in an additive, multiplicative, or weighted additive form (Cadwallader 1979c).

In particular, the following three models were tested:

$$P_i = \sum_{j=1}^{n} A_{ij} \tag{6.3}$$

$$P_i = \prod_{j=1}^{n} A_{ij} \tag{6.4}$$

$$P_i = \sum_{j=1}^{n} A_{ij} W_j \tag{6.5}$$

where P_i is the relative attractiveness of neighborhood i, A_{ij} is the attractiveness rating of neighborhood i on attribute j, and W_j is the relative importance of attribute j. These models represent additive, multiplicative, and weighted additive forms, respectively, and all the constituent variables, such as overall neighborhood preference, the attractiveness ratings on each of the three dimensions, and the relative weightings, were measured on the previously defined seven-point scales that were then averaged across subjects.

Multiattribute attitude models such as these have proved useful in a wide variety of decision-making contexts where a particular spatial alternative can be viewed as a bundle of attributes (Cadwallader 1981a). The weighted additive model represents a linear compensatory model with weighted components. It is compensatory in the sense that low ratings on one attribute can be compensated for by high ratings on another attribute. Such models tend to perform particularly well in those situations where a relatively large variance exists across the weightings. As is usual, the weighting of the items in the weighted additive model has been accomplished by using simple numbers, al-

Table 6.10. Comparison of neighborhood choice models

	Actual	Additive	Multiplicative	Weighted additive
Shorewood Hills	16	14	19	14
Nakoma	16	14	16	14
Maple Bluff	13	13	13	13
Hilldale	12	14	16	14
Odana	12	13	13	13
Middleton	11	11	9	11
Indian Hills	11	11	8	11
Monona	9	10	6	10
		$D = 4$	$D = 8$	$D = 4$

Source: Cadwallader 1979c.
Note: D refers to the index of dissimilarity.

though the weighting function could also be calibrated by incorporating some kind of sliding scale, to reflect the widespread phenomenon of decreasing marginal utilities associated with higher attainment levels. The simple additive model is also a linear compensatory model and is like the weighted additive version, except that the weighting term is omitted. Finally, a multiplicative version of the model was also tested, as evidence exists that subjective judgments often conform to a multiplying rule between factors (Lieber 1979).

The results for this particular context and sample of subjects indicate that the additive model is more appropriate than its multiplicative counterpart but that there is no difference between the additive versions. The first column in table 6.10 shows the actual percentage of subjects who preferred each of the eight neighborhoods, while the remaining columns show the percentages predicted by each of the three models. The goodness of fit associated with each model is measured by the index of dissimilarity, which ranges from zero, indicating a perfect fit, to one hundred.

At first glance all three models appear to provide reasonably good fits, with the two additive formulations being only marginally superior. In this particular situation, however, the maximum possible value of one hundred is a little misleading. If we knew nothing about the underlying decision-making process, our best prediction would be that an equal proportion of subjects would rate highest each of the eight neighborhoods. A comparison of this prediction and the observed behavior leads to a value of 7.5 for the index of dissimilarity. Viewed in this light, then, the results suggest that the additive models are genuinely superior to the multiplicative version.

A major reason for the excellent performance of the additive for-

mulations is the fact that whenever the predictor variables are monotonically related to the dependent variable, as in the present instance,
the linear model tends to fit well (Louviere and Norman 1977). Also,
the predictor variables were genuinely independent, as they had been
derived from an orthogonal factor analysis. On the other hand, one of
the major problems with the multiplicative model is that if any attribute
is at a near-zero psychological value, the overall utility value will be
very low, irrespective of how high the other attributes might be rated.

Nevertheless, it is somewhat surprising that the simple additive
model performed as well as the weighted additive model, given the
greater information content of the latter. In the present context, however, this situation is perhaps understandable, as the individual indicators for the evaluative dimenions did not vary markedly in relative
importance. In those situations where a greater variance in the weightings occurs, one could expect the weighted additive model to perform
better than the simple additive model. This issue emphasizes the significance of distinguishing between determinant as opposed to important attributes, as attributes rated as important by subjects will not be
pivotal in the decision-making process if the levels associated with
such attributes are relatively invariant across the alternatives.

Finally, the simple additive model was retested by incorporating a
familiarity variable, as previous research has suggested the importance
of familiarity, or information levels, in the formation of preferences
(Cadwallader 1978). This reformulation provided the following equation:

$$P_i = \sum_{j=1}^{n} A_{ij} + F_i \qquad (6.6)$$

where the notation is the same as in equations 6.3, 6.4, and 6.5 and F_i is
the level of familiarity associated with neighborhood i, as measured by
a seven-point rating scale. The index of dissimilarity for equation 6.6 is
3, so the equation is a slightly better predictor than the simple additive
model. It should be noted, however, that the utility functions used to
evaluate the alternatives might change during the course of the decision-making process (Phipps 1983).

Researchers have also offered a number of other approaches to the
problem of determining how individual evaluative dimensions are
combined into some kind of overall utility value (Ellis and Mackay
1990; Golledge and Rushton 1984; Louviere and Timmermans 1990b).
The revealed preference approach, as the name implies, involves the
examination of observed behavior in order to uncover the underlying

preference structure (Clark 1982c). Ideally, however, only purely discretionary behavior should be analyzed via revealed preferences. Since desired but unattainable choices are never observed, one runs the risk of confounding preferences and constraints (Desbarats 1983b). Moreover, models relying on revealed behavior restrict themselves to the domain of experience, and thus one must extrapolate beyond the observed types of spatial alternatives. That is, such models are ineffective in predicting an individual's level of satisfaction for an alternative with attribute levels outside the range of prior experience (Maclennan and Williams 1980).

As a result of these problems with the revealed preference paradigm, other researchers have argued for a more experimental approach, whereby simulated choice data are used to present a wider range of alternatives. Such an approach allows the researcher to make observations over repeated, experimentally controlled trials and to estimate parameters that are context-free. For example, information integration theory, or functional measurement, involves an algebraic model of human information processing (Anderson 1981, 1982; Louviere and Timmermans 1990a). Individuals assign values to levels of atrributes and then combine those values into an overall utility value. Analysis of variance is used to discriminate between the alternative functional forms and thus to uncover the underlying combination rules. Within the context of residential choice, Louviere and Meyer (1976) provide evidence for a combination rule involving linear averaging.

In a similar vein, the conjoint measurement approach also requires subjects to evaluate multiattribute alternatives by comparing predetermined levels of the supposedly important attributes (Phipps and Carter 1985). The subjective rankings of various combinations of these experimental levels are then decomposed into preference functions. For example, Knight and Menchik (1976) explored individual preferences for a variety of residential forms based on the evaluation of hypothetical levels of such attributes as distance between houses, view from the backyard, and price. In conjoint measurement, however, the subjects are simply asked to rank order the stimulus combinations, which is a less-demanding task than producing the numerical responses that are used in functional measurement. On the other hand, since conjoint measurement only involves ordinal-level data, its diagnostic value for identifying alternative composition rules is rather weak. In addition, a number of problems are associated with the experimental approach in general. First, the use of factorial designs restricts the number of attributes that can be easily processed by the subjects. Second, specifying appropriate levels of the attributes—deciding how the levels should be spaced—is problematic. Third and most important, decision-making under experimental conditions may well differ from decision-making in the real world (Timmermans 1984).

Given these disadvantages of working with experimental data, discrete choice models based upon observed behavior have become increasingly popular (Wrigley and Longley 1984; Deurloo, Dieleman, and Clark 1988; Maier and Weiss 1991). Researchers have contributed to this literature in at least three major areas: microeconomic theories of consumer behavior, psychological theories of choice, and new statistical methods for analyzing categorical data (Clark, Deurloo, and Dieleman 1988). Discrete multivariate analysis allows a large number of parameters to be estimated, including those for each of the category levels and those describing the interactions among them. These interactions are usually of central concern, although models containing third- or higher-order interactions are often extremely difficult to interpret (Alba 1987). The most that can be said in such situations is that the association structure is extremely complex. Whitney and Boots (1979) have used a log-linear modeling approach to assess the impact of selected household characteristics on residential mobility in the twin cities of Kitchener and Waterloo, Ontario. In a similar vein, Segal (1979) has provided an example of log-linear modeling in the context of neighborhood choice, and Friedman (1981), Boehm (1982), and Fischer and Aufhauser (1988) have used multinomial logit models.

To date, most decision-making models have been compensatory, in the sense that individuals are assumed to trade off attributes. An alternative perspective, however, suggests that a low value on one attribute cannot be compensated for by a high value on another attribute. Although there are a variety of such non-compensatory choice models, the major ones for discrete choice modeling have been the elimination-by-aspects (EBA) models proposed by Tversky (1972). Such models treat decision-making as a process of elimination and so do not require the simultaneous consideration of every attribute for every alternative. Rather, the important attributes are considered sequentially. At each stage the individual selects a particular attribute, and all the alternatives which do not possess that attribute are eliminated. The decision is thus decomposed into a series of steps, and individuals can eliminate a large number of alternatives after only a few attributes have been considered. The decision-maker selects one aspect, or attribute, and then eliminates all alternatives that are unsatisfactory with respect to that single attribute. Then a second attribute is chosen, and so on, until only one alternative remains. In this way the decision-maker is not expected to integrate all the pertinent information before arriving at one ultimate decision.

For example, within the context of residential mobility we can hypothesize at least two such steps. First, the household will collect information to help select an appropriate neighborhood. Second, the household will obtain information in order to choose a specific house within that neighborhood. Using data from Syracuse, New York, Talarchek (1982) found that the behavioral patterns of residential search and selection are highly individualized but that the sequence in which information is acquired does indicate a general two-stage process of the kind just described. When investigating the locational choice process of some new residents in Melbourne, Australia, Young (1984) also found that the elimination-by-aspects model provided an acceptable statistical fit to the data. Such success is not achieved without cost, however, as the elimination-by-aspects approach involves estimating a large number of parameters.

A wide range of approaches, therefore, have been used to address the issue of residential choice. No single approach, however, has successfully captured the potential complexity of this process. In particular, insufficient attention has been given to identifying possible interaction effects among the constituent attributes. Such interaction effects were the focus of a study by the present author (Cadwallader 1992), in which log-linear procedures were used to calibrate a variety of decision-making models, using the previously described data on Madison, Wisconsin.

Regression analysis is the most convenient methodology for identifying possible interaction effects. If two variables interact in their effect upon some response variable, then the effect of either explanatory variable on the response variable depends on the value of the other explanatory variable. That is, the variables X_1 and X_2 interact in the determination of a third variable Y if the effect of X_1 on Y depends upon the level of X_2. Similarly, the effect of X_2 on Y will depend on the level of X_1. For example, a common type of theoretical situation involves the assumption that a given phenomenon will occur when both factors are present but that it is unlikely to occur whenever either of these factors is absent (Blalock 1965). If we have three continous variables, with Y representing neighborhood attractiveness, then such a situation arises when we postulate that Y values will be large only when both X_1 and X_2 are large and that Y values will be small if either X_1 or X_2 approaches zero.

The presence or absence of this interaction effect is usually tested by including product terms as additional variables in a multiple regression model (Allison 1977). For example, the three-variable case described above would generate the following equation:

$$Y = a + b_1X_1 + b_2X_2 + b_3X_1X_2 \qquad (6.7)$$

where b_3 is the coefficient associated with the product of variables X_1 and X_2. The necessity of including the interaction term can be assessed by using the t statistic to test the null hypothesis that b is zero. If b_3 is significantly different from zero, then the interaction should be included.

A comparable test for interaction effects involves comparing the complete and reduced models by using the F statistic (Agresti and Agresti 1979:383–85). A model with three independent variables, containing all possible first-order interactions, would have the following form:

$$Y = a + b_1X_1 + b_2X_2 + b_3X_3 + b_4X_1X_2 + b_5X_1X_3 + b_6X_2X_3 \qquad (6.8)$$

In order to test the hypothesis of no first-order interaction, this model would be compared with the following reduced model:

$$Y = a + b_1X_1 + b_2X_2 + b_3X_3 \qquad (6.9)$$

We are thus testing the null hypothesis that the coefficients b_4, b_5, and b_6 are all zero.

The F test statistic can be expressed via the coefficients of multiple determination for the two models, as follows:

$$F = \frac{(R_c^2 - R_r^2)/(k - g)}{(1 - R_c^2)/[n - (k + 1)]} \qquad (6.10)$$

where R_c^2 refers to the complete model and R_r^2 refers to the reduced model; k and g represent the number of independent variables in the complete and reduced models, respectively; and $(k - g)$ and $[n - (k + 1)]$ are the associated degrees of freedom. If the calculated value of this statistic for a given sample is significant when compared with the tabulated F distribution, then we infer that interaction is present. So, while the t test can be used for individual coefficients, the complete-versus-reduced model F test can be used to test a number of regression parameters simultaneously, in order to decide if any of them are nonzero.

In the present example, there are three independent variables, representing the three evaluative scales, for each of the three neighborhoods. The reduced models, those without any interaction terms, all fit the data reasonably well (table 6.11). As expected, all the coefficients

Table 6.11. The standardized regression models

Indian Hills
Attractiveness = .139 park facilities* + .185 distinctiveness** + .373 reputation***
$R^2 = .267$

Middleton
Attractiveness = .150 distinctiveness* + .253 spaciousness*** + .315 location***
$R^2 = .237$

Hilldale
Attractiveness = .276 housing*** + .279 distinctiveness*** + .266 quiet***
$R^2 = .415$

Note: * indicates signifiance at .10; **, significance at .05; and ***, significance at .01.

are positive, indicating that an increase in any individual attribute leads to an increase in overall attractiveness. In addition, most of the coefficients are different from zero at the .01 significance level. These reduced models were then compared with complete models containing all three first-order interaction terms. The results were inconclusive, as the *t* tests on individual coefficients suggested some interaction effects for Indian Hills and Middleton, but the F test described in equation 6.10 was insignificant for all three neighborhoods.

For a number of reasons, however, the use of multiple regression to analyze statistical interaction can prove problematic (Fisher 1988). First, some hypotheses concerning interaction cannot be meaningfully tested unless the variables are measured on ratio scales (Allison 1977). Second, in equations containing interaction terms, the partial correlations and standarized regression coefficients cannot be interpreted, and thus it becomes misleading to evaluate the relative importance of the main effects and interaction effects (Marsden 1981). For example, given the functional relationship between the interaction term and its constituent variables, it is not possible to hold X_1 and X_2 constant while investigating the effect of X_1X_2. Third, the use of regression models to identify interaction is especially difficult when measurement error occurs in one or more of the variables (Bohrnstedt and Marwell 1977). In particular, the reliability of the cross-products term can be low even when the constituent variables have high reliability. For these reasons, the present author (Cadwallader 1992) undertook further analysis, using a series of log-linear models. These models involved converting the seven-point rating scales into dichotomous categories, indicating either a low or a high value for each neighborhood on each particular scale, as perceived by individual subjects.

Regression analysis is not appropriate for analyzing categorical data, as the observations are not drawn from populations that are normally distributed with constant variance. A special class of statistical techniques, called log-linear models, however, has recently been developed for the analysis of such data (Wrigley 1985). Log-linear models can be used to identify the relationships among a set of categorical variables when the aim is to predict the number of cases in each cell of a multidimensional contingency table. More specifically, a linear model represents the log of the frequencies in each cell as a function of the various combinations of the categorical variables. The smaller the difference between the predicted and observed frequencies, the better the model fits the data. In a sense, log-linear models are similar to multiple regression models; the dependent variable is the number of cases in each cell of the contingency table, and the categorical variables function as independent variables.

A saturated model, which contains all main effects and interaction terms, will exactly reproduce all the observed cell frequencies. That is, it will fit the data perfectly. But a log-linear model with as many parameters as there are cells does not constitute a parsimonious description of the relationships among the variables. Rather, models should be identified that contain as few parameters as possible, while still providing an adequate fit to the data. For example, models that do not contain higher-order interaction terms are usually preferable, as such terms are often difficult to interpret. Although it is possible to delete any particular term from a saturated model, most researchers tend to focus on the so-called hierarchical models. In a hierarchical model, if a term exists for the interaction of a group of variables, then lower-order terms must also exist for all possible combinations of those variables. Thus, if the interaction term ABC is included in a three-variable model, then the terms A, B, C, AB, AC, and BC must also be included.

The likelihood-ratio chi-square statistic can be used to assess the goodness-of-fit associated with competing hierarchical models. The degrees of freedom for a particular model are calculated by subtracting the number of independent parameters from the number of cells in the contingency table. Small values of chi-square indicate a good-fitting model (for a saturated model the chi-square statistic is always zero). Alternatively, in those instances where the observed significance level associated with the chi-square statistic is very small, the model can be rejected. The likelihood-ratio statistic can also be used to assess the contribution of individual terms, as the decrease in value of this statistic when a particular term is added to a model indicates the relative contribution of that term. In other words, two models differing only in the presence of a particular effect can be fit to the data; the difference between the two likelihood-ratio chi-square values, called a partial chi-

Table 6.12. Tests of hypotheses that particular k-way effects are zero

		Likelihood-ratio chi-square and probability level		
k	$d.f.$	Indian Hills	Middleton	Hilldale
1	4	154.55 (.000)	172.84 (.000)	69.84 (.000)
2	6	38.45 (.000)	26.20 (.000)	107.81 (.000)
3	4	1.41 (.842)	1.48 (.831)	1.71 (.789)
4	1	3.05 (.081)	0.09 (.766)	5.23 (.022)

Source: Cadwallader 1992: table 1.

square, also has a chi-square distribution and can thus be used to test the hypothesis that the effect is zero.

In the present instance, the saturated model for each of the three neighborhoods can be expressed as follows:

$$\log_e m_{ijkl} = \lambda + \lambda_i^A + \lambda_j^B + \lambda_k^C + \lambda_l^D + \lambda_{ij}^{AB} + \lambda_{ik}^{AC} + \lambda_{il}^{AD} + \lambda_{jk}^{BC} + \lambda_{jl}^{BD}$$
$$+ \lambda_{kl}^{CD} + \lambda_{ijk}^{ABC} + \lambda_{ijl}^{ABD} + \lambda_{ikl}^{ACD} + \lambda_{jkl}^{BCD} + \lambda_{ijkl}^{ABCD} \qquad (6.11)$$

Where m_{ijkl} is the expected frequency of the $ijkl$ cell; λ is the grand mean; A–D are main effects; AB–CD are two-way interaction effects; ABC–BCD are three-way interaction effects; and $ABCD$ is a four-way interaction effect. Such a model would, of course, fit the data perfectly, as a saturated model has as many parameters as there are cells in the four-dimensional contingency table. To obtain a more parsimonious model while still maintaining an adequate fit to the observed data, we must eliminate those parameters which are not necessary to describe the structural relationships among the four variables in the contingency table (Wrigley 1985:173).

With this aim in mind, it is often useful to test whether interaction terms of a particular order are zero. Table 6.12 provides results for the tests that first-, second-, third-, or fourth-order interaction effects are zero, for each neighborhood. For example, the test that third-order effects are zero is based on the difference between the likelihood-ratio chi-square for a model without third-order terms and that for a model with third-order terms. If the observed probability level is large, it means that the hypothesis that third-order terms are zero cannot be rejected. In the present case, it can be seen that first- and second-order terms should be included in the final model for each neighborhood but that the third- and fourth-order interactions are not significantly different from zero at the .05 level. The only exception is Hilldale, where the fourth-order interaction term is significantly different from zero.

While the results in table 6.12 indicate the overall importance of

Table 6.13. The partial chi-squares for Indian Hills

Effect	Partial chi-square	Probability
ARD	.273	.601
ARP	.892	.345
ADP	.124	.725
RDP	.654	.419
AR	8.936	.003
AD	8.567	.003
AP	2.144	.143
RD	5.616	.018
RP	.402	.526
DP	.701	.403
A	40.740	.000
R	24.718	.000
D	67.702	.000
P	21.394	.000

Source: Cadwallader 1992: table 2.
Note: A represents attractiveness; *R*, reputation;
D, distinctiveness; and *P*, park facilities.

effects of various orders, they do not test the individual terms. In many instances, even if the hypothesis that all second-order terms are zero is rejected, not all second-order terms will be needed for a parsimonious description of the data. In this context, partial chi-squares can be used to assess the contribution of individual terms. A partial chi-square is the difference between the likelihood-ratio chi-square values for two models that differ only with respect to the presence or absence of the effect to be tested. For example, to test the partial association of variables *A* and *B*, the complete second-order model would be fitted, and then the same model without the *AB* interaction term would also be fitted. The difference in the chi-square value for these two models represents the partial chi-square associated with the second-order interaction *AB* (Wrigley 1985:197).

In the present instance, partial test statistics were computed for each term in the saturated log-linear model. When the partial values are small, with correspondingly high probability levels, it means that those particular effects are not necessary to adequately represent the data. For Indian Hills (table 6.13), as expected from the testing of particular *k*-way effects, none of the third-order terms are significantly different from zero. Three of the six second-order effects are significant, however, as are the four main effects. Similarly, for Middleton (table 6.14) the third-order effects are all insignificant, but two of the second-order effects and three of the first-order effects are significantly differ-

Table 6.14. The partial chi-squares for Middleton

Effect	Partial chi-square	Probability
ALS	.254	.614
ALD	.012	.915
ASD	1.221	.269
LSD	.164	.686
AL	11.599	.001
AS	6.168	.013
AD	.929	.335
LS	.020	.889
LD	.541	.462
SD	2.303	.129
A	47.957	.000
L	18.327	.000
S	1.998	.158
D	104.560	.000

Note: A represents attractiveness; *L*, location;
S, spaciousness; and *D*, distinctiveness.

ent from zero. Finally, the partial chi-squares for Hilldale (table 6.15) indicate the presence of four second-order effects and four main effects.

Stepwise selection strategies can also be used to identify the most appropriate model. Starting with a saturated model, a backwards elimination procedure can be used to successively delete the various inter-

Table 6.15. The partial chi-squares for Hilldale

Effect	Partial chi-square	Probability
AHD	.009	.926
AHQ	.083	.774
ADQ	.841	.359
HDQ	.230	.632
AH	9.032	.003
AD	5.653	.017
AQ	13.326	.000
HD	2.344	.126
HQ	11.516	.001
DQ	2.214	.137
A	5.839	.016
H	3.052	.081
D	55.896	.000
Q	5.057	.025

Note: A represents attractiveness; *H*, housing;
D, distinctiveness; and *Q*, quiet.

action parameters. For example, if only the saturated model adequately fits the data, then the model selection procedure stops at this point. Otherwise, terms are deleted in a hierarchical fashion. At the first step, the interaction term whose removal results in the least significant change in the likelihood-ratio chi-square statistic is deleted, as long as the observed significance level is larger than the criterion for remaining in the model. In the present context, a significance level of .05 was used as the cutoff for remaining in the model. This cutoff meant that for Hilldale the analysis stopped with the saturated model, as the fourth-order interaction could not be deleted.

The final acceptable model for Indian Hills was as follows:

$$\log_e m_{ijkl} = \lambda + \lambda_i^A + \lambda_j^R + \lambda_k^D + \lambda_l^P + \lambda_{ij}^{AR} + \lambda_{ik}^{AD} + \lambda_{jk}^{RD} \qquad (6.12)$$
$$L.R. \; X^2 = 6.889 \quad d.f. = 8 \quad P = .549$$

where $L.R.$ X^2 is the likelihood-ratio chi-square statistic, $d.f.$ is the degrees of freedom, and P is the associated probability level. This model contains all four main effects, plus the second-order interactions involving attractiveness and distinctiveness, attractiveness and reputation, and reputation and distinctiveness. It thus contains all the terms indicated by the analysis of partial chi-squares. The absence of any three-variable interaction parameters implies that when two variables are associated, that association is unaffected by the level of a third variable. Similarly, the final acceptable model for Middleton contained the following terms:

$$\log_e m_{ijkl} = \lambda + \lambda_i^A + \lambda_j^L + \lambda_k^S + \lambda_l^D + \lambda_{ij}^{AL} + \lambda_{ik}^{AS} \qquad (6.13)$$
$$L.R. \; X^2 = 7.154 \quad d.f. = 9 \quad P = .621$$

Again, there are no third-order effects, but there are two second-order effects, involving attractiveness and location and attractiveness and space, and all four main effects. Also, as with Indian Hills, this is the same model for Middleton that was suggested by the partial chi-square analysis.

Thus far we have concentrated on describing the structural relationships among all four categorical variables. An alternative approach involves treating neighborhood attractiveness as a response variable, with the remaining three variables being explanatory. This distinction between response and explanatory variables generates a set of log-linear models that are simply a special case of the general class of log-

Table 6.16. Hierarchical log-linear models with attractiveness as a response variable for Indian Hills

Model	Likelihood-ratio chi-square	Degrees of freedom	Probability
1 *RDP + A*	29.976	7	.000
2 *RDP + AR*	14.289	6	.027
3 *RDP + AD*	15.294	6	.018
4 *RDP + AP*	28.293	6	.000
5 *RDP + AR + AD*	6.209	5	.286
6 *RDP + AR + AP*	12.632	5	.027
7 *RDP + AD + AP*	13.001	5	.023
8 *RDP + AR + AD + AP*	4.125	4	.389
9 *RDP + ARD*	6.112	4	.191
10 *RDP + ARP*	12.115	4	.017
11 *RDP + ADP*	12.910	4	.012
12 *RDP + ARD + AP*	3.968	3	.265
13 *RDP + ARP + AD*	3.427	3	.330
14 *RDP + ADP + AR*	4.108	3	.250
15 *RDP + ARD + ARP*	3.177	2	.204
16 *RDP + ARD + ADP*	3.946	2	.139
17 *RDP + ARP + ADP*	3.327	2	.189
18 *RDP + ARD + ARP + ADP*	3.054	1	.081

Source: Cadwallader 1992: table 3.
Note: Notation is the same as in table 6.13.

linear models we have considered thus far (Wrigley 1985:216–23). In other words, the same principles of parameter estimation, hierarchical structure, and model selection also apply to this more-restricted set of models.

In models that imply a distinction between respone and explanatory variables, the structural relationships between the explanatory variables are treated as given and are automatically included in all the models (Fingleton 1981). For example, in the present context we are analyzing four-dimensional tables in which variable A is the response variable and the remaining three variables, B, C, and D, are explanatory. In any model, then, we must automatically include the interaction BCD and all its lower-order relatives: BC, BD, CD, B, C, and D. That is, these parameters cannot be excluded from any of the models, irrespective of their statistical significance. In this way, all of our attention during the process of model selection is focused on the parameters associated with the relationship between the response and explanatory variables.

The hierarchical structure of log-linear models for this situation can be seen in table 6.16, which describes the results for Indian Hills. The first and simplest model states that the response variable A is independent of the explanatory variables *RDP*, and it obviously does not provide a very good fit to the data. Rather, in this case the most likely candiates for best model are models 5, 8, and 13. If more than one model provides an acceptable fit to the data, it has been suggested that the best model is the simplest model which fits the data adequately and to which no single parameter can be added which provides a significant improvement in fit (Upton and Fingleton 1979). In other words, one can calculate the difference in the likelihood-ratio chi-square for each additional parameter.

As neither Model 8 nor Model 13 involves a significant improvement over Model 5, Model 5 is the chosen model. This model contains interactions between attractiveness and reputation, and attractiveness and distinctiveness. In its full form this model is represented as follows:

$$\log_e m_{ijkl} = \lambda + \lambda_j^R + \lambda_k^D + \lambda_l^P + \lambda_{jk}^{RD} + \lambda_{jl}^{RP} + \lambda_{kl}^{DP} + \lambda_{jkl}^{RDP} \qquad (6.14)$$
$$+ \lambda_i^A + \lambda_{ij}^{AR} + \lambda_{ik}^{AD}$$

This formulation is different from that shown in equation 6.12, of course, as it is constrained to include the interaction *RDP* and its lower-order relatives. More important, both equations contain the same interactions involving the response variable, neighborhood attractiveness. It should be remembered, however, that Model 13, which suggests a third-order interaction between attractiveness, reputation, and park facilities, also provides an acceptable fit to the data.

For Middleton (table 6.17), again a number of models fit the data adequately. In particular, models 5, 8, 14, and 16 are the best models associated with different degrees of freedom. Of these, Model 5 is the most parsimonious, and none of the other models exhibit a significant improvement of fit for each additional parameter. In its full form the chosen model is represented as follows:

$$\log_e m_{ijkl} = \lambda + \lambda_j^L + \lambda_k^S + \lambda_l^D + \lambda_{jk}^{LS} + \lambda_{jl}^{LD} + \lambda_{kl}^{SD} + \lambda_{jkl}^{LSD} \qquad (6.15)$$
$$+ \lambda_i^A + \lambda_{ij}^{AL} + \lambda_{ik}^{AS}$$

This structure is the same as that in equation 6.13, except that it is constrained to include the third-order interaction between the explanatory variables *LSD* and its lower-order relatives. Again, however, there is confirmation of the two second-order interactions involving the response variable, that is, attractiveness and location, and attractiveness

Table 6.17. Hierarchical log-linear models with attractiveness as a response variable for Middleton

Model	Likelihood-ratio chi-square	Degrees of freedom	Probability
1 *LSD* + *A*	22.432	7	.002
2 *LSD* + *AL*	9.512	6	.147
3 *LSD* + *AS*	14.738	6	.022
4 *LSD* + *AD*	19.671	6	.003
5 *LSD* + *AL* + *AS*	2.463	5	.782
6 *LSD* + *AL* + *AD*	7.702	5	.173
7 *LSD* + *AS* + *AD*	13.133	5	.022
8 *LSD* + *AL* + *AS* + *AD*	1.551	4	.818
9 *LSD* + *ALS*	2.217	4	.696
10 *LSD* + *ALD*	7.699	4	.103
11 *LSD* + *ADS*	12.132	4	.016
12 *LSD* + *ALS* + *AD*	1.332	3	.722
13 *LSD* + *ALD* + *AS*	1.542	3	.673
14 *LSD* + *ADS* + *AL*	.348	3	.951
15 *LSD* + *ALS* + *ALD*	1.310	2	.519
16 *LSD* + *ALS* + *ADS*	.100	2	.951
17 *LSD* + *ALD* + *ADS*	.342	2	.843
18 *LSD* + *ALS* + *ALD* + *ADS*	.088	1	.767

Source: Cadwallader 1992: table 4.
Note: Notation is the same as in table 6.14.

and spaciousness. As with Indian Hills, however, models for Middleton containing higher-order interactions involving attractiveness also provide acceptable fits to the data.

Finally, for Hilldale (table 6.18), as implied by the previous stepwise analysis, none of the models provide exceptionally good fits to the data. Model 8, perhaps the best, contains second-order interactions between attractiveness and each of the explanatory variables. This model is represented as follows:

$$\log_e m_{ijkl} = \lambda + \lambda_j^H + \lambda_k^D + \lambda_l^Q + \lambda_{jk}^{HD} + \lambda_{jl}^{HQ} + \lambda_{kl}^{DQ} + \lambda_{jkl}^{HDQ} \quad (6.16)$$
$$+ \lambda_i^A + \lambda_{ij}^{AH} + \lambda_{ik}^{AD} + \lambda_{il}^{AQ}$$

It is noteworthy that the second-order interactions involving attractiveness were also suggested by the partial chi-squares (table 6.15). The results for models 12–14 again suggest, however, the possibility of third-order effects when attractiveness is treated as a response variable.

The purpose of this discussion has been to address the issue of interaction effects in models of residential choice. Both regression and

Table 6.18. Hierarchical log-linear models with attractiveness as a response variable for Hilldale

Model	Likelihood-ratio chi-square	Degrees of freedom	Probability
1 *HDQ + A*	60.863	7	.000
2 *HDQ + AH*	29.390	6	.000
3 *HDQ + AD*	41.439	6	.000
4 *HDQ + AQ*	23.784	6	.001
5 *HDQ + AH + AD*	19.623	5	.001
6 *HDQ + AH + AQ*	11.951	5	.035
7 *HDQ + AD + AQ*	15.329	5	.009
8 *HDQ + AH + AD + AQ*	6.256	4	.181
9 *HDQ + AHD*	19.382	4	.001
10 *HDQ + AHQ*	11.743	4	.019
11 *HDQ + ADQ*	13.715	4	.008
12 *HDQ + AHD + AQ*	6.188	3	.103
13 *HDQ + AHQ + AD*	6.110	3	.106
14 *HDQ + ADQ + AH*	5.328	3	.149
15 *HDQ + AHD + AHQ*	6.070	2	.048
16 *HDQ + AHD + ADQ*	5.310	2	.070
17 *HDQ + AHQ + ADQ*	5.236	2	.073
18 *HDQ + AHD + AHQ + ADQ*	5.228	1	.022

Source: Cadwallader 1992: table 5.
Note: Notation is the same as in table 6.15.

log-linear approaches were used for this purpose, although the log-linear models provided a more detailed analysis of the data. As a result of calibrating a variety of models, one can suggest that interaction effects might well play a role in the residential decision-making process but that such effects will generally involve only lower-order terms. At the very least, however, those researchers undertaking empirical investigations of residential choice should be alert to the possibility of significant interaction effects.

An obvious extension of the approach used here involves the construction of structural equation models. When using continuous data, structural equation models allow one to quantify the direct and indirect effects of predetermined variables on endogenous variables (Cadwallader 1986b). Goodman's (1979) suggestions about how causal interpretations might be imposed on systems of discrete variables by the use of log-linear or logit approaches have not met with universal acceptance, however. In particular, the assignment of numerical values to the causal arrows in the path diagram has proved problematic. First, it has been argued that there is no calculus of path coefficients to calculate the magnitude of effects along indirect paths (Fienberg 1980:120). Second, variables with multiple categories will lead to a variety of estimated path coefficients for a given arrow in the path diagram. Third, the presence of higher-order interaction terms in log-linear models can lead to very complex path diagrams.

Recently, however, considerable progress has been made in the treatment of causal models containing discrete variables. Winship and Mare (1983) present several alternative approaches to the formulation of structural equation models for discrete data and demonstrate that such models can be as analytically flexible as their continuous counterparts. In particular, they show how direct and indirect effects can be calculated by applying Stolzenberg's (1979) methods for the analysis of nonlinear models in general. Although they consider only recursive models with two-category variables, their approach can be extended to systems involving simultaneity and ordered response variables. To date, however, no reliable computer program exists for the maximum-likelihood estimation of structural equations with discrete data that matches the flexibility of LISREL for continuous variables (Cadwallader 1987).

References

Index

References

Abler, R.; Adams, J. S.; and Gould, P. 1971. *Spatial organization: The geographer's view of the world.* Englewood Cliffs, N.J.: Prentice-Hall.

Abu-Lughod, J., and Foley, M. M. 1960. The consumer votes by moving. In *Housing choices and housing constraints,* ed. N. N. Foote, J. Abu-Lughod, M. M. Foley, and L. Winnick, 134–78. New York: McGraw-Hill.

Adams, J. S. 1970. Residential structure of midwestern cities. *Annals of the Association of American Geographers* 60:37–62.

Adams, J. S., and Gilder, K. A. 1976. Household location and intra-urban migration. In *Social areas in cities,* vol. 1, *Spatial processes and forms,* ed. D. T. Herbert and R. J. Johnston, 159–92. New York: Wiley.

Agnew, J., and Duncan, J. 1981. The transfer of ideas into Anglo-American geography. *Progress in Human Geography* 5:42–57.

Agresti, A., and Agresti, B. 1979. *Statistical methods for the social sciences.* San Francisco: Dellen.

Alba, R. 1987. Interpreting the parameters of log-linear models. *Sociological Methods and Research* 16:45–77.

Alexander, S. 1983. A model of population change with new and return migration. *Environment and Planning A* 15:1231–57.

Allison, P. 1977. Testing for interaction in multiple regression. *American Journal of Sociology* 83:144–53.

Allison, P. 1984. *Event history analysis: Regression for longitudinal event data.* Beverly Hills: Sage.

Almon, S. 1965. The distributed lag between capital appropriations and expenditures. *Econometrica* 33:178–96.

Alonso, W. 1964. The historic and structural theories of urban form: Their implications for urban renewal. *Land Economics* 40:227–31.

Alperovich, G. 1983. Lagged response in intra-urban migration of home owners. *Regional Studies* 17:297–304.

Alperovich, G.; Bergsman, J.; and Ehemann, C. 1977. An econometric model of migration between U.S. metropolitan areas. *Urban Studies* 14:135–45.

Althauser, R. 1971. Multicollinearity and non-additive regression models. In *Causal models in the social sciences*, ed. H. Blalock, Jr., 453–72. Chicago: Aldine.

Alwin, D., and Hauser, R. 1981. The decomposition of effects in path analysis. In *Linear models in social research*, ed. P. V. Marsden, 123–40. Beverly Hills: Sage.

Amrhein, C. G. 1985. Interregional labor migration and information flows. *Environment and Planning A* 17:1111–26.

Anderson, N. H. 1974. Algebraic models in perception. In *Psychophysical judgment and measurement*, vol. 2 of *Handbook of Perception*, ed. E. C. Carterette and M. P. Friedman, 215–98. New York: Academic Press.

Anderson, N. H. 1981. *Foundations of information integration theory*. New York: Academic Press.

Anderson, N. H. 1982. *Methods of information integration theory*. New York: Academic Press.

Archer, M. S. 1982. Morphogenesis versus structuration: On combining structure and action. *British Journal of Sociology* 33:455–83.

Asher, H. B. 1976. *Causal modeling*. Beverly Hills: Sage.

Baerwald, T. J. 1981. The site selection process of suburban residential builders. *Urban Geography* 2:339–57.

Baird, J. C. 1970. *Psychophysical analysis of visual space*. New York: Pergamon Press.

Baird, J. C.; Wagner, M.; and Noma, E. 1982. Impossible cognitive spaces. *Geographical Analysis* 14:204–16.

Ballard, K., and Clark, G. 1981. The short-run dynamics of inter-state migration: A space-time economic adjustment model of in-migration to fast growing states. *Regional Studies* 15:213–28.

Baran, P., and Sweezy, P. 1966. *Monopoly capital*. Harmondsworth, Eng.: Penguin.

Barber, G. M., and Milne, W. J. 1988. Modelling internal migration in Kenya: An econometric analysis with limited data. *Environment and Planning A* 20:1185–96.

Barff, R. A. 1989. Migration and labor supply in New England. *Geoforum* 20:293–301.

Barff, R. A. 1990. The migration response to the economic turnaround in New England. *Environment and Planning A* 22:1497–516.

Barrett, F. 1976. The search process in residential relocation. *Environment and Behavior* 8:169–98.

Barsby, S. L., and Cox, D. R. 1975. *Interstate migration of the elderly: An economic analysis*. Lexington, Mass.: Lexington Books.

Bassett, K., and Short, J. R. 1980. *Housing and residential structure: Alternative approaches*. Boston: Routledge and Kegan Paul.

Becker, G. S. 1964. *Human capital*. New York: Columbia University Press.

Bell, D. N. F., and Kirwan, F. X. 1979. Return migration in a Scottish context. *Regional Studies* 13:101–11.

Bell, W. 1955. Economic, family, and ethnic status: An empirical test. *American Sociological Review* 20:45–52.

Bentler, P. 1980. Multivariate analysis with latent varibles: Causal modeling. *Annual Review of Psychology* 31:419–56.

Bentler, P. 1982. Linear systems with multiple levels and types of latent variables. In *Systems under indirect observation*, pt. 1, ed. K. Jöreskog and H. Wold, 101–30. Amsterdam: North-Holland.

Bentler, P., and Weeks, D. 1980. Linear structural equations with latent variables. *Psychometrika* 45:289–308.

Berry, B. J. L. 1968. A synthesis of formal and functional regions using a general field theory of spatial behavior. In *Spatial analysis: A reader in statistical geography*, ed. B. J. L. Berry and D. F. Marble, 419–28. Englewood Cliffs, N.J.: Prentice-Hall.

Bielby, W., and Hauser, R. 1977. Structural equation models. *Annual Review of Sociology* 3:137–61.

Blalock, H. M., Jr. 1964. *Causal inferences in nonexperimental research*. Chapel Hill: University of North Carolina Press.

Blalock, H. M., Jr. 1965. Theory building and the concept of interaction. *American Sociological Review* 30:374–81.

Blalock, H. M., Jr. 1969. *Theory construction: From verbal to mathematical formulations*. Englewood Cliffs, N.J.: Prentice-Hall.

Blaug, M. 1976. The empirical status of human capital theory: A slightly jaundiced view. *Journal of Economic Literature* 14:827–55.

Blumner, S. M., and Johnson, V. M. 1975. The effects of selected variables on housing values in Pomona, California. *Geographical Analysis* 7:303–10.

Boehm, T. 1982. A hierarchical model of housing choice. *Urban Studies* 19:17–31.

Bohrnstedt, G., and Marwell, G. 1977. The reliability of products of two random variables. In *Sociological methodology, 1978*, ed. K. Schuessler, 254–73. San Francisco: Jossey-Bass.

Boomsma, A. 1982. The robustness of LISREL against small sample sizes in factor analysis models. In *Systems under indirect observation*, pt. 1, ed. K. Jöreskog and H. Wold, 149–73. Amsterdam: North-Holland.

Borchert, J. 1983. Instability in American metropolitan growth. *Geographical Review* 73:127–49.

Borts, G. H., and Stein, J. L. 1964. *Economic growth in a free market*. New York: Columbia University Press.

Bourne, L. S. 1976. Housing supply and housing market behavior in residential development. In *Social areas in cities*, vol. 1, *Spatial processes and form*, ed. D. T. Herbert and R. J. Johnston, 111–58. New York: Wiley.

Bourne, L. S. 1981. *The geography of housing*. New York: Wiley.

Bourne, L. S., and Murdie, R. A. 1972. Interrelationships of social and physical space: A multivariate analysis of metropolitan Toronto. *Canadian Geographer* 16:211–29.

Boyce, R. R. 1969. Residential mobility and its implications for urban spatial change. *Proceedings of the Association of American Geographers* 1:22–26.

Bradbury, J. 1985. Regional and industrial restructuring processes in the new international division of labor. *Progress in Human Geography* 9:38–63.

Browett, J. 1984. On the necessity and inevitability of uneven development under capitalism. *International Journal of Urban and Regional Research* 8:155–77.

Brown, K. 1981. Race, class and culture: Towards a theorization of the "choice/constraint" concept. In *Social interaction and ethnic segregation*, ed. P. Jackson and S. J. Smith, 185–203. Institute of British Geographers Special Publication no. 12. London: Academic Press.

Brown, L. A. 1981. *Innovation diffusion: A new perspective*. New York: Methuen.

Brown, L. A., and Gustavus, S. 1977. Place attributes in a migration decision context. *Environment and Planning* 9:529–48.

Brown, L. A., and Holmes, J. 1971. Search behavior in an intra-urban migration context: A spatial perspective. *Environment and Planning* 3:307–26.

Brown, L. A., and Moore, E. G. 1971. The intra-urban migration process: A perspective. In *Internal structure of the city: Readings on space and environment*, ed. L. S. Bourne, 200–209. New York: Oxford University Press.

Brown, W. H., Jr. 1972. Access to housing: The role of the real estate industry. *Economic Geography* 48:66–78.

Browne, M. 1982. Covariance structures. In *Topics in applied multivariate analysis*, ed. D. Hawkins, 72–141. Cambridge: Cambridge University Press.

Brummell, A. C. 1981. A method of measuring residential stress. *Geographical Analysis* 13:248–61.

Bunge, M. 1959. *Causality*. Cambridge, Mass.: Harvard University Press.

Bunting, T., and Guelke, L., 1979. Behavioral and perception geography: A critical appraisal. *Annals of the Association of American Geographers* 69:448–62.

Burnley, I. H. 1988. Population turnaround and the peopling of the countryside?: Migration from Sydney to country districts of New South Wales. *Australian Geographer* 19:268–83.

Burns, L. 1982. Metropolitan growth in transition. *Journal of Urban Economics* 11:112–29.

Cadwallader, M. T. 1976. Cognitive distance in intraurban space. In *Environmental knowing: Theories, research, and methods*, ed. G. Moore and R. G. Golledge, 316–24. Stroudsburg, Pa.: Dowden, Hutchinson, and Ross.

Cadwallader, M. T. 1977. Frame dependency in cognitive maps: An analysis using directional statistics. *Geographical Analysis* 9:284–92.

Cadwallader, M. T. 1978. Urban information and preference surfaces: Their patterns, structures, and interrelationships. *Geografiska Annaler* 60B:97–106.

Cadwallader, M. T. 1979a. Neighborhood evaluation in residential mobility. *Environment and Planning A* 11:393–401.

Cadwallader, M. T. 1979b. Problems in cognitive distance: Implications for cognitive mapping. *Environment and Behavior* 11:559–76.

Cadwallader, M. T. 1979c. The process of neighborhood choice. Paper presented at the International Conference on Environmental Psychology, University of Surrey, Guildford, Eng.

Cadwallader, M. T. 1981a. Towards a cognitive gravity model: The case of consumer spatial behavior. *Regional Studies* 15:275–84.

Cadwallader, M. T. 1981b. A unified model of urban housing patterns, social patterns, and residential mobility. *Urban Geography* 2:115–30.

Cadwallader, M. T. 1982. Urban residential mobility: A simultaneous equations approach. *Transactions of the Institute of British Geographers,* n.s., 7:458–73.

Cadwallader, M. T. 1985a. *Analytical urban geography: Spatial patterns and theories.* Englewood Cliffs, N.J.: Prentice-Hall.

Cadwallader, M. T. 1985b. Structural equation models of migration: An example from the Upper Midwest USA. *Environment and Planning A* 17:101–13.

Cadwallader, M. T. 1986a. Migration and intra-urban mobility. In *Population geography: Progress and prospect,* ed. M. Pacione, 257–83. London: Croom Helm.

Cadwallader, M. T. 1986b. Structural equation models in human geography. *Progress in Human Geography* 10:24–47.

Cadwallader, M. T. 1987. Linear structural relationships with latent variables: The LISREL model. *Professional Geographer* 39:317–26.

Cadwallader, M. T. 1988. Urban geography and social theory. *Urban Geography* 9:227–51.

Cadwallader, M. T. 1989a. A conceptual framework for analysing migration behavior in the developed world. *Progress in Human Geography* 13:494–511.

Cadwallader, M. T. 1989b. A synthesis of macro and micro approaches to explaining migration: Evidence from inter-state migration in the United States. *Geografiska Annaler* 71B:85–94.

Cadwallader, M. T. 1991. Metropolitan growth and decline in the United States: An empirical analysis. *Growth and Change* 22:1–16.

Cadwallader, M. T. 1992. Log-linear models of residential choice. *Area* 24: in press.

Campbell, D. T., and Fiske, D. W. 1959. Convergent and discriminant validation by the multitrait-multimethod matrix. *Psychological Bulletin* 56:81–105.

Carmines, E. G. 1986. The analysis of covariance structure models. In *New tools for social scientists: Advances and applications in research methods,* ed W. D. Berry and M. S. Lewis-Beck, 23–55. Beverly Hills: Sage.

Castells, M. 1977. *The urban question: A Marxist approach.* London: Edward Arnold.

Castells, M. 1983. *The city and the grassroots: A cross-cultural theory of urban social movements.* London: Edward Arnold.

Cebula, R. J. 1974. Local government policies and migration: An analysis for SMSA's in the United States, 1965–70. *Public Choice* 19:85–93.

Cebula, R. J. 1979. *The determinants of human migration.* Lexington, Mass.: Lexington Books.

Cebula, R. J. 1980a. Geographic mobility and the cost of living: An explanatory note. *Urban Studies* 17:353–55.

Cebula, R. J. 1980b. Voting with one's feet: A critique of the evidence. *Regional Science and Urban Economics* 10:91–107.

Cebula, R. J. 1983. *Geographic living-cost differentials.* Lexington, Mass.: Lexington Books.

Chalmers, J. A., and Greenwood, M. J. 1977. Thoughts on the rural to urban migration turnaround. *International Regional Science Review* 2:167–70.

Chalmers, J. A., and Greenwood, M. J. 1985. The regional labor market adjustment process: Determinants of changes in rates of labor force participation, unemployment, and migration. *Annals of Regional Science* 19:1–17.

Chapin, F. S. 1974. *Human activity patterns in the city.* New York: Wiley.

Chatfield, C. 1984. *The analysis of time series: An introduction.* 3d ed. London: Chapman and Hall.

Chouinard, V.; Fincher, R.; and Webber, M. 1984. Empirical research in scientific human geography. *Progress in Human Geography* 8:347–80.

Clark, G. L. 1982a. Dynamics of interstate labor migration. *Annals of the Association of American Geographers* 72:297–313.

Clark, G. L. 1982b. Volatility in the geographical structure of U.S. interstate migration. *Environment and Planning A* 14:145–67.

Clark, G. L. 1983. *Interregional migration, national policy, and social justice.* Totowa, N.J.: Rowman and Allanheld.

Clark, G. L., and Ballard, K. P. 1980. Modeling out-migration from depressed regions: The significance of origin and destination characteristics. *Environment and Planning A* 12:799–812.

Clark, G. L., and Dear, M. 1984. *State apparatus: Structures and langauge of legitimacy.* Boston: Allen and Unwin.

Clark, G. L., and Gertler, M. 1983. Migration and capital. *Annals of the Association of American Geographers* 73:18–34.

Clark, W. A. V. 1971. A test of directional bias in residential mobility. In *Models of spatial variation,* ed. H. McConnell and D. W. Yaseen, 2–27. DeKalb: Northern Illinois University Press.

Clark, W. A. V. 1972. Behaviour and the constraints of spatial structure. *New Zealand Geographer* 28:171–80.

Clark, W. A. V. 1975. Locational stress and residential mobility in a New Zealand context. *New Zealand Geographer* 31:67–79.

Clark, W. A. V. 1976. Migration in Milwaukee. *Economic Geography* 52:171–80.

Clark, W. A. V. 1981a. On modelling search behavior. In *Dynamic spatial models,* ed. D. Griffith and R. MacKinnon, 102–31. Alphen aan den Rijn, Neth.: Sijthoff en Noordhoff.

Clark, W. A. V. 1981b. Residential mobility and behavioral geography: Parallelism or interdependence?" In *Behavioral problems in geography revisited,* ed. K. R. Cox and R. G. Golledge, 182–205. New York: Methuen.

Clark, W. A. V. ed. 1982a. *Modelling housing market search.* London: Croom Helm.

Clark, W. A. .V. 1982b. Recent research on migration and mobility: A review and interpretation. *Progress in Planning* 18:1–56.

Clark, W. A. V. 1982c. A revealed preference analysis of intraurban migration choices. In *Proximity and preference: Problems in the multidimensional analysis of large data sets,* ed. R. Golledge and J. Rayner, 144–68. Minneapolis: University of Minnesota Press.

Clark, W. A. V. 1986. *Human migration.* Beverly Hills: Sage.

Clark, W. A. V., and Avery, K. L. 1978. Patterns of migration: A macroanalytic case study. In *Geography and the urban environment,* vol. 1, ed. D. T. Herbert and R. J. Johnston, 135–96. Chichester, Eng.: Wiley.

Clark, W. A. V., and Burt, J. E. 1980. The impact of workplace on residential relocation. *Annals of the Association of American Geographers* 70:59–67.

Clark, W. A. V., and Cadwallader, M. T. 1973a. Locational stress and residential mobility. *Environment and Behavior* 5:29–41.

Clark, W. A. V., and Cadwallader, M. T. 1973b. Residential preferences: An alternate view of intraurban space. *Environment and Planning* 5:693–703.

Clark, W. A. V.; Deurloo, M. C.; and Dieleman, F. M. 1984. Housing consumption and residential mobility. *Annals of the Association of American Geographers* 74:29–43.

Clark, W. A. V.; Deurloo, M. C.; and Dieleman, F. M. 1986. Residential mobility in Dutch housing markets. *Environment and Planning A* 18:763–88.

Clark, W. A. V.; Deurloo, M. C.; and Dieleman, F. M. 1988. Modeling strategies for categorical data: Examples from housing and tenure choice. *Geographical Analysis* 20:198–219.

Clark, W. A. V., and Hosking, P. L. 1986. *Statistical methods for geographers.* New York: Wiley.

Clark, W. A. V., and Huff, J. O. 1977. Some empirical tests of duration-of-stay effects in intraurban migration. *Environment and Planning A* 9:1357–74.

Clark, W. A. V.; Huff, J. O.; and Burt, J. E. 1979. Calibrating a model of the decision to move. *Environment and Planning A* 11:689–704.

Clark, W. A. V., and Onaka, J. L. 1983. Life cycle and housing adjustment as explanations of residential mobility. *Urban Studies* 20:47–57.

Clark, W. A. V., and Smith, T. R. 1979. Modeling information use in a spatial context. *Annals of the Association of American Geographers* 69:575–88.

Clark, W. A. V., and Smith, T. R. 1982. Housing market search behavior and expected utility theory: 2. The process of search. *Environment and Planning A* 14:717–37.

Clark, W. A. V., and White, K. 1990. Modeling elderly mobility. *Environment and Planning A* 22:909–24.

Clayton, C. 1977a. Interstate population migration process and structure in the United States, 1935 to 1970. *Professional Geographer* 29:177–81.

Clayton, C. 1977b. The structure of interstate and interregional migration, 1965–1970. *Annals of Regional Science* 11:109–22.

Cliff, A. D.; Haggett, P.; Ord, J. K.; Bassett, K. A.; and Davies, R. B. 1975. *Elements of spatial structure: A quantitative approach.* Cambridge: Cambridge University Press.

Comrey, A. L. 1973. *A first course in factor analysis.* New York: Academic Press.

Congdon, P. 1988. The interdependence of geographical migration with job and housing mobility in London. *Regional Studies* 22:81–93.

Cordey-Hayes, M. 1978. Migration within a system of post-industrial cities. In *Systems of cities: Readings on structure, growth, and policy,* ed. L. S. Bourne and J. W. Simmons, 394–401. New York: Oxford University Press.

Costner, H. L. 1985. Theory, deduction, and rules of correspondence. In *Causal models in the social sciences,* 2d ed., ed. H. M. Blalock, Jr., 229–50. New York: Aldine.

Couclelis, H., and Golledge, R. G. 1983. Analytic research, positivism, and behavioral geography. *Annals of the Association of American Geographers* 73:331–39.

Cox, K. R. 1981. Bourgeois thought and the behavioral geography debate. In *Behavioral problems in geography revisited,* ed. K. R. Cox and R. G. Golledge, 256–79. New York: Methuen.

Cromartie, J., and Stack, C. 1989. Reinterpretation of black return and non-return migration to the South, 1975–1980. *Geographical Review* 79:297–310.

Cronin, F. J. 1982. Racial differences in the search for housing. In *Modelling housing market search,* ed. W. A. V. Clark, 81–105. London: Croom Helm.

Curran, C. 1977. Migration and welfare: An analysis of their relationship. *Indian Journal of Economics* 58:1–16.

Cushing, B. J. 1987a. Location-specific amenities, topography, and population migration. *Annals of Regional Science* 21:74–85.

Cushing, B. J. 1987b. A note on specification of climate variables in models of population migration. *Journal of Regional Science* 27:641–48.

Dahlberg, A., and Holmlund, B. 1978. The interaction of migration, income, and employment in Sweden. *Demography* 15:259–66.

Dahmann, D. C. 1986. Geographical mobility research with panel data. *Growth and Change* 17:35–48.

Darden, J. T. 1980. Lending practices and policies affecting the American metropolitan system. In *The American metropolitan system: Present and future,* ed. S. D. Brunn and J. O. Wheeler, 93–110. New York: Wiley.

DaVanzo, J. S. 1978. Does unemployment affect migration? Evidence from micro data. *Review of Economics and Statistics* 60:504–14.

DaVanzo, J. S. 1981. Microeconomic approaches to studying migration decisions. In *Migration decision making,* ed. G. F. DeJong and R. W. Gardner, 90–129. New York: Pergamon.

DaVanzo, J. S., and Morrison, P. A. 1981. Return and other sequences of migration in the United States. *Demography* 18:85–101.

Davies, R. B. 1991. The analysis of housing and migration careers. In *Migration models: Macro and micro approaches,* ed. J. Stillwell and P. Congdon, 207–27. London: Belhaven Press.

Davies, R. B., and Pickles, A. R. 1985. A panel study of life-cycle effects in residential mobility. *Geographical Analysis* 17:199–216.

Davies, W. 1984. *Factorial ecology.* Aldershot, Eng.: Gower.

Dawes, R. M., and Corrigan, B. 1974. Linear models in decision making. *Psychological Bulletin* 81:95–106.

Day, R. A., and Walmsley, D. J. 1981. Residential preferences in Sydney's inner suburbs: A study in diversity. *Applied Geography* 1:185–97.

Dear, M. J. 1986. Theory and object in political geography. *Political Geography Quarterly* 5:295–97.

Dear, M. J., and Moos, A. I. 1986. Structuration theory in urban analysis: 2. Empirical application. *Environment and Planning A* 18:351–73.

Demko, D. 1974. Cognition of southern Ontario cities in a potential migration context. *Economic Geography* 50:20–34.

Desbarats, J. M. 1977. Estimating external constraints to migration. *Professional Geographer* 29:283–89.

Desbarats, J. M. 1983a. Constrained choice and migration. *Geografiska Annaler* 65B:11–22.

Desbarats, J. M. 1983b. Spatial choice and constraints on behavior. *Annals of the Association of American Geographers* 73:340–57.

Deurloo, M. C.; Dieleman, F. M.; and Clark, W. A. V. 1988. Generalized log-linear models of housing choice. *Environment and Planning A* 20:55–69.

Deutscher, T. 1982. Issues in data collection and reliability in marketing multidimensional scaling studies: Implications for large stimulus sets. In *Proximity and preference: Problems in the multidimensional analysis of large data sets,* ed. R. G. Golledge and J. N. Rayner, 272–88. Minneapolis: University of Minnesota Press.

Dhrymes, P. J. 1971. *Distributed lags: Problems of estimation and formulation.* San Francisco: Holden-Day.

Dierx, A. H. 1988a. Estimation of a human capital model of migration. *Annals of Regional Science* 22:99–110.

Dierx, A. H. 1988b. A life-cycle model of repeat migration. *Regional Science and Urban Economics* 18:383–97.

Doling, J., and Williams, P. 1983. Building societies and local lending behavior. *Environment and Planning A* 15:663–73.

Donaldson, B. 1973. An empirical investigation into the concept of sectoral bias in the mental maps, search spaces and migration patterns of intra-urban migrants. *Geografiska Annaler* 55B:13–33.

Donaldson, B., and Johnston, R. J. 1973. Intraurban sectoral mental maps: Further evidence from an extended methodology. *Geographical Analysis* 5:45–54.

Doorn, P. K., and Van Rietbergen, A. 1990. Lifetime mobility: Interrelationships of labor mobility, residential mobility and household cycle. *Canadian Geographer* 34:33–48.

Doreian, P., and Hummon, N. 1977. Estimates for differential equation models of social phenomena. In *Sociological methodology, 1977,* ed. D. Heise, 180–208. San Francisco: Jossey-Bass.

Dorigo, G., and Tobler, W. 1983. Push-pull migration laws. *Annals of the Association of American Geographers* 73:1–17.

Downs, R. M. 1970. The cognitive structure of an urban shopping center. *Environment and Behavior* 2:13–39.

Downs, R. M. 1981. Cognitive mapping: A thematic analysis. In *Behavioral problems in geography revisited,* ed. K. R. Cox and R. G. Golledge, 95–122. New York: Methuen.

Downs, R. M., and Stea, D., eds. 1973. *Image and environment: Cognitive mapping and spatial behavior.* Chicago: Aldine.

Downs, R. M., and Stea, D., eds. 1977. *Maps in minds: Reflections on cognitive mapping.* New York: Harper and Row.

Draper, N. R., and Smith, H. 1966. *Applied regression analysis.* New York: Wiley.

Duncan, J. 1985. Individual action and political power: A structuration perspective. In *The future of geography,* ed. R. J. Johnston, 174–89. New York: Methuen.

Duncan, J. 1988. Commentary on Martin Cadwallader's urban geography and social theory. *Urban Geography* 9:265–68.

Duncan, J., and Ley, D. 1982. Structural Marxism and human geography: A critical assessment. *Annals of the Association of American Geographers* 72:30–59.

Duncan, O. D. 1966. Path analysis: Sociological examples. *American Journal of Sociology* 72:1–16.

Duncan, O. D. 1975. *Introduction to structural equation models.* New York: Academic Press.

Dwyer, J. H. 1983. *Statistical models for the social and behavioral sciences.* New York: Oxford University Press.

Elliot, B., and McCrone, D. 1975. Landlords in Edinburgh: Some preliminary findings. *Sociological Review* 23:539–62.

Ellis, M., and Mackay, D. B. 1990. Modelling individual residential preferences using vector and ideal point logit models. *Tijdschrift voor Economische en Sociale Geografie* 81:123–32.

Entrikin, J. N. 1976. Contemporary humanism in geography. *Annals of the Association of American Geographers* 66:615–32.

Ermuth, F. 1974. *Residential satisfaction and urban environmental preferences.* Geographic Monograph no. 3, Atkinson College, York University, Toronto.

Evans, A. W. 1990. The assumption of equilibrium in the analysis of migration and interregional differences: A review of some recent research. *Journal of Regional Science* 30:515–31.

Evans, G. 1980. Environmental cognition. *Psychological Bulletin* 88:259–87.

Everitt, B. 1984. *An introduction to latent variable models.* New York: Chapman and Hall.

Ewing, G. O. 1981. On the sensitivity of conclusions about the bases of cognitive distance. *Professional Geographer* 33:311–14.

Fielding, A. J. 1985. Migration and the new spatial division of labour. In *Contemporary studies of migration,* ed. G. A. Van der Knaap and P. E. White, 173–80. Norwich, Eng.: Geo Books.

Fields, G. S. 1976. Labor force migration, unemployment and job turnover. *Review of Economics and Statistics* 58:407–15.

Fields, G. S. 1979. Place-to-place migration: Some new evidence. *Review of Economics and Statistics* 61:21–32.

Fienberg, S. 1980. *The analysis of cross-classified categorical data.* 2d ed. Cambridge, Mass.: M.I.T. Press.

Fincher, R. 1983. The inconsitency of eclecticism. *Environment and Planning A* 15:607–22.

Fingleton, B. 1981. Log-linear modelling of geographical contingency tables. *Environment and Planning A* 13:1539–51.

Finney, J. M. 1972. Indirect effects in path analysis. *Sociological Methods and Research* 1:175–86.

Fischer, M. M., and Aufhauser, E. 1988. Housing choice in a regulated market: A nested multinomial logit analysis. *Geographical Analysis* 20:47–69.

Fisher, F. M. 1966. *The identification problem in econometrics*. New York: McGraw-Hill.

Fisher, F. M. 1985. The choice of instrumental variables in the estimation of economy-wide econometric models. In *Causal models in the social sciences*. 2d ed., ed. H. M. Blalock, Jr., 159–88. New York: Aldine.

Fisher, G. A. 1988. Problems in the use and interpretation of product variables. In *Common problems / proper solutions: Avoiding error in quantitative research*, ed. J. S. Long, 84–107. Beverly Hills: Sage.

Flowerdew, R. 1976. Search strategies and stopping rules in residential mobility. *Transactions of the Institute of British Geographers*, n.s., 1:47–57.

Flowerdew, R. 1982. Institutional effects on internal migration. In *Institutions and geographical patterns*, ed. R. Flowerdew, 209–27. New York: St. Martin's Press.

Flowerdew, R., and Amrhein, C. 1989. Poisson regression models of Canadian census division migration flows. *Papers of the Regional Science Association* 67:89–102.

Flowerdew, R., and Salt, J. 1979. Migration between labour market areas in Great Britain, 1970–1971. *Regional Studies* 13:211–31.

Fotheringham, S. 1981. Spatial structure and distance-decay parameters. *Annals of the Association of American Geographers* 71:425–36.

Fotheringham, S. 1991. Migration and spatial structure: The development of the competing destinations model. In *Migration models: Macro and micro approaches*, ed. J. Stillwell and P. Congdon, 57–72. London: Belhaven Press.

Fredland, D. R. 1974. *Residential mobility and home purchase: A longitudinal perspective on the family life cycle and the housing market*. Lexington, Mass.: Lexington Books.

Frey, W. H., and Speare, A., Jr. 1988. *Regional and metropolitan growth and decline in the United States*. New York: Russell Sage Foundation.

Friedman, J. 1981. A conditional logit model of the role of local public services in residential choice. *Urban Studies* 18:347–58.

Fuguitt, G. V. 1985. The nonmetropolitan population turnaround. *Annual Review of Sociology* 11:159–280.

Gaile, G., and Hanink, D. 1985. Relative stability in American metropolitan growth. *Geographical Analysis* 17:341–48.

Gescheider, G. A. 1988. Psychophysical scaling. *Annual Review of Psychology* 39:169–200.

Giddens, A. 1979. *Central problems in social theory: Action, structure, and contradiction in social analysis*. Berkeley: University of California Press.

Giddens, A. 1981. *A contemporary critique of historical materialism*. London: Macmillan.

Giddens, A. 1984. *The constitution of society: Outline of the theory of structuration*. Cambridge, Eng.: Polity Press.

Giddens, A. 1985. Time, space and regionalization. In *Social relations and spatial structures*, ed. D. Gregory and J. Urry, 265–95. London: Macmillan.

Gober-Meyers, P. 1978a. Employment-motivated migration and economic growth in post-industrial market economies. *Progress in Human Geography* 2:207–29.

Gober-Meyers, P. 1978b. Interstate migration and economic growth: A simultaneous equations approach. *Environment and Planning A* 10:1241–52.

Gober-Meyers, P. 1978c. Migration analysis: The role of geographic scale. *Annals of Regional Science* 12:52–61.

Gober, P.; McHugh, K. E.; and Reid, N. 1991. Phoenix in flux: Household instability, residential mobility, and neighborhood change. *Annals of the Association of American Geographers* 81:80–88.

Goldberger, A. S. 1972. Structural equation methods in the social sciences. *Econometrica* 40:979–1001.

Goldberger, A. S. 1973. Structural equation models: An overview. In *Structural equation models in the social sciences,* ed. A. S. Goldberger and O. D. Duncan, 1–18. New York: Seminar Press.

Golledge, R. G. 1980. A behavioral view of mobility and migration research. *Professional Geographer* 32:14–21.

Golledge, R. G. 1981. Misconceptions, misinterpretations, and misrepresentations of behavioral approaches in human geography. *Environment and Planning A* 13:1325–44.

Golledge, R. G.; Rivizzigno, V. L.; and Spector, A. 1976. Learning about a city: Analysis by multidimensional scaling. In *Spatial choice and spatial behavior: Geographic essays on the analysis of preferences and perceptions,* ed. R. G. Golledge and G. Rushton, 95–116. Columbus: Ohio State University Press.

Golledge, R. G., and Rushton, G. 1972. *Multidimensional scaling: Review and geographical applications.* Commission on College Geography Technical Paper no. 10. Washington, D.C.: Association of American Geographers.

Golledge, R. G., and Rushton, G. 1984. A review of analytic behavioural research in geography. In *Geography and the urban environment: Progress in research and applications,* vol. 6, ed. D. T. Herbert and R. J. Johnston, 1–43. New York: Wiley.

Golledge, R. G., and Stimson, R. J. 1987. *Analytical behavioural geography.* London: Croom Helm.

Golledge, R. G., and Timmermans, H. 1990. Applications of behavioral research on spatial problems: 1. Cognition. *Progress in Human Geography* 14:57–99.

Goodman, J. L., Jr. 1982. Linking local mobility rates to migration rates: Repeat movers and place effects. In *Modelling housing market search,* ed. W. A. V. Clark, 209–23. London: Croom Helm.

Goodman, L. 1979. A brief guide to the causal analysis of data from surveys. *American Journal of Sociology* 84:1078–95.

Goss, E., and Chang, H. S. 1983. Changes in elasticities of interstate migration: Implication of alternative functional forms. *Journal of Regional Science* 23:223–32.

Gould, P. R. 1973. The black boxes of Jonkoping: Spatial information and preference. In *Image and environment: Cognitive mapping and spatial behavior,* ed. R. M. Downs and D. Stea, 235–45. Chicago: Aldine.

Gould, P. R. 1975a. Acquiring spatial information. *Economic Geography* 51:87–99.

Gould, P. R. 1975b. *People in information space: The mental maps and information surfaces of Sweden.* Lund Studies in Geography, ser. B, Human Geography, no. 42.

Gould, P. R., and White, R. 1986. *Mental maps.* 2d ed. Boston: Allen and Unwin.

Grant, K. E., and Vanderkamp, J. 1980. The effects of migration on income: A micro study with Canadian data, 1965–71. *Canadian Journal of Economics* 13:381–406.

Graves, P. 1980. Migration and climate. *Journal of Regional Science* 20:227–37.

Greenwood, M. J. 1973. Urban economic growth and migration: Their interaction. *Environment and Planning* 5:91–112.

Greenwood, M. J. 1975. Research on internal migration in the United States: A survey. *Journal of Economic Literature* 13:397–433.

Greenwood, M. J. 1981. *Migration and economic growth in the United States: National, regional, and metropolitan perspectives.* New York: Academic Press.

Greenwood, M. J. 1985. Human migration: Theory, models, and empirical studies. *Journal of Regional Science* 25:521–44.

Greenwood, M. J., and Hunt, G. L. 1989. Jobs versus amenities in the analysis of metropolitan migration. *Journal of Urban Economics* 25:1–16.

Gregory, D. 1981. Human agency and human geography. *Transactions of the Institute of British Geographers,* n.s., 6:1–18.

Gregson, N. 1986. On duality and dualism: The case of structuration and time geography. *Progress in Human Geography* 10:184–205.

Gregson, N. 1987. Structuration theory: Some thoughts on the possibilities for empirical research. *Environment and Planning D: Society and Space* 5:73–91.

Grigg, D. B. 1977. E. G. Ravenstein and the "laws of migration." *Journal of Historical Geography* 3:41–54.

Hagerstrand, T. 1957. Migration and area. In *Migration in Sweden,* ed. D. Hannerberg, T. Hagerstrand, and B. Odeving, 27–158. Lund Studies in Geography no. 13. Lund: Gleerup.

Haggett, P.; Cliff, A. D.; and Frey, A. 1977. *Locational analysis in human geography.* 2d ed. London: Edward Arnold.

Hanson, P. O.; Marble, D. F.; and Pitts, F. R. 1972. Individual movement and communication fields: A preliminary examination. *Regional Science Perspectives* 2:80–94.

Hanushek, E. A., and Jackson, J. E. 1977. *Statistical methods for social scientists.* New York: Academic Press.

Harkman, A. 1989. Migration behavior among the unemployed and the role of unemployment benefits. *Papers of the Regional Science Association* 66:143–50.

Harman, E., and Betak, J. 1976. Behavioral geography, multidimensional scaling, and the mind. In *Spatial choice and spatial behavior: Geographic essays on the analysis of preferences and perceptions,* ed. R. G. Golledge and G. Rushton, 3–20. Columbus: Ohio State University Press.

Harman, H. H. 1967. *Modern factor analysis.* 2d ed. Chicago: University of Chicago Press.

Harris, J. R., and Todaro, M. P. 1970. Migration, unemployment and development: A two-sector model. *American Economic·Review* 60:126–42.

Hart, R. A. 1973. Economic expectations and the decision to migrate: An analysis by socio-economic group. *Regional Studies* 7:271–85.

Harvey, D. 1973. *Social justice and the city.* London: Edward Arnold.

Harvey, D. 1974. Class-monopoly rent, finance capital and the urban revolution. *Regional Studies* 8:239–55.

Harvey, D. 1975. The political economy of urbanization in advanced capitalist societies: The case of the United States. In *The social economy of cities,* ed. G. Gappert and H. M. Rose, 119–63. Beverly Hills: Sage.

Harvey, D. 1976. The Marxian theory of the state. *Antipode* 8:80–89.

Harvey, D. 1978. The urban process under capitalism: A framework for analysis. *International Journal of Urban and Regional Research* 2:101–31.

Harvey, D. 1981. Conceptual and measurement problems in the cognitive-behavioral approach to location theory. In *Behavioral problems in geography revisited,* ed. K. R. Cox and R. G. Golledge, 18–42. New York: Methuen.

Harvey, D. 1982. *The limits to capital.* Chicago: University of Chicago Press.

Hauser, R. M. 1973. Disaggregating a social-psychological model of educational attainment. In Structural equation models in the social sciences, ed. A. S. Goldberger and O. D. Duncan, 255–84. New York: Seminar Press.

Hauser, R. M., and Goldberger, A. S. 1971. The treatment of unobservable variables in path analysis. In *Sociological methodology, 1971,* ed. H. L. Costner, 81–117. San Francisco: Jossey-Bass.

Haynes, K. E., and Fotheringham, A. S. 1984. *Gravity and spatial interaction models.* Beverly Hills: Sage.

Haynes, R. M. 1974. Application of exponential distance decay to human and animal activities. *Geografiska Annaler* 56B:90–104.

Hefner, R.; Levy, S. G.; and Warner, H. L. 1967. A survey of internationally relevant attitudes and behaviors. *Peace Research Society Papers (International)* 7:139–50.

Herting, J. R. 1985. Multiple indicator models using LISREL. In *Causal models in the social sciences,* 2d ed., ed. H. M. Blalock, Jr., 263–319. New York: Aldine.

Herting, J. R., and Costner, H. L. 1985. Respecification in multiple indicator models. In *Causal models in the social sciences,* 2d ed., ed. H. M. Blalock, Jr., 321–93. New York: Aldine.

Herzog, H., and Schlottmann, A. 1984. Labor force mobility in the United States: Migration, unemployment, and remigration. *International Regional Science Review* 9:43–58.

Hill, F. 1973. Spatio-temporal trends in urban population density: A trend surface analysis. In *The form of cities in central Canada: Selected papers,* ed. L. S. Bourne, R. D. MacKinnon, and J. W. Simmons, 103–19. Department of Geography Research Pulication no. 11, University of Toronto.

Hirschman, A. 1958. *The strategy of economic development.* New Haven, Conn.: Yale University Press.

Hirst, M. A. 1976. A Markovian analysis of inter-regional migration in Uganda. *Geografiska Annaler* 58B:79–94.

Horton, F. E., and Reynolds, D. R. 1971. Action space differentials in cities. In

Perspectives in geography, vol. 1, *Models of spatial variation,* ed. H. McConnell and D. W. Yaseen, 83–102. DeKalb: Northern Illinois University Press.

Hotelling, H. 1936. Relations between two sets of variates. *Biometrica* 28:321–29.

Hourihan, K. 1979a. The evaluation of urban neighborhoods: 1. Perception. *Environment and Planning A* 11:1337–53.

Hourihan, K. 1979b. The evaluation of urban neighborhoods: 2. Preference. *Environment and Planning A* 11:1355–66.

Hourihan, K. 1984. Residential satisfaction, neighborhood attributes, and personal characteristics: An exploratory path analysis in Cork, Ireland. *Environment and Planning A* 16:425–36.

Huff, J. O. 1982. Spatial aspects of residential search. In *Modelling housing market search,* ed. W. A. V. Clark, 106–29. London: Croom Helm.

Huff, J. O. 1984. Distance-decay models of residential search. In *Spatial statistics and models,* ed. G. L. Gaile and C. J. Willmott, 345–66. Dordrecht, Neth.: D. Reidel.

Huff, J. O. 1986. Geographic regularities in residential search behavior. *Annals of the Association of American Geographers* 76:208–27.

Huff, J. O., and Clark, W. A. V. 1978a. Cumulative stress and cumulative inertia: A behavioral model of the decision to move. *Environment and Planning A* 10:1101–19.

Huff, J. O., and Clark, W. A. V. 1978b. The role of stationarity in Markov and opportunity models of intraurban migration. In *Population mobility and residential change,* ed. W. A. V. Clark and E. G. Moore, 183–213. Studies in Geography no. 25. Northwestern University, Evanston, Ill.

Huggett, R. 1980. *Systems analysis in geography.* New York: Oxford University Press.

Hughes, J. W., and Carey, G. W. 1972. Factorial ecologies: Oblique and orthogonal solutions. A case study of the New York SMSA. *Environment and Planning* 4:147–62.

Intriligator, M. D. 1978. *Econometric models, techniques, and applications.* Englewood Cliffs, N.J.: Prentice-Hall.

Isaac, P. D. 1982. Considerations in the selection of stimulus pairs for data collection in multidimensional scaling. In *Proximity and preference: Problems in the multidimensional analysis of large data sets,* ed. R. G. Golledge and J. N. Rayner, 80–89. Minneapolis: University of Minnesota Press.

Islam, M. N., and Choudhury, S. A. 1990. Self-selection and intermunicipal migration in Canada. *Regional Science and Urban Economics* 20:459–72.

Isserman, A. M. 1985. Economic-demographic modeling with endogenously determined birth and migration rates: Theory and prospects. *Environment and Planning A* 17:25–45.

Izraeli, O., and Lin, A. 1984. Recent evidence on the effect of real earnings on net migration. *Regional Studies* 18:113–20.

Jackson, P., and Smith, S. J., eds. 1981. *Social interaction and ethnic segregation.* Institute of British Geographers, Special Publication no. 12. London: Academic Press.

James, L., and Singh, B. 1978. An introduction to the logic, assumptions, and basic analytic procedures of two-stage least squares. *Psychological Bulletin* 85:1104–22.

Jessop, B. 1982. *The capitalist state.* Oxford: Robertson.

Johnston, J. 1972. *Econometric methods.* 2d ed. New York: McGraw-Hill.

Johnston, R. J. 1970. Latent migration potential and the gravity model: A New Zealand study. *Geographical Analysis* 2:387–97.

Johnston, R. J. 1972. Activity spaces and residential preferences: Some tests of the hypothesis of sectoral mental maps. *Economic Geography* 48:199–211.

Johnston, R. J. 1973. Spatial patterns in suburban evaluations. *Environment and Planning* 5:385–95.

Johnston, R. J. 1976. Residential area characteristics: Research methods for identifying urban sub-areas; social area analysis and factorial ecology. In *Social areas in cities,* vol. 1, *Spatial processes and form,* ed. D. T. Herbert and R. J. Johnston, 193–235. New York: Wiley.

Johnston, R. J. 1978. *Multivariate statistical analysis in geography: A primer on the general linear model.* London: Longman.

Johnston, R. J. 1980. On the nature of explanation in human geography. *Transactions of the Institute of British Geographers,* n.s., 5:402–12.

Johnston, R. J. 1982a. *Geography and the state: An essay in political geography.* New York: St. Martin's Press.

Johnston, R. J. 1982b. On the nature of human geography. *Transactions of the Institute of British Geographers,* n.s., 7:123–25.

Johnston, R. J. 1983. *Philosophy and human geography: An introduction to contemporary approaches.* London: Edward Arnold.

Johnston, R. J. 1984. Marxist political economy, the state and political geography. *Progress in Human Geography* 8:473–92.

Johnston, R. J. 1985. To the ends of the earth. In *The future of geography,* ed. R. J. Johnston, 326–38. New York: Methuen.

Jones, C., and Maclennan, D. 1987. Building societies and credit rationing: An empirical examination of redlining. *Urban Studies* 24:205–16.

Jones, R. 1978. Myth maps and migration in Venezuela. *Economic Geography* 54:75–91.

Jones, R. 1980. The role of perception in urban in-migration: A path analytic model. *Geographical Analysis* 12:98–108.

Jones, R., and Zannaras, G. 1976. Perceived versus objective urban opportunities and the migration of Venezuelan youths. *Annals of Regional Science* 10:83–97.

Jöreskog, K. 1973. A general method for estimating a linear structural equation system. In *Structural equation models in the social sciences,* ed. A. S. Goldberger and O. D. Duncan, 85–112. New York: Seminar Press.

Jöreskog, K. 1982. The LISREL approach to causal model-building in the social sciences. In *Systems under indirect observation,* pt. 1, ed. K. Jöreskog and H. Wold, 81–99. Amsterdam: North-Holland.

Jöreskog, K., and Sorbom, D. 1981. *LISREL: Analysis of structural relationships by the method of maximum likelihood.* Version 5. Chicago: National Educational Resources.

Joseph, G. 1975. A Markov analysis of age/sex differences in inter-regional migration in Great Britain. *Regional Studies* 9:69–78.

Joshi, T. R. 1972. Toward computing factor scores. In *International geography,* vol. 2, ed. W. P. Adams and F. M. Helleiner, 906–8. Toronto: University of Toronto Press.

Kachigan, S. K. 1986. *Statistical analysis: An interdisciplinary introduction to univariate and multivariate methods.* New York: Radius Press.

Kain, J. F., and Quigley, J. M. 1970. Measuring the value of housing quality. *Journal of the American Statistical Association* 65:532–48.

Katz, D. A. 1982. *Econometric theory and applications.* Englewood Cliffs, N.J.: Prentice-Hall.

Kau, J., and Sirmans, C. 1977. The influence of information cost and uncertainty on migration: A comparison of migrant types. *Journal of Regional Science* 17:89–96.

Kau, J., and Sirmans, C. 1979. A recursive model of the spatial allocation of migrants. *Journal of Regional Science* 19:47–56.

Kenny, D. A. 1979. *Correlation and causality.* New York: Wiley.

Keown, P. A. 1971. The career cycle and the stepwise migration process. *New Zealand Geographer* 27:175–84.

King, R. 1978. Return migration: A neglected aspect of population geography. *Area* 10:175–82.

King, R., ed. 1986. *Return migration and regional economic problems.* London: Croom Helm.

Kipnis, B. A. 1985. Graph analysis of metropolitan residential mobility: Methodology and theoretical implications. *Urban Studies* 22:179–87.

Kirk, W. 1963. Problems of geography. *Geography* 48:357–71.

Klecka, W. 1980. *Discriminant analysis.* Beverly Hills: Sage.

Kleiner, M., and McWilliams, W. 1977. An analysis of alternative labor force population forecasting models. *Annals of Regional Science* 11:74–85.

Knapp, T. A., and Graves, P. E. 1989. On the role of amenities in models of migration and regional development. *Journal of Regional Science* 29:71–87.

Knight, R., and Menchik, M. 1976. Conjoint preference estimation for residential land use policy evaluation. In *Spatial choice and spatial behavior: Geographic essays on the analysis of preferences and perceptions,* ed. R. G. Golledge and G. Rushton, 135–55. Columbus: Ohio State University Press.

Knox, P. L. 1987. *Urban social geography: An introduction.* 2d ed. New York: Longman.

Knox, P. L., and MacLaran, A. 1978. Values and perceptions in descriptive approaches to urban social geography. In *Geography and the urban environment,* vol. 1, ed. D. Herbert and R. J. Johnston, 197–246. Chichester, Eng.: Wiley.

Kontuly, T., and Bierens, H. J. 1990. Testing the recession theory as an explanation for the migration turnaround. *Environment and Planning A* 22:253–70.

Koopmans, T. C. 1985. Identification problems in economic model construction. In *Causal models in the social sciences,* 2d ed., ed. H. M. Blalock, Jr., 103–23. New York: Aldine.

Koyck, L. M. 1954. *Distributed lags and investment analysis.* Amsterdam: North-Holland.

Krumm, R. 1983. Regional labor markets and the household migration decision. *Journal of Regional Science* 23:361–75.

Kuz, T. 1978. Quality of life, an objective and subjective variable analysis. *Regional Studies* 12:409–17.

Landale, N. S., and Guest, A. M. 1985. Constraints, satisfaction and residential mobility: Speare's model reconsidered. *Demography* 22:199–222.

Lee, E. S. 1966. A theory of migration. *Demography* 3:47–57.

Leonard, S. 1982. Urban managerialism: A period of transition? *Progress in Human Geography* 6:190–215.

Ley, D. 1981. Behavioral geography and the philosophies of meaning. In *Behavioral problems in geography revisited,* ed. K. R. Cox and R. G. Golledge, 209–30. New York: Methuen.

Liaw, K. L. 1990. Joint effects of personal factors and ecological variables on the interprovincial migration pattern of young adults in Canada: A nested logit analysis. *Geographial Analysis* 22:189–208.

Lieber, S. R. 1978. Place utility and migration. *Geografiska Annaler* 60B:16–27.

Lieber, S. R. 1979. An experimental approach for the migration decision process. *Tijdschrift voor Economische en Sociale Geografie* 70:75–85.

Linneman, P., and Graves, P. 1983. Migration and job change: A multinomial logit approach. *Journal of Urban Economics* 14:263–79.

Liu, B. 1973. *The quality of life in the United States, 1970: Index, rating and statistics.* Kansas City, Mo.: Midwest Research Institute.

Liu, B. 1975. Differential net migration rates and the quality of life. *Review of Economics and Statistics* 57:329–37.

Liu, B. 1977. Local government finance and metropolitan employment growth: A simultaneous equations model. *Southern Economic Journal* 43:1379–85.

Lloyd, R. E. 1976. Cognition, preference, and behavior in space: An examination of the structural linkages. *Economic Geography* 52:241–53.

Lodge, M. 1981. *Magnitude scaling: Quantitative measurement and opinions.* Beverly Hills: Sage.

Loehman, E., and Emerson, R. 1985. A simultaneous equation model of local government expenditure dicisions. *Land Economics* 61:419–32.

Long, J. S. 1981. Estimation and hypothesis testing in linear models containing measurement error: A review of Jöreskog's model for the analysis of covariance structures. In *Linear models in social research,* ed. P. V. Marsden, 209–56. Beverly Hills: Sage.

Long, J. S. 1983. *Covariance structure models: An introduction to LISREL.* Beverly Hills: Sage.

Long, L. H. 1972. The influence of number and ages of children on residential mobility. *Demography* 9:317–82.

Long, L. H. 1988. *Migration and residential mobility in the United States.* New York: Russell Sage Foundation.

Long, L. H., and Hansen, K. A. 1975. Trends in return migration to the South. *Demography* 12:601–14.

Louviere, J. J. 1978. Modeling individual residential preferences: A totally dis-aggregate approach. *Transportation Research* 13A:1–15.

Louviere, J. J. 1982. Applications of functional measurement to problems in spatial decision making. In *Proximity and preference: Problems in the multidimensional analysis of large data sets,* ed. R. G. Golledge and J. N. Rayner, 191–213. Minneapolis: University of Minnesota Press.

Louviere, J. J., and Meyer, R. 1976. A model for residential impression formation. *Geographical Analysis* 8:479–86.

Louviere, J. J., and Norman, K. L. 1977. Applications of information-processing theory to the analysis of urban travel demand. *Environment and Behavior* 9:91–106.

Louviere, J. J., and Timmermans, H. 1990a. Hierarchical information integration applied to residential choice behavior. *Geographical Analysis* 22:127–44.

Louviere, J. J., and Timmermans, H. 1990b. A review of recent advances in decompositional preference and choice models. *Tijdschrift voor Economische en Sociale Geografie* 81:214–24.

Lowry, I. 1966. *Migration and metropolitan growth: Two analytical models.* San Francisco: Chandler.

Lueck, V. M. 1976. Cognitive and affective components of residential preferences for cities: A pilot study. In *Spatial choice and spatial behavior: Geographic essays on the analysis of preferences and perceptions,* ed. R. G. Golledge and G. Rushton, 273–300. Columbus: Ohio State University Press.

Mabogunje, A. L. 1970. Systems approach to a theory of rural-urban migration. *Geographical Analysis* 2:1–18.

McCracken, K. W. J. 1975. Household awareness spaces and intraurban migration search behavior. *Professional Geographer* 27:166–70.

Macdonald, K. 1977. Path analysis. In *The analysis of survey data,* vol. 2, ed. C. O'Muircheartaigh and C. Payne, 81–104. London: Wiley.

MacEachren, A. M. 1980. Travel time as the basis of cognitive distance. *Professional Geographer* 32:30–36.

McFadden, D. 1973. Conditional logit analysis of qualitative choice behavior. In *Frontiers in econometrics,* ed. P. Zarembka, 105–42. New York: Academic Press.

McGinnis, R. 1968. A stochastic model of social mobility. *American Sociological Review* 33:712–22.

McGrath, J. E., ed. 1970. *Social and psychological factors in stress.* New York: Holt, Rinehart and Winston.

McHugh, K. E. 1984. Explaining migration intentions and destination selection. *Professional Geographer* 36:315–25.

McHugh, K. E. 1987. Black migration reversal in the United States. *Geographical Review* 77:171–82.

McHugh, K. E. 1988. Determinants of black interstate migration, 1965–70 and 1975–80. *Annals of Regional Science* 22:36–48.

McKay, J., and Whitelaw, J. S. 1977. The role of large private and government organizations in generating flows of inter-regional migrants: The case of Australia. *Economic Geography* 53:28–44.

Maclennan, D., and Williams, N. 1980. Revealed-preference theory and spatial choices: Some limitations. *Environment and Planning A* 12:909–19.

Madden, M. 1978. The perception of distance in migration on Merseyside. *Area* 10:167–73.

Maher, C. A. 1982. Population turnover and spatial change in Melbourne, Australia. *Urban Geography* 3:240–57.

Maier, G., and Weiss, P. 1991. The discrete choice approach to migration modelling. In *Migration models: Macro and micro approaches*, ed. J. Stillwell and P. Congdon, 17–33. London: Belhaven Press.

Mark, J. 1977. Determinants of urban house prices: A methodological comment. *Urban Studies* 14:359–63.

Marsden, P. V. 1981. Conditional effects in regression models. In *Linear models in social research*, ed. P. V. Marsden, 97–116. Beverly Hills: Sage.

Massey, D. 1985. New directions in space. In *Social relations and spatial structures*, ed. D. Gregory and J. Urry, 9–19. London: Macmillan.

Meyer, R. 1980. A descriptive model of constrained residential search. *Geographical Analysis* 12:21–32.

Michelson, W. 1977. *Environmental choice, human behavior and residential satisfaction*. New York: Oxford University Press.

Miliband, R. 1969. *The state in capitalist society*. London: Quartet.

Milne, W. 1991. The human capital model and its econometric estimation. In *Migration models: Macro and micro approaches*, ed. J. Stillwell and P. Congdon, 137–51. London: Belhaven Press.

Mincer, J. 1978. Family migration decisions. *Journal of Political Economy* 86:749–73.

Miron, J. 1979. Migration and urban economic growth. *Regional Science and Urban Economics* 9:159–83.

Moore, E. G. 1971. Comments on the use of ecological models in the study of residential mobility in the city. *Economic Geography* 47:73–85.

Moore, E. G. 1986. Mobility intention and subsequent relocation. *Urban Geography* 7:497–514.

Moore, E. G., and Clark, W. A. V. 1986. Stable structure and local variation: A comparison of household flows in four metropolitan areas. *Urban Studies* 23:185–96.

Moos, A., and Dear, M. 1986. Structuration theory in urban analysis: 1. Theoretical exegesis. *Environment and Planning A* 18:231–52.

Morrill, R. L. 1963. The distribution of migration distances. *Papers and Proceedings of the Regional Science Association* 11:75–84.

Morrill, R. L. 1988. Intra-metropolitan demographic structure: A Seattle example. *Annals of Regional Science* 22:1–16.

Morrill, R. L., and Pitts, F. R. 1967. Marriage, migration, and the mean information field: A study in uniqueness and generality. *Annals of the Association of American Geographers* 57:401–22.

Murdie, R. A. 1986. Residential mortgage lending in metropolitan Toronto: A case study of the resale market. *Canadian Geographer* 30:98–110.

Murie, A.; Niner, P.; and Watson, C. 1976. *Housing policy and the housing system*. London: Allen and Unwin.

Myrdal, G. 1957. *Economic theory and underdeveloped regions*. London: Duckworth.

Nakosteen, R. A., and Zimmer, M. 1980. Migration and income: The question of self-selection. *Southern Economic Journal* 46:840–51.

Namboodiri, N. K.; Carter, L. F.; and Blalock, H. M., Jr. 1975. *Applied multivariate analysis and experimental designs*. New York: McGraw-Hill.

Nicholson, B.; Brinkley, I.; and Evans, A. 1981. The role of the inner city in the development of manufacturing industry. *Urban Studies* 18:57–71.

Norcliffe, G. B. 1969. On the use and limitations of trend surface models. *Canadian Geographer* 13:338–48.

Norcliffe, G. B. 1974. Territorial influences in urban political space: A study of perception in Kitchener-Waterloo. *Canadian Geographer* 18:311–29.

Odland, J. 1988a. Migration and occupational choice among young labor force entrants: A human capital model. *Geographical Analysis* 20:281–96.

Odland, J. 1988b. Sources of change in the process of population redistribution in the United States, 1955–1980. *Environment and Planning A* 20:789–809.

Odland, J., and Bailey, A. J. 1990. Regional out-migration rates and migration histories: A longitudinal analysis. *Geographical Analysis* 22:158–70.

Okun, B. 1968. Interstate population migration and state income inequality: A simultaneous equation approach. *Economic Development and Cultural Change* 16:297–313.

Olvey, L. 1972. Regional growth and inter-regional migration: Their pattern of interaction. *Review of Regional Studies* 2:139–63.

Osgood, C. E.; Suci, G. J.; and Tannenbaum, P. H. 1957. *The measurement of meaning*. Urbana: University of Illinois Press.

Owen, D. W., and Green, A. E. 1989. Spatial aspects of labor mobility in the 1980's. *Geoforum* 20:107–26.

Pacione, M. 1982. The use of objective and subjective measures of life quality in human geography. *Progress in Human Geography* 6:495–514.

Pack, J. 1973. Determinants of migration to central cities. *Journal of Regional Science* 13:249–60.

Pahl, R. E. 1969. Urban social theory and research. *Environment and Planning* 1:143–53.

Pahl, R. E. 1979. Socio-political factors in resource allocation. In *Social problems and the city*, ed. D. T. Herbert and D. M. Smith, 33–46. London: Oxford University Press.

Palm, R. I. 1976. The role of real estate agents as information mediators in two American cities. *Geografiska Annaler* 58B:28–41.

Palm, R. I. 1979. Financial and real estate institutions in the housing market. In *Geography and the urban environment*, vol. 2, ed. D. T. Herbert and R. J. Johnston, 83–123. New York: Wiley.

Palm, R. I. 1985. Ethnic segmentation of real estate agent practice in the urban housing market. *Annals of the Association of American Geographers* 75:58–68.

Palm, R. I., and Caruso, D. 1972. Factor labeling in factorial ecology. *Annals of the Association of American Geographers* 62:122–33.

Parkin, F. 1979. *Marxism and class theory: A bourgeois critique*. London: Tavistock.

Parr, J. 1966. Out-migration and the depressed area problem. *Land Economics* 2:149–59.

Phipps, A. G. 1983. Utility function switching during residential search. *Geografiska Annaler* 65B:23–38.

Phipps, A. G. 1989. Residential stress and consumption disequilibrium in the Saskatoon housing market. *Papers of the Regional Science Association* 67:71–87.

Phipps, A. G., and Carter, J. E. 1984. An individual-level analysis of the stress-resistance model of household mobility. *Geographical Analysis* 16:176–89.

Phipps, A. G., and Carter, J. E. 1985. Individual differences in the residential preferences of inner-city homeowners. *Tijdschrift voor Economische en Sociale Geografie* 76:32–42.

Phipps, A. G., and Laverty, W. H. 1983. Optimal stopping and residential search behavior. *Geographical Analysis* 15:187–204.

Pickles, A., and Rogerson, P. 1984. Wage distributions and spatial preferences in competitive job search and migration. *Regional Studies* 18:131–42.

Pickvance, C. G. 1974. Life cycle, housing tenure and residential mobility: A path analytic approach. Urban Studies 11:171–88.

Pindyck, R. S., and Rubinfeld, D. L. 1976. *Econometric models and economic forecasts.* New York: McGraw-Hill.

Pipkin, J. S. 1981. Cognitive behavioral geography and repetitive travel. In *Behavioral problems in geography revisited,* ed. K. R. Cox and R. G. Golledge, 145–81. New York: Methuen.

Pipkin, J. S. 1982. Some remarks on multidimensional scaling in geography. In *Proximity and preference: Problems in the multidimensional analysis of large data sets,* ed. R. G. Golledge and J. N. Rayner, 214–32. Minneapolis: University of Minnesota Press.

Plane, D. A. 1987. The geographical components of change in a migration system. *Geographical Analysis* 19:283–99.

Plane, D. A., and Rogerson, P. A. 1986. Dynamic flow modeling with inter-regional dependency effects: An aplication to structural change in the U.S. migration system. *Demography* 23:91–104.

Plaut, T. 1981. An econometric model for forecasting regional population growth. *International Regional Science Review* 6:53–70.

Pocock, D., and Hudson, R. 1978. *Images of the urban environment.* London: Macmillan.

Poot, J. 1987. Estimating duration-of-residence distributions: Age, sex and occupational differentials in New Zealand. *New Zealand Geographer* 43:23–32.

Popp, H. 1976. The residential location decison process: Some empirical and theoretical considerations. *Tijdschrift voor Economische en Sociale Geografie* 67:300–305.

Porell, F. 1982. Intermetropolitan migration and quality of life. *Journal of Regional Science* 22:137–58.

Preston, V. 1982. A multidimensional scaling analysis of individual differences in residential area evaluation. *Geografiska Annaler* 64B:17–26.

Preston, V. 1984. A path model of residential stress and inertia among older people. *Urban Geography* 5:146–64.

Preston, V. 1986. A case study of context effects and residential area evaluation in Hamilton, Canada. *Environment and Planning A* 18:41–52.

Pringle, D. 1980. *Causal modelling: The Simon-Blalock approach.* Concepts and Techniques in Modern Geography no. 27. Norwich, Eng.: Geo Abstracts.

Quigley, J. M. 1976. Housing demand in the short run: An analysis of polytomous choice. *Explorations in Economic Research* 3:76–102.

Quigley, J. M., and Weinberg, D. H. 1977. Intra-metropolitan residential mobility: A review and synthesis. *International Regional Science Review* 2:41–66.

Ravenstein, E. G. 1885. The laws of migration. *Journal of the Royal Statistical Society* 48:167–227.

Ravenstein, E. G. 1889. The laws of migration. *Journal of the Royal Statistical Society* 52:214–301.

Rayner, J. N. 1971. *An introduction to spectral analysis.* London: Pion.

Rees, P. H. 1970. Concepts of social space: Toward an urban social geography. In *Geographic perspectives on urban systems,* ed. B. J. L. Berry and F. E. Horton, 306–94. Englewood Cliffs, N.J.: Prentice-Hall.

Rees, P. H. 1983. Multiregional mathematical demography: Themes and issues. *Environment and Planning A* 15:1571–83.

Rees, P. H., and Wilson, A. G. 1977. *Spatial population analysis.* London: Edward Arnold.

Reitsma, R. F., and Vergoossen, D. 1988. A causal typology of migration: The role of commuting. *Regional Studies* 22:331–40.

Renas, S., and Kumar, R. 1981. The cost of living, labor market opportunities, and the migration decision: Some additional evidence, *Annals of Regional Science* 15:74–79.

Renas, S., and Kumar, R. 1983. Climatic conditions and migration: An econometric inquiry. *Annals of Regional Science* 17:69–78.

Riddell, J. B. 1970. On structuring a migration model. *Geographical Analysis* 2:403–9.

Riddell, J. B., and Harvey, M. E. 1972. The urban system in the migration process: An evaluation of step-wise migration in Sierra Leone. *Economic Geography* 48:270–83.

Ritchey, P. N. 1976. Explanations of migration. *Annual Review of Sociology* 2: 363–404.

Robson, B. T. 1973. *Urban growth: An approach.* London: Methuen.

Rodgers, A. 1970. Migration and industrial development: The southern Italian experience. *Economic Geography* 46:111–35.

Rogers, A. 1967. A regression analysis of interregional migration in California. *Review of Economics and Statistics* 49:262–67.

Rogers, A. 1979. Migration patterns and population redistribution. *Regional Science and Urban Economics* 9:275–310.

Rogers, A. 1990. Requiem for the net migrant. *Geographical Analysis* 22:283–300.

Rogers, A., and Belanger, A. 1990. The importance of place of birth in migration and population redistribution analysis. *Environment and Planning A* 22:193–210.

Rogers, A., and Willekens, F., eds. 1986. *Migration and settlement: A comparative study.* Dordrecht, Neth.: D. Reidel.

Rogerson, P. A. 1984. New directions in the modelling of interregional migration. *Economic Geography* 60:111–21.

Rogerson, P. A. 1987. Changes in U.S. national mobility levels. *Professional Geographer* 39:344–51.

Rogerson, P. A. 1990. Migration analysis using data with time intervals of differing widths. *Papers of the Regional Science Association* 68:97–106.

Root, J. D. 1975. Intransitivity of preferences: A neglected concept. *Proceedings of the Association of American Geographers* 7:185–89.

Roseman, C. C. 1971. Channelization of migration flows from the rural South to the industrial Midwest. *Proceedings of the Association of American Geographers* 3:140–46.

Roseman, C. C. 1977. *Changing migration patterns within the United States.* Washington, D.C.: Association of American Geographers.

Roseman, C. C. 1983. A framework for the study of migration destination selection. *Population and Environment: Behavioral and Social Issues* 6:151–65.

Roseman, C. C., and McHugh, K. E. 1982. Metropolitan areas as redistributors of population. *Urban Geography* 3:22–33.

Rossi, P. H. 1980. *Why families move.* 2d ed. Beverly Hills: Sage.

Rummell, R. J. 1970. *Applied factor analysis.* Evanston, Ill.: Northwestern University Press.

Rushton, G. 1981. The scaling of locational preferences. In *Behavioral problems in geography revisited,* ed. K. R. Cox and R. G. Golledge, 67–92. New York: Methuen.

Sandefur, G. D., and Scott, W. J. 1981. A dynamic analysis of migration: An assessment of the effects of age, family and career variables. *Demography* 18:355–68.

Sandefur, G. D., and Tuma, N. B. 1987. How data type affects conclusions about individual mobility. *Social Science Research* 16:301–28.

Sandefur, G. D.; Tuma, N. B.; and Kephart, G. 1991. Race, local labour markets and migration in the United States, 1975–1983. In *Migration models: Macro and micro approaches,* ed. J. Stillwell and P. Congdon, 187–206. London: Belhaven Press.

Sandell, S. H. 1977. Women and the economics of family migration. *Review of Economics and Statistics* 59:406–14.

Saunders, P. 1979. *Urban politics: A sociological interpretation.* London: Hutchinson.

Saunders, P. 1981. *Social theory and the urban question.* New York: Holmes and Meier.

Saunders, P., and Williams, P. 1986. The new conservatism: Some thoughts on recent and future developments in urban studies. *Environment and Planning D: Society and Space* 4:393–99.

Sayer, A. 1984. *Method in social science: A realist approach.* London: Hutchinson.

Sayer, A. 1985. Realism and geography. In *The future of geography,* ed. R. J. Johnston, 159–73. New York: Methuen.

Schultz, T. W. 1963. *The economic value of education.* New York: Columbia University Press.

Schusky, J. 1966. Public awareness and concern with air pollution in the St. Louis metropolitan area. *Journal of Air Pollution Control Association* 16:72–76.

Schwartz, A. 1973. Interpreting the effect of distance on migration. *Journal of Political Economy* 81:1153–69.

Schwind, P. J. 1971. Spatial preferences of migrants for regions: The example of Maine. *Proceedings of the Association of American Geographers* 3:150–56.

Schwind, P. J. 1975. A general field theory of migration: United States, 1955–1960. *Economic Geography* 51:1–16.

Scott, A. J. 1980. *The urban land nexus and the state.* London: Pion.

Segal, D. 1979. A quasi-loglinear model of neighborhood choice. In *The economics of neighborhood,* ed. D. Segal, 57–82. New York: Academic Press.

Sell, R. R. 1983. Analyzing migration decisions: The first step—whose decisions? *Demography* 20:299–311.

Selye, H. 1956. *The stress of life.* New York: McGraw-Hill.

Shaw, R. P. 1975. *Migration theory and fact.* Philadelphia: Regional Science Research Institute.

Shaw, R. P. 1985. *Intermetropolitan migration in Canada: Changing determinants over three decades.* Toronto: NC Press.

Sheppard, E. S. 1978. Theoretical underpinnings of the gravity hypothesis. *Geographical Analysis* 10:386–402.

Sheppard, E. S. 1984. The distance-decay gravity model debate. In Spatial statistics and models, ed. G. L. Gaile and C. J. Willmott, 367–88. Dordrecht, Neth.: D. Reidel.

Sheppard, E. S. 1988. The search for flexible theory: Comments on Cadwallader. *Urban Geography* 9:255–64.

Short, J. R. 1978. Residential mobility. *Progress in Human Geography* 2:419–47.

Simmons, J. W. 1968. Changing residence in the city: A review of intra-urban mobility. *Geographical Review* 58:622–51.

Simon, H. A. 1957. *Models of man.* New York: Wiley.

Simon, H. A. 1985. Spurious correlation: A causal interpretation. In Causal models in the social sciences, 2d ed., ed. H. M. Blalock, Jr., 7–21. New York: Aldine.

Sjaastad, L. 1962. The costs and returns of human migration. *Journal of Political Economy* 70:80–93.

Slater, P. B. 1984. A partial hierarchical regionalization of 3140 U.S. counties on the basis of 1965–1970 intercounty migration. *Environment and Planning A* 16:545–50.

Slater, P. B. 1989. A field theory of spatial interaction. *Environment and Planning A* 21:121–26.

Smith, C. 1983. A case study of structuration: The pure-bred beef business. *Journal for the Theory of Social Behavior* 13:3–17.

Smith, G. C., and Ford, R. G. 1985. Urban mental maps and housing estate preferences of council tenants. *Geoforum* 16:25–36.

Smith, N. 1982. Gentrification and uneven development. *Economic Geography* 58:139-55.

Smith, N. 1984. *Uneven development: Nature, capital and the production of space.* Oxford: Blackwell.

Smith, T. R., and Clark, W. A. V. 1980. Housing market search: Information constraints and efficiency. In *Residential mobility and public policy,* ed. W. A. V. Clark and E. G. Moore, 100-125. Beverly Hills: Sage.

Smith, T. R.; Clark, W. A. V.; Huff, J. O.; and Shapiro, P. 1979. A decision-making and search model for intraurban migration. *Geographical Analysis* 11:1-22.

Smith, T. R.; Clark, W. A. V.; and Onaka, J. 1982. Information provision: An analysis of newspaper real estate advertisements. In *Modelling housing market search,* ed. W. A. V. Clark, 160-86. London: Croom Helm.

Sonnenfeld, J. 1976. Multidimensional measurement of environmental personality. In *Spatial choice and spatial behavior: Geographic essays on the analysis of preferences and perceptions,* ed. R. G. Golledge and G. Rushton, 51-66. Columbus: Ohio State University Press.

Speare, A., Jr. 1971. A cost-benefit model of rural to urban migration in Taiwan. *Population Studies* 25:117-30.

Speare, A., Jr. 1974. Residential satisfaction as an intervening variable in residential mobility. *Demography* 11:173-88.

Speare, A., Jr.; Goldstein, S.; and Frey, W. H. 1974. *Residential mobility, migration, and metropolitan change.* Cambridge, Mass.: Ballinger.

Spence, I. 1982. Incomplete experimental designs for multidimensional scaling. In *Proximity and preference: Problems in the multidimensional analysis of large data sets,* ed. R. G. Golledge and J. N. Rayner, 29-46. Minneapolis: University of Minnesota Press.

Spencer, M. 1977. History and sociology: An analysis of Weber's "The City." *Sociology* 11:507-25.

Stapleton, C. M. 1980. Reformulation of the family life-cycle concept: Implications for residential mobility. *Environment and Planning A* 12:1103-18.

Stapleton-Concord, C. M. 1982. Sex differentials in recent U.S. migration rates. *Urban Geography* 3:142-65.

Stapleton-Concord, C. M. 1984. A mover/stayer approach to residential mobility of the aged. *Tijdschrift voor Economische en Sociale Geografie* 75:249-62.

Stevens, S. S. 1975. *Psychophysics: Introduction to its perceptual, neural, and social prospects.* New York: Wiley.

Stillwell, J. 1991. Spatial interaction models and the propensity to migrate over distance. In *Migration models: Macro and micro approaches,* ed. J. Stillwell and P. Congdon, 34-56. London: Belhaven Press.

Stillwell, J., and Congdon, P., eds. 1991. *Migration models: Macro and micro approaches.* London: Belhaven Press.

Stolzenberg, R. 1979. The measurement and decomposition of causal effects in nonlinear and nonadditive models. In *Sociological methodology, 1980,* ed. K. Schuessler, 459-88. San Francisco: Jossey-Bass.

Stone, L. O. 1971. On the correlation between metropolitan area in- and out-migration by occupation. *Journal of the American Statistical Association* 66:693–701.

Tabuchi, T. 1988. Interregional income differentials and migration: Their inter-relationships. *Regional Studies* 22:1–10.

Talarchek, G. M. 1982. Sequential aspects of residential search and selection. *Urban Geography* 3:34–57.

Taylor, S. M. 1979. Personal dispositions and human spatial behavior. *Economic Geography* 55:184–95.

Thomas, R. N., and Catau, J. C. 1974. Distance and the incidence of step-wise migration in Guatemala. *Proceedings of the Association of American Geographers* 6:113–16.

Thorndyke, P. W. 1981. Distance estimation from cognitive maps. *Cognitive Psychology* 13:526–50.

Thrift, N. J. 1983. On the determination of social action in space and time. *Environment and Planning D: Society and Space* 1:23–57.

Timmermans, H. 1984. Decompositional multiattribute preference models in spatial choice analysis: A review of some recent developments. *Progress in Human Geography* 8:189–221.

Timmermans, H., and Golledge, R. G. 1990. Applications of behavioral research on spatial problems: 2. Preference and choice. *Progress in Human Geography* 14:311–54.

Tinkler, K. J. 1969. Trend surface with "low explanations": The assessment of their significance. *American Journal of Science* 267:114–23.

Tobler, W. R. 1978. Migration fields. In *Population mobility and residential change,* ed. W. A. V. Clark and E. G. Moore, 215–32. Studies in Geography no. 25. Northwestern University, Evanston, Ill.

Tobler, W. R. 1979. Estimation of attractivities from interactions. *Environment and Planning A* 11:121–27.

Tobler, W. R. 1982. Surveying multidimensional measurement. In *Proximity and preference: Problems in the multidimensional analysis of large data sets,* ed. R. G. Golledge and J. N. Rayner, 3–9. Minneapolis: University of Minnesota Press.

Todd, D. 1979. *An introduction to the use of simultaneous-equation regression analysis in geography.* Concepts and Techniques in Modern Geography no. 21. Norwich, Eng.: Geo Abstracts.

Todd, D. 1981. Rural out-migration in southern Manitoba: A simple path analysis of "push" factors. *Canadian Geographer* 25:252–66.

Todd, D. 1982. Subjective correlates of small-town population change. *Tijdschrift voor Economische en Sociale Geografie* 73:109–21.

Tolman, E. C. 1948. Cognitive maps in rats and men. *Psychological Review* 55:189–208.

Townsend, A. R. 1980. The role of returned migrants in England's poorest region. *Geoforum* 11:353–69.

Trowbridge, C. C. 1913. On fundamental methods of orienting and imaginary maps. *Science* 38:888–97.

Tuan, Y. F. 1977. *Space and place: The perspective of experience.* Minneapolis: University of Minnesota Press.

Tuma, N. B.; Hannan, M. T.; and Groeneveld, L. P. 1979. Dynamic analysis of event histories. *American Journal of Sociology* 84:820–54.

Turner, M. E., and Stevens, C. D. 1971. The regression analysis of causal paths. In *Causal models in the social sciences,* ed. H. M. Blalock, Jr., 75–100. Chicago: Aldine.

Tversky, A. 1972. Elimination-by-aspects: A theory of choice. *Psychological Review* 79:281–99.

Unwin, D. J. 1970. Percentage RSS in trend surface analysis. *Area* 2:25–28.

Unwin, D. J. 1981. *Introductory spatial analysis.* New York: Methuen.

Upton, G., and Fingleton, B. 1979. Log-linear models in geography. *Transactions of the Institute of British Geographers,* n.s., 4:103–15.

Urry, J. 1987. Some social and spatial aspects of services. *Environment and Planning D: Society and Space* 5:5–26.

Van Arsdol, M. D., Jr.; Camilleri, S. F.; and Schmid, C. F. 1958. The generality of urban social area indexes. *American Sociological Review* 23:277–84.

Vanderkamp, J. 1970. The effects of out migration on regional employment. *Canadian Journal of Economics* 3:541–50.

Vanderkamp, J. 1989. Regional adjustment and migration flows in Canada, 1971 to 1981. *Papers of the Regional Science Association* 67:103–19.

Walker, R. A. 1981. A theory of suburbanization: Capitalism and the construction of urban space in the United States. In *Urbanization and urban planning in capitalist society,* ed. M. Dear and A. J. Scott, 383–429. New York: Methuen.

Walker, R. A., and Storper, M. 1981. Capital and industrial location. *Progress in Human Geography* 5:473–509.

Walmsley, D. J. 1982. Personality and regional preference structures: A study of introversion-extroversion. *Professional Geographer* 34:279–88.

Webber, M. J. 1983. Life-cycle stages, mobility, and metropolitan change: 1. Theoretical issues. *Environment and Planning A* 15:293–306.

Webber, M. J.; Symanski, R.; and Root, J. 1975. Toward a cognitive spatial theory. *Economic Geography* 51:100–116.

Weidlich, W., and Haag, G., eds. 1988. *Interregional migration: Dynamic theory and comparative analysis.* Berlin: Springer-Verlag.

Weiss, L., and Williamson, J. 1972. Black education, earnings, and interregional migration: Some new evidence. *American Economic Review* 62:372–83.

White, S. E. 1974. Residential preference and urban in-migration. *Proceedings of the Association of American Geographers* 6:47–50.

White, S. E. 1978. Mental map variability: A migration modeling problem. *Annals of Regional Science* 12:89–97.

White, S. E. 1980a. Awareness, preference, and interurban migration. *Regional Science Perspectives* 10:71–86.

White, S. E. 1980b. A philosophical dichotomy in migration research. *Professional Geographer* 32:6–13.

White, S. E. 1981. The influence of urban residential preferences on spatial behavior. *Geographical Review* 71:176–87.

Whitney, J. B., and Boots, B. N. 1979. An examination of residential mobility through the use of the log-linear model. *Regional Science and Urban Economics* 9:393–409.

Williams, P. R. 1976. The role of institutions in the inner London housing market: The case of Islington. *Transactions of the Institute of British Geographers,* n.s., 1:72–82.

Williams, P. R. 1978. Urban managerialism: A concept of relevance? *Area* 10: 236–40.

Williams, P. R. 1982. Restructuring urban managerialism: Towards a political economy of urban allocation. *Environment and Planning A* 14:95–105.

Wilson, A. G. 1971. A family of spatial interaction models, and associated developments. *Environment and Planning* 3:1–32.

Wilson, D. 1989. Toward a revised urban managerialism: Local managers and community development block grants. *Political Geography Quarterly* 8:21–41.

Wilson, F. D. 1987. Metropolitan and nonmetropolitan migration streams: 1935–1980. *Demography* 24:211–28.

Winship, C., and Mare, R. 1983. Structural equations and path analysis for discrete data. *American Journal of Sociology* 89:54–110.

Wolpert, J. 1965. Behavioral aspects of the decision to migrate. *Papers and Proceedings of the Regional Science Association* 15:159–69.

Woods, R. 1982. *Theoretical population geography.* Harlow, Eng.: Longman.

Woods, R. 1985. Towards a general theory of migration? in *Contemporary studies of migration,* ed. G. A. Van der Knaap and P. E. White, 1–5. Norwich, Eng.: Geo Books.

Wright, E. O. 1983. Giddens' critique of Marxism. *New Left Review* 139:11–35.

Wright, S. 1934. The method of path coefficients. *Annals of Mathematical Statistics* 5:161–215.

Wright, S. 1985. Path coefficients and path regressions: Alternative or complementary concepts? In *Causal models in the social sciences,* 2d ed., ed. H. M. Blalock, Jr., 39–53. New York: Aldine.

Wrigley, N. 1985. *Categorical data analysis for geographers and environmental scientists.* New York: Longman.

Wrigley, N., and Longley, P. 1984. Discrete choice modelling in urban analysis. In *Geography and the urban environment,* vol. 6, ed. D. T. Herbert and R. J. Johnston, 45–94. New York: Wiley.

Yeates, M. 1974. *An introduction to quantitative analysis in human geography.* New York: McGraw-Hill.

Yezer, A. M. J., and Thurston, L. 1976. Migration patterns and income change: Implications for the human capital approach to migration. *Southern Economic Journal* 42:693–702.

Young, W. 1984. Modelling residential location choice. *Australian Geographer* 16:21–28.

Zeller, R. A., and Carmines, E. G. 1980. *Measurement in the social sciences: The link between theory and data.* Cambridge: Cambridge University Press.

Index